More Day to Dawn

MORE DAY TO DAWN

Thoreau's Walden *for the Twenty-first Century*

Edited by

Sandra Harbert Petrulionis

and

Laura Dassow Walls

UNIVERSITY OF MASSACHUSETTS PRESS

AMHERST AND BOSTON

Compilation copyright © 2007 by the
University of Massachusetts Press
ALL RIGHTS RESERVED
Printed in the United States of America

Published by arrangement with *Nineteenth-Century Prose*,
San Diego State University

LC 2006028847
ISBN 10: 1-55849-576-2
ISBN 13: 978-1-55849-576-0

Designed by Steve Dyer
Set in Fairfield by dix!
Printed and bound by The Maple-Vail Book Manufacturing Group

Library of Congress Cataloging-in-Publication Data

More day to dawn : Thoreau's Walden for the twenty-first century /
edited by Sandra Harbert Petrulionis and Laura Dassow Walls.
p.   cm.
ISBN-13: 978-1-55849-576-0 (cloth : alk. paper)
ISBN-10: 1-55849-576-2 (cloth : alk. paper)
1. Thoreau, Henry David, 1817–1862. Walden.
2. Thoreau, Henry David, 1817–1862—Criticism and interpretation.
I. Petrulionis, Sandra Harbert, 1959–.   II. Walls, Laura Dassow.
PS3048.M67   2007
818'.303—dc22
2006028847

British Library Cataloguing in Publication data are available.

In Memory of
Bradley P. Dean

"Drive a nail home
and clinch it so faithfully
that you can wake up in the night
and think of your work
with satisfaction."

Contents

Acknowledgments

THIS COLLECTION originated as a double session at the 2003 MLA annual convention, sponsored by the Thoreau Society and organized by Sandra Harbert Petrulionis and Laura Dassow Walls. As interest gathered, others joined the original contributors, and the resulting collection of essays was published in *Nineteenth-Century Prose,* volume 31 (Fall 2004), in a special issue commemorating the 150th anniversary of the publication of *Walden.* We thank its editor and publisher, Barry Tharaud, for permission to reprint them here. Three of these essays have appeared in whole or in part in other books, and we thank the following for permission to republish them here: Lance Newman for his article from *Our Common Dwelling: Henry Thoreau, Transcendentalism, and the Class Politics of Nature* (Palgrave, 2005), and the publishers for H. Daniel Peck's essay in *Midwest Studies in Philosophy* 28.1 (2004): 85–101 (Blackwell) and David M. Robinson's chapter in *Natural Life: Thoreau's Worldly Transcendentalism* (Cornell University Press, 2004).

For their excellent contributions to this volume, we also thank Robert Cummings, Robert Lopez, Lance Newman, Daniel Peck, Dana Phillips, Larry Reynolds, David Robinson, William Rossi, Robert Sattelmeyer, Sarah Wider, and Michael Ziser. Our special thanks to Nina Baym for writing the Introduction; to Lance Newman for suggesting such a fitting title for the book; to Joel Myerson for his assistance and encouragement in seeking a publisher for this collection in book form; and to Mila Tasseva-Kurktchieva for help with reformatting the essays for republication. Finally, we thank Paul Wright, Bruce Wilcox, and Carol Betsch of University of Massachusetts Press for their insights, guidance, and editorial expertise.

SANDY PETRULIONIS AND
LAURA DASSOW WALLS

Abbreviations of Works by Henry David Thoreau

Corr   *The Correspondence of Henry David Thoreau,* ed. Walter Harding and Carl Bode. New York: New York University Press, 1958.

MW   *The Maine Woods,* ed. Joseph J. Moldenhauer. Princeton: Princeton University Press, 1972.

RP   *Reform Papers,* ed. Wendell Glick. Princeton: Princeton University Press, 1973.

W   *Walden,* ed. J. Lyndon Shanley. Princeton: Princeton University Press, 1971.

Wk   *A Week on the Concord and Merrimack Rivers,* ed. Carl F. Hovde, William L. Howarth, and Elizabeth Witherell. Princeton: Princeton University Press, 1980.

WF   *Wild Fruits: Thoreau's Rediscovered Last Manuscript,* ed. Bradley P. Dean. New York: Norton, 2000.

Introduction

Walden *Sesquicentennial Essays*

NINA BAYM

H ENRY DAVID THOREAU's *Walden* appeared in 1854, 153 years ago. When the untried author built his tiny cabin on Ralph Waldo Emerson's wood lot near the shore of Walden Pond—he started building the cabin in spring 1845, made his official move on July 4 of that year, and stayed for twenty-six months—he had no idea that his contemplated work might ever be widely distributed. The 1854 book addressed itself quite narrowly to "you who read these pages, who are said to live in New England" concerning "your outward condition or circumstances in this world, in this town," by which he meant Concord, Massachusetts. He could not have imagined his chronicle becoming a national treasure capable of delighting, irritating, and inspiring compatriots from Maine to California for well over a century. But, schooled in the Emersonian idea that books exist to inspire their readers, he would have been delighted at the prospect. *Walden* projects the image of a man withdrawing for a time from frenetic, materialistic, superficial modernity into rejuvenating communion with timeless nature. Thoreau's gesture has been imitated by countless thousands across the nation. The site of his cabin has become virtually a shrine. The book is a repository of memorable phrases, remarkable descriptions, literary allusion, and acerbic social criticism that still rings true to American life—perhaps even more now than in its own relatively rustic age.

Thoreau moved to the pond to read, think, stroll, perhaps plant a crop (at least one critic thinks his claim to have grown beans was a hoax), and launch a literary career by completing two books. The first book would memorialize his beloved older brother John, who had died painfully from tetanus in 1842, by narrating a two weeks' trip the duo made in a home-made boat, paddling down the Concord and Merrimack rivers in 1839. The second would address residents of Concord and its environs, exposing the spiritual poverty of their daily existence as well as the stupidity of their economic arrangements—both understood as the result of their idolizing market capitalism. The critique would be brought home by pointed contrasts between his neighbors' empty lives and his own plenitude at the pond, paradoxically achieved through thoughtful simplification.

He needed solitude to write the first book (published in 1849 as *A Week on the Concord and Merrimack Rivers*), time and space away from the noise of his father's pencil business and his mother's boarding house. He required a place on the margins of Concord to write the second, where he could watch his neighbors and they could watch him. He needed both distance and proximity. He said (in a sentence used as the caption for *Walden*'s frontispiece—now usually printed as an epigraph): "I do not propose to write an ode to dejection, but to brag as lustily as chanticleer in the morning, standing on his roost, if only to wake my neighbors up." The rooster is a barnyard fowl who, despite domestication, has not lost his intuitive knowledge of such eternal verities as darkness and dawn. Human beings need his infallible timekeeping. *Walden*'s Thoreau is a chanticleer who wants to be needed.

What he sought at the pond for himself, ultimately, was a kind of working vacation. The fusion of and contradiction between vacation and work constitute only one of the many converging paradoxes by which *Walden* is complicated and enlivened. When Thoreau moved back to Concord in September 1847, he had virtually completed *A Week* and had in hand an early draft of *Walden*. But his planned literary career was derailed by *A Week*'s utter failure to sell. In the "Economy" chapter of *Walden* he memorably compares himself to an Indian basket-weaver unable to market his wares: "I too had woven a kind of basket of a delicate texture, but I had not made it worth any one's while to buy them. Yet not the less, in my case, did I think it worth my while to weave them, and instead of studying how to make it worth men's while to buy my baskets, I studied rather how to avoid the necessity of selling them" (*W* 19). Brave words, not entirely sincere. The seven more years Thoreau put into the weaving of *Walden* certainly had publication as an aim, and in fact the book sold moderately well, although its wide impact had to wait until after the Civil War.

Walden was much longer, more subtle, more artistically self-aware, more variegated in subject matter, and more tonally flexible than what he brought back from the pond. It consists of twenty chapters neatly paired in oppositions: reading and sounds, solitude and visitors, the bean-field and the village, the ponds and Baker Farm, higher laws and brute neighbors. These chapters are arranged in a seasonal sequence, collapsing Thoreau's sojourn at the pond into a year and adding journal observations from years after he left the pond as well. Although Thoreau concealed neither the length of his stay nor his use of later observations, the power of the seasonal organization is such that he is popularly remembered for having spent one single, complete year at the pond. Thoreau's seasonal shape departed from the standard calendar pattern by beginning in summer—after the planting season—and ending with the arrival of spring. This pattern aligned his stay with myths of death and rebirth, allowing him to identify his narrative with world religions as well as with a psychic journey from joy (summer) through depression and despair (winter) into renewal (spring).

This pattern does not so much constrict observation as allow Thoreau the freedom to stray associatively without losing the main path. Emerson had taught him that a record of one's life ("life passed through the fire of thought," as he put it in the "Divinity School Address"), despite all its twists and turns, would inevitably compose itself into a whole. But even so, Thoreau labored over every sentence. One can read the book uncritically for its remarkable prose, for its moving set pieces of natural description or its invigorating (often amusing) polemic, for its curmudgeonly advice on what to read and what to ignore, for its chronicle of a year in a nature both wild and cultivated, for its testimony to the meanings of life. One can also identify patterns of metaphor, trace Thoreau's extensive repertory of literary allusion, find signs of personal biography, recognize submerged currents of anger and doubt, note the use or rejection of representational conventions of Thoreau's day, and consider specific historical events to which the book responded. The book contains the sort of multiplicity that allows for continual interpretation and reinterpretation.

The essays collected here are implicit tributes to *Walden's* variety. Each approaches the book from a particular angle, although all point to and unpack versions of the dualism that scholars have identified as its thematic engine. In so doing, the essays all grant authority to the book itself; they neither treat it as a cultural product nor pipe it through one or another uncongenial theoretical container. The split between action and contemplation, the opposition between nature as it is in detail and as it is made to serve the generalizing imagination, the clash between theology and science as these are applied to the natural world, the struggle between materialism and idealism, the use and rejection of literary predecessors, the conflict between wild nature and nature brought under the plow, the desire to transcend earth versus the desire to dig into it, the wish to escape one's body versus the yearning to live fully through one's body, the need to communicate versus the desire to say something never uttered before, the gap between the world and its representation in language—all these concerns so central to *Walden* are treated with refreshing originality and admirable precision in this collection. Too, the question of whether the persona is a provocateur or a crank (or whether these two personae are perhaps identical), which every teacher of *Walden* must deal with in the classroom, appears and reappears throughout.

The first essay, Robert Sattelmeyer's "*Walden*: Climbing the Canon," follows *Walden's* history from advance publicity in Horace Greeley's *New York Tribune* on to recent critical analysis, showing how *Walden* entered the literary canon and stayed there. Recognizing how much Thoreau the man and *Walden* the book have been conflated in the public mind, so that Thoreau is well known to (and admired by) people who have never read a word he wrote, Sattelmeyer adroitly extricates *Walden* from the author's biography to narrate the book's life. He shows how *Walden* was admired by British critics in the 1890s, and how it has been reinterpreted over the decades in such landmarks of analysis as Emerson's ambivalent, paradigm-establishing eulogy first published in 1862 but many times reprinted, V. L. Parrington's *Main Currents of American Thought* (1927), Van Wyck Brooks's *The Flowering of New England* (1937), F. O. Matthiessen's *American Renaissance* (1941), Sherman Paul's *The Shores of America* (1958), and Stanley Cavell's *The Senses of Walden* (1972). In the 1890s it figured in the genteel canon, in the 1920s it became a dissenting book, in the 1930s a left-wing book, in the 1940s a testament to democracy, in the 1950s a triumph of literary formalism and mythic archetype, in the 1960s a brief for dropping out of the mainstream, and in recent decades a primer for conservationists. Among all these changing emphases, Sattelmeyer sees three continuing approaches: it is a book about nature or living in nature, a book of dissent from dominant cultural values, and a work of deliberate literary art.

Taking up *Walden* as a book about nature, H. Daniel Peck in "Lakes of Light: Modes of Representation in *Walden*" shows, with a focus on the "Ponds" chapter, how little natural description *Walden* actually contains overall, how sparse are the descriptions it offers of Walden Pond itself. The chapter—ninth out of twenty—comes surprisingly late, and Walden is only one of the ponds Thoreau describes. Peck's analysis complicates the habit of reading the pond as a symbol of Thoreau's inner, transcendental self, and as that only. Reminding us that *Walden* began as a book of social criticism rather than an account of a life in nature, and that the redemptive possibilities of nature-study emerge only (and incompletely) in the later drafts, he suggests that the additions of the seasonal structure and its mythical overlays do not control the book or even dominate the descriptions of the pond. Nor is description controlled by questions of transcendent meaning or scientific accuracy. Rather, Thoreau's concern is to represent the natural world as landscape, without falling victim to conventional modes of landscape description. Close reading of Thoreau's language in "The Ponds" chapter reveals how thoroughly he knew the paradigms of literary landscape available in his day, and how rigorously he worked both to exploit and to escape them.

Environmentalist critics who admire Thoreau tend to celebrate his post-*Walden* work for its increasing factuality. Such critics understand Thoreau either as an emergent scientist who concomitantly rejected the Transcendental idealizing exemplified in Emerson's *Nature,* or as one who rejected both science and Transcendentalism in favor of unmediated contact with nature. From these perspectives, *Walden* is read chronologically as the last text before Thoreau began openly to quarrel with the Transcendental premises of Emerson's early work. In "Thoreau and Idealism: 'Face to Face to a Fact,'" David M. Robinson revisits Emerson's *Nature* to clarify Emerson's actual position and then shows how the ethos of observational fidelity and the problems of generalizing from natural observation (which for Emerson were seemingly not problems) already figure in *Walden.* But while *Walden* appears to reject Emerson's glib dismissal of natural specifics in favor of generalities, it never discards Emerson's sense that generalizing is a human habit of divine origin. Even as Thoreau rejected Emerson in part, he adapted Emersonian ideas as he found them in translations of the Hindu *Vishnu Purana* and the

Bhagavat Gita. Through these texts, however, he could propose in opposition to Emerson that connecting fact to meaning takes work, requires preparation. Robinson points out that for Thoreau, the challenges posed by matter to mind are made still more difficult by the fallibility of the observer as a perceiver of phenomena who must also organize data into larger wholes.

Larry J. Reynolds's "The Cimiter's 'Sweet' Edge: Thoreau, Contemplation, and Violence" also considers Thoreau's reading of the *Bhagavat Gita* in *Walden,* but from a very different angle, focusing on its justification, even celebration, of violence. He asks whether Thoreau's attraction to the Hindu text might not represent a powerful attraction to violent action, which his morality rejects unless it can be rationalized by attaching it to a righteous cause. Reynolds's discussion notes the way Thoreau takes aggression in the animal world as something natural and hence beyond the reach of human morality, in effect something God-ordained and therefore good. He also notes Thoreau's recognition of the human potential for brutality, as in the over-whelming instance of slavery, an evil whose existence might sanction princi-pled counter-violence as another sort of good. In due time Thoreau would celebrate John Brown's impetus to employ violence in a cause he considered just, but in "Civil Disobedience" directly (his night in jail for antislavery civil disobedience occurred in 1846, during his time at the pond) and in *Walden* implicitly, he elects a conscientious pacifism as the appropriate human re-sponse to injustice. Yet Reynolds finds constant signs of the "inner fire, the violent aggression" that roils the placid surface of *Walden* in excess of any cause that might be invoked to explain it. This makes *Walden* in important ways a visible exercise in repressing violence in favor of contemplation. The persona of *Walden* is thus drawn to peaceful meditation not so much for its own sake as for its function as a defense against violent impulses.

For William Rossi in the next essay, "Following Thoreau's Instincts," ac-counts of animals in *Walden* invite a more scientific line of inquiry. He pro-poses that Thoreau's text is responding to the Scotsman Robert Chambers's 1844 bestseller, *Vestiges of the Natural History of Creation,* which brought evo-lutionary thought into transatlantic discourse fifteen years before Darwin. Rossi explicates Chambers's ideas, connects them to Coleridge's influential 1825 *Aids to Reflection,* and shows how they inflect Thoreau's consideration of the vexed connection between animal instinct and human intuition. To the Transcendentalist, instinct is the lowest faculty, intuition the highest; but to the crypto-evolutionist, instinct and intuition are much the same. Thoreau's chanticleer, after all, is a Transcendentalist. Rossi shows how changes in the various drafts of *Walden* indicate awareness of Chambers and the debates his ideas were inspiring among educated people. Especially in *Walden's* chapters "Higher Laws" and "Brute Neighbors," Thoreau wavers between representations of animals whose instinct is identical to intuition (so that they remain attuned to what humans have forgotten), and representations in which animals lack self-understanding and self-control and are thus far below humans in the chain of being. From the latter perspective, humans are ethically required to overcome, to transcend, their kinship to animals; in the former, they are ethically required to cultivate that same kinship. More generally, Thoreau is not able to accept any science that might extract the natural world from a creation that is foundationally ethical.

Lance Newman's "Thoreau's Materialism: From *Walden* to *Wild Fruits*" merges ethics, evolution, and environmentalism. Putting *Walden* within a narrative of Thoreau's development, Newman sees the text as formulating a problem to which the very late (1862) manuscript (not published as a book until *Wild Fruits* came out in 2000) is the solution. As well as demonstrating Thoreau's move from the Transcendental to scientific mode of apprehending natural fact—from idealism to materialism—Newman documents Thoreau's sociopolitical move from critiquing the capitalist logic of individualist selves in a market economy to expressing an ideal of communal selves living in respectful relation to the land. The chapter wherein materialist analysis begins to show how "capitalist social and economic relations have destroyed humankind's immediate collective relationship with nature" is "Economy." Questions just barely asked in *Walden* are fully formulated in *Wild Fruits,* which describes "much more particularly than in *Walden* the concrete ways in which the specific institutions of private property and competitive commerce prevent the citizens of a no longer classless republic from experiencing wild land either aesthetically or devotionally." Newman's approach is not a classical Marxism that discredits aesthetics and the devotional as forms of false consciousness. For him, Thoreau's gain in scientific sophistication does not come at the cost of a belief that human life on earth should be a spiritual celebration.

In "Thoreau, Homer, and Community," Robert Oscar López looks at a different form of community, that of affective human relations, the connections of one to one. Thoreau not only kept much to himself in "real life" after his brother's death, he features his need for solitude and escape from other human beings prominently in *Walden*. Yet he also seeks authentic connection to others, looking for relations characterized by respect for personal autonomy. In the "Visitors" chapter he establishes such a relation, briefly, with an illiterate Canadian woodchopper. (The man is not named in *Walden*, but Thoreau's journals identify him as Alex Therien.) Therien knows a little Greek, which leads Thoreau to label him a true Homeric man, and to entertain him by translating part of Achilles' reproof to Patroclus from Homer's *Iliad*. The passage expresses a martial ideal, showing that male bonds depend on rejecting effeminacy. López points out that the Therien episode dramatizes this ideal, because Thoreau is standing so close to Therien when he translates that the two must be touching each other. López is not interested in biographical homoeroticism, but studies the episode for insight into Thoreau's attraction to the classical. The *Iliad* exhibits a culture that is bolder, stronger, simpler, more poetic, and more masculine than Thoreau's own New England. It is also more brutal and far less rational. Its appeals to atavistic elements within the modern self must be recognized, appreciated, and overcome in favor of a more mature, impersonal, abstract ideal of global community linked by principle and conscience. For Reynolds, Rossi, and López, *Walden* asks the question: how can one withdraw to nature without reverting, how can one use nature to rise rather than sink?

Affective bonds are also the focus of Sarah Ann Wider's essay, " 'And What Became of Your Philosophy Then?': Women Reading *Walden*." The bonds considered here are between Thoreau and women readers. Women might be expected to resist *Walden*'s misogyny; that they do not is evidenced through a variety of examples, from Wider's own encounters with the book, through jottings found in diverse scrapbooks and copybooks kept by women, with a brief mention of Virginia Woolf's appreciation, on to a full discussion of Elizabeth von Arnim's *Solitary Summer* (1899), much influenced by and often referencing *Walden*. Wider's chief example of *Walden*'s chronic denigration of women and women's work is from "Reading," where the spoken tongue is identified with the brutish mother, thus seeming to exclude women from the realm of literacy itself, and therefore from reading *Walden*. Wider hypothesizes that "advocacy of distance is perhaps the greatest gift Thoreau offers his marginalized readers, for within that space lies the large, revolutionary prospect that a markedly different perspective can successfully challenge the dominant one." The gift Thoreau offers to male readers, then, is exactly the gift he offers to women as well. If Thoreau did not himself imagine women within his implied audience, Wider shows that women have refused to accept their exclusion.

The female responses Wider analyzes take Thoreau's distance as symbolic. It does not require an actual retreat to nature. Such readers may not think of *Walden* as a book of nature, and may not even have much interest in the natural world. A quite different view of the relationship of *Walden*'s persona to the natural setting is provided by Michael G. Ziser in "Thoreau: *Walden* and the Georgic Mode." Ziser begins by considering and rejecting the habit of reading *Walden* as an updated version of the classical pastoral, a reading associated especially with Leo Marx's 1967 *Machine in the Garden.* He proposes that *Walden* is better thought of as an updated version of the classical georgic (a genre in which Thoreau read widely), which he defines as "didactic writing about the natural world as apprehended through human labor practices." Above all, the georgic's relation to labor differs from the pastoral's because it is an agricultural genre dominated by and directed to busy farmers, not idle shepherds. Whether shepherds are in fact idle is another question, outside the pastoral purview, because pastoral is produced by gentlemen on holiday for other gentlemen on holiday, rather than folk who need to make any sort of living from the soil. The chapter of *Walden* central to Ziser's analysis is "The Bean-Field," which shows Thoreau as a physical and mental laborer, but always a worker. In "The Bean-Field" Thoreau rejects the pastoral assumption that work always involves a degree of inauthenticity by refusing to take life easy and let things be what they are. Recognizing that those who take life easy are privileged rather than objective observers, he argues in "The Bean-Field" that labor is a means of truly connecting people to the earth, which is the human way to make life meaningful.

The contemporary environmental conflict between those who work the land for profit and professional environmentalists who want to remove land from the market is inherent in the imagined dispute between shepherds and farmers, pastoral and georgic. In "Thoreau's Divide: Rediscovering the Environmental Activist/Agriculturalist Debate in *Walden*'s 'Baker Farm,'" Robert Cummings makes this timely conflict his focus, arguing that *Walden* proleptically represents a "divide of consciousness" wherein an ethos born from the "everyday, necessary, hands-on practice" of surviving on the land struggles to occupy the same theoretic ground claimed by "a distanced, circumspect, informed, and privileged land-use perspective." In contrast to the standard environmental approach, Cummings takes the agriculturalist side. He contests the standard reading of "Baker Farm" as a "misanthropic diatribe against the poor, ignorant, working-class bogger," presenting the authorial persona in that chapter as a humorous satire on officious pretension: "Thoreau satirizes his theories on simple living by placing the narrator's advice to 'go a-huckleberry-ing' against the stark relief of family responsibilities." As well as offering a new approach toward this problematic chapter, Cummings reminds us of the current of humor that runs through *Walden,* and of the extent to which perspectives presented as global, as above the particularity of concrete experience, are no less partial than their more obviously incomplete competitors.

Dana Phillips's "Leaving *Walden*" looks at both *Walden* and *The Maine Woods,* using Thoreau's extravagant irascibility in *Walden* to identify him with the long parade of American social satirists working within the tradition of the tall tale. But Phillips also reminds us that Thoreau fits in with the long line of American slackers, from Rip Van Winkle forward, whose programmatic idleness constitutes a reproach to the inane busywork of their compatriots. Yet again, Phillips considers *Walden* from the perspective of recent theories of social construction, especially as these have been enunciated by Bruno Latour, Stephen Shapin, Simon Shaffer, and other sociologists of science. There is a sense, he argues, in which Thoreau too is a social constructionist. But he finds Thoreau "more hopeful and much less passive" than these contemporary thinkers. Thoreau "would have regarded resting in the conviction that all facts are socially constructed as an outright begging of one of the most important questions we can ask ourselves about our lives." Phillips uses Thoreau to speak back to, to satirize those who imagine that calling a fact a social construction will stop discussion. Even if a fact is recognized as value-laden, its status (and the value it represents) will continue to be "live issues." Because he recognizes at once the social constructedness and the real existence of facts, Thoreau resorts to the flexible strategies of satire to keep himself from settling into any one observational stance. This makes satire not merely an attack mode, but also a philosophical choice.

The tendency of all these essays is to see *Walden* as an account of struggle rather than a peaceful, genteel narrative of escaping life's responsibilities by withdrawing to nature. Responsive to philosophy, science, predecessor texts, theology, social trends, economic life, local culture, and contemporary intellectual currents, the book exemplifies as well as narrates its attempts to encompass all these materials into a formal structure. In *Walden,* nature is the key that unlocks the universe; the universe is infinite.

Walden

Climbing the Canon

ROBERT SATTELMEYER

W*alden*'s rise to canonical status and something more, which I attempt to trace in this essay, is coeval with the rise of American literature itself as an academic discipline in the twentieth century, and yet the book's shifting reputation is difficult to disentangle from the larger fact of Thoreau himself as a controversial and iconic figure in American culture. The latter phenomenon actually had its beginnings in publicity about Thoreau's Walden experiment that appeared even before *Walden* was published in 1854, and the reception of the book a hundred and fifty years later is still highly colored (*pace* the much-heralded death of the author) by Thoreau's public stature as a voice of political, social, and economic dissent within the dominant culture as well as what Lawrence Buell terms an "environmental saint"—an originating source of conservation and preservation movements that have had a profound impact on the American landscape as well as its culture.[1]

Not even Mark Twain, I would argue, Thoreau's only serious American rival as a writer claimed at once by diverse publics and academic specialists, presents so thoroughgoing a conflation of literary artist and cultural property. And this conflation is largely centered in one book, *Walden,* whose narrative voice is ineluctably identified as Thoreau's own, and not diffused, as in Twain's case, through many books, fictional characters, and public pronouncements over a long and highly visible career.

But if this complex overlay of reputations and constituencies presents difficulties, its intrinsic interest has led a number of scholars to plot the larger trajectories of Thoreau's reputation in studies that are helpful to the task at hand. Extended treatments include Wendell Glick's *The Recognition of Henry David Thoreau* (1969), Michael Meyer's *Several More Lives to Live: Thoreau's Political Reputation in America* (1977), Meyer and Walter Harding's chapter "Thoreau's Reputation" in their *New Thoreau Handbook* (1980), Raymond R. Borst's *Henry David Thoreau: A Reference Guide, 1835–1899* (1987), Gary Scharnhorst's *Henry David Thoreau: A Case Study in Canonization* (1993), and Buell's chapter "The Canonization and Recanonization of the Green Thoreau" in *The Environmental Imagination: Thoreau, Nature Writing, and the Formation of American Culture* (1995).[2] As their titles suggest, these studies concern themselves primarily with the growth and shifting fortunes of Thoreau as author and cultural icon rather than with the reception of *Walden,* though because of the conflation of the man and the book there is a great deal of overlap. Thoreau's friend Daniel Ricketson was emblematic of the general tendency: he began one of his first letters to Thoreau "Dear Mr. Walden."[3]

For the first half of *Walden*'s life, sparked by ambivalent and at least partially negative portraits by Emerson and Lowell following his death, the principal issue of Thoreau criticism was the character of the man himself; detractors and hagiographers took turns, generally citing Thoreau's writings only briefly and in passing. This part of the story may be sketched in relatively brief terms, for it was not until the 1930s and 1940s, when American literature gained a purchase in the academy, that a coherent strain of thoughtful and analytical criticism of *Walden* itself began to appear.

I

Unlike Thoreau's first book, *A Week on the Concord and Merrimack Rivers,* *Walden* appeared with some fanfare, sold reasonably well, and generated numerous and mostly positive reviews. *Walden* was published by Ticknor and Fields, the most prestigious American publishing firm during the middle part of the nineteenth century. Its junior partner and guiding force, James T. Fields, energetically promoted the work of American writers such as Emerson, Hawthorne, Longfellow, and Lowell. The Ticknor and Fields imprint carried a certain cachet, and Fields saw to it that advance sheets of *Walden* were sent to influential reviewers, magazines, and newspapers.[4] Horace Greeley, who had been acting informally as Thoreau's literary agent for several years, provided additional publicity. Greeley had called attention to Thoreau's early *Walden* lectures in his *New York Tribune* in 1849—in correspondence that was reprinted in a number of other papers—and he ran a notice of the book along with lengthy extracts in advance of its publication in the summer of 1854.[5] The title of this piece on the appearance of *Walden*, "A Massachusetts Hermit," conveys some sense of how the book was promoted and at the same time misrepresented, emphasizing its against-the-grain qualities and drawing attention to the eccentric characteristics and critical notions of its author. The popular myth of Thoreau as someone who permanently withdrew from society and lived in the woods has its origins in publicity for Thoreau and for *Walden* reaching back five years before it was published.

In response to these efforts, sales and reviews were generally strong. In its first year, about 1,750 copies out of a printing of 2,000 were sold or given to reviewers (*A Week* had only sold about 200 copies), and there were a number of positive reviews by well-known literary figures in important magazines and newspapers.[6] As Gary Scharnhorst summarizes the contemporary reception of *Walden*, we can see that it was received much as it was promoted:

> Of the total of sixty-nine contemporary reviews, forty-nine were strongly favorable. Many of these notices also included excerpts from the book; that is, literally hundreds of thousands of readers may have come across at least part of *Walden* in their local papers. For the record, too, these notices had the effect of cementing Thoreau's contemporary reputation as a "quaint" writer or "eccentric" thinker: one or both of these terms appear in over half of the reviews.[7]

After its initially favorable reception, the first edition of *Walden* was out of print by 1859. But only briefly: a second edition was issued in 1862, the year of Thoreau's death, and it has been in print ever since, having been reprinted more than 150 times during its first hundred years of life.[8] Still, after Thoreau's death circumstances conspired to throw *Walden* further into the shadow cast by its author's shifting reputation and larger-than-life public image.

A modest outpouring of new articles and books followed Thoreau's death, both deflecting attention from the reissue of *A Week* and *Walden* and highlighting Thoreau as nature writer, eccentric thinker, and travel writer. The major essays "Walking," "Autumnal Tints," and "Wild Apples" appeared in the *Atlantic Monthly* in 1862 (now edited by James T. Fields and owned by

Ticknor and Fields, so that it served to showcase the firm's authors and pro-
mote its books), and then in the collection *Excursions* in 1863. This volume
was followed by *The Maine Woods* in 1864, *Cape Cod* and *Letters to Various
Persons* in 1865, and *A Yankee in Canada, with Anti-Slavery and Reform Papers*
in 1866. These works, along with the seasonal selections from Thoreau's Journals that H. G. O. Blake edited during the 1880s and 1890s, ensured that his
posthumous reputation was primarily as a nature writer. *Walden* continued to
sell, of course, but in light of its twentieth-century reputation it is interesting
to note that its cumulative sales by 1880 were only a couple of hundred copies
greater than those of the more recently issued *Maine Woods* and *Cape Cod*.[9]

Negative assessments of Thoreau by Emerson and Lowell also affected
his literary reputation and, by extension, *Walden's* stature among American
books. Lowell's well-known critique, published in the *North American Review*
in 1865 and reprinted in *My Study Windows* (1871), was a workmanlike piece
of character assassination that probably stemmed at least in part from Lowell's
lingering resentment of Thoreau for having flamed him over the "mean and
cowardly" expurgation of a sentence from "Chesuncook" when Lowell was
editing the *Atlantic Monthly* in 1857.[10] This review probably injured Thoreau's
reputation less than has been supposed—not only in the sense that no
publicity is bad publicity, but also because it roused Thoreau's partisans
(T. W. Higginson, for example) to his defense.[11]

More subtle and damaging, probably, was Emerson's putatively favorable
eulogy, which was printed in the *Atlantic Monthly* in the year of Thoreau's
death. Perhaps the most ambivalent eulogy in literary history, Emerson's
praise of his long-time friend's character is balanced by an account of his
faults and an insinuation that Thoreau's life was essentially a failure. Apparently never having given up his early expectation that Thoreau would have an
influential career or role in public affairs (his disappointment is evident as
early as "Experience"), Emerson left Thoreau's future reading public to ponder his famous pronouncement that his younger friend, "instead of engineering for all America . . . was the captain of a huckleberry-party." Even more
remarkably, from the standpoint of Thoreau's literary reputation, Emerson's
eulogy-cum-essay says absolutely nothing about Thoreau's writings. Nothing.
As a kind of afterthought, Emerson "subjoin[s] a few sentences from his
unpublished manuscripts" (emphasis added), further reinforcing the clear
sense of the overall essay (by virtue of its silence on this score) that in the

overall summing up, Thoreau's aims and works as a writer are not worth mentioning.

Such was the boost into posthumous fame that Thoreau received from his oldest friend and mentor, America's preeminent literary figure. To make matters worse, the essay was reprinted as the Introduction to the first of Thoreau's posthumous volumes, *Excursions* (1863). It persisted as a part of the first collected (Riverside) edition of Thoreau's works in 1894, moving to the beginning of the *Miscellanies* volume of that set, only to return as the Introduction to the twenty-volume Walden Edition (1906) that was standard for most of the twentieth century. Thus it provided the portal, as it were, through which untold thousands of readers encountered Thoreau's writings; and to the extent that it shaped their horizon of expectations, it suggested that Thoreau was chiefly to be regarded as a noble if eccentric soul whose life was a failure, whose work in natural history was a "broken task," and whose writings might chiefly be appreciated insofar as they could be mined for small gems of vivid description.

Houghton Mifflin evolved from Ticknor and Fields around 1880, and thereafter played the major role (along with such Thoreauvian disciples as H. G. O. Blake, Franklin Sanborn, and H. S. Salt) in promoting Thoreau's writings. *Walden,* however, was not accorded any particular priority of place in these efforts, and in general Thoreau's reputation in the late nineteenth century was chiefly as a nature writer and descriptive stylist. Neither the book's overall themes nor its trenchant critiques of American culture were represented, for example, in the influential anthologies of *American Prose* that Horace Scudder edited for Houghton Mifflin in the 1880s and beyond. Thoreau was by this time a canonical figure, but the same could not be said of *Walden* as a canonical work. The anthology's selections (by which most readers would have known Thoreau's work) included "Sounds" and "Brute Neighbors" from *Walden* (beginning the tradition that would last over a century of having Thoreau known by students chiefly as the author of the "Battle of the Ants") and "The Highland Light" from *Cape Cod.* As Lawrence Buell summarizes the effect of late nineteenth-century anthologizing, "Thoreau would have become first known to American readers . . . as the author of comparatively descriptive and scientific, nonmystical, and non-pugnacious essays, and through Emerson's representation of him as 'the bachelor of thought and nature.'"[12]

II

Although criticism continued to focus on its author's character and cultural representativeness, *Walden* began to emerge from this endless and endlessly reductive argument in the early decades of the twentieth century. Chief among the forces that would foster its reputation as a seminal American book were the influence of socially progressive British admirers of Thoreau, important changes in the publication and copyright status of *Walden,* and the beginnings of what Lawrence Buell terms "the gradual displacement of the first 'genteel canon' by the conception of an 'oppositional canon'" of great artists whose works tend to dissent from the prevailing values of their times.[13] This transition boosted *Walden's* fame at the same time that it led to the beginnings of a long bear market in many of the New England worthies once ranked high above Thoreau, such as Lowell, Longfellow, Whittier, and Holmes.

The importance of British criticism in shifting perceptions of Thoreau and *Walden* reaches back into the last decades of the nineteenth century when Thoreau was promoted and admired by influential literary figures and leaders of the British labor movement. Sir Walter Scott had overseen the first British edition of *Walden* in 1886. Robert Blatchford's *Merrie England,* a popular early Labor treatise, urged its proletarian audience to read *Walden,* and the party distributed cheap paperbound editions to its members.[14] The utopian socialist H. S. Salt was especially dogged and effective in promoting Thoreau in a number of essays, editions, and an influential biography in 1890. Salt drew attention to Thoreau's political thought and writing—especially "Civil Disobedience"—which had been largely ignored in America. He acknowledged *Walden* as Thoreau's masterpiece, and although his critique of the book was not systematic, he was perhaps the first to point out its pervasive humor, which he characterized as "grave, dry, pithy, sententious, almost saturnine in its tone, yet perhaps for that very reason the more racy and suggestive to those readers who have the faculty for appreciating it."[15] As was the case with the revival of Melville and the acknowledgment of Whitman's importance, British critics were the first to recognize the complexity and reach, the radical implications, and the literary merits, of *Walden.*

Meanwhile, in its native country, though Thoreau had been to an extent co-opted by the genteel tradition as a nonthreatening nature writer, *Walden* prospered from publishing decisions and copyright issues during the first de-

cade of the twentieth century. In 1906, urged by Bliss Perry, a successor
to Fields as editor of the *Atlantic* and a senior editor of the firm, Houghton
Mifflin brought out the twenty-volume "Walden Edition" of Thoreau's complete writings, including for the first time fourteen volumes of his journal,
making Thoreau the first American writer to have his (supposedly) complete
journal printed. For the carriage trade, there was a special large-format "Manuscript Edition" printed from the same plates that contained a leaf of original
manuscript tipped in to the first volume of each set (thereby scattering 600
leaves of manuscript from drafts of various works in progress). This event
marked Houghton Mifflin's last opportunity to capitalize upon and commod-
ify Thoreau, for their copyright to *Walden* expired in 1910. The production of
a handsome edition of an author's collected works certainly neither signifies
nor guarantees canonical stature, and in Thoreau's case it seems chiefly to
indicate the high-water mark of his bourgeois respectability as a nature writer
and member of the New England literary company. The Walden Edition, in
fact, was almost identical in format to the twenty-three-volume edition of
the works of John Burroughs that Houghton Mifflin brought out two years
earlier in 1904. But whether the edition was named for the pond, the book, or
both, the Walden Edition also instantiates the preeminence of that title and
that work in Thoreau publication, and probably reflects a growing sense
among both readers and publishers that *Walden* was the single work by which
Thoreau would primarily be known and celebrated.

The fact that the Houghton Mifflin copyright to *Walden* expired in 1910
meant of course that it was then in the public domain for reprints and anthology selections. As Gary Scharnhorst reports, at least eight new editions of
Walden were published in 1910 alone, and within a few years lesson plans for
teaching the book in high schools began to appear.[16] Selections from *Walden*
in anthologies, too, now began to reflect a less sanitized and genial version of
Thoreau the nature writer. Norman Foerster's influential *Chief American
Prose Writers* of 1916 is notable not only for including Thoreau in its list of
the nine most important American prose writers (Melville, Mark Twain,
Howells, and James don't make the cut), but also for its diverse selections
from *Walden,* including "Where I Lived, and What I Lived For," "Solitude,"
and the "Conclusion."

Walden is unusual among nineteenth-century American texts in the richness of manuscript material that survives, documenting the revisions that the
book underwent between Thoreau's years at the pond and 1854. Unfortu-

nately, the first edition of the book to make use of these materials, Franklin B. Sanborn's Bibliophile Society edition of 1909, served only to distort and corrupt the text beyond recognition. Taking the tradition of the high-handed Victorian editor to ludicrous lengths, Sanborn added 12,000 words he alleged (without evidence) that Thoreau had been forced to cut, reordered the chapter arrangement, and cut up "Economy" and moved numerous passages from it to other chapters to make them come out to a more uniform length.[17]

Catching up to British appreciations, American critics of the teens and twenties began to move away from what might be termed, using the title of Ellery Channing's eccentric biography of his friend, the "poet-naturalist" Thoreau, and to recognize more facets of his writing and character. Most of this recognition, however, is still generalized and not specifically tied to sustained analysis of *Walden*. Especially notable was John Macy's 1913 *The American Spirit in Literature,* an attack on the genteel tradition in American letters in which Thoreau figures (along with Mark Twain and Whitman) as one of our "most stalwart men of genius" and as "the one anarchist of great literary power in a nation of slavish conformity to legalism." Macy saw *Walden* as "one of those whole, profound books in which the best of an author is distilled,"[18] and his study is a sort of precursor, as Lawrence Buell observes, "to the so-called antinomian theory of American literature—the theory that the major American writers have been visionary dissenters."[19] This estimation paved the way not only for Thoreau's wider acceptance in the academy in the 1930s, but also for the acceptance of *Walden* as a cynosure of the oppositional canon.

During the teens, Thoreau's reputation (if not *Walden*'s specifically) was also bolstered by the beginnings of serious academic criticism by Mark Van Doren and Norman Foerster, and translations of *Walden* (which appeared in German as early as 1897) were issued in Russian in 1910, in Japanese in 1911, in Italian in 1920, and French in 1922.[20]

The twenties did little to enhance *Walden*'s reputation, the conventional wisdom being that the boom years of the Jazz Age were less than conducive to contemplation of the sort of plain living and high thinking inscribed in the text. Nevertheless, the book had by now secured a place in the American canon, and the Depression era would enhance its reputation and its visibility as a reformist document. The most notable development of the twenties, in fact, was a kind of preview of the tone of thirties' criticism, V. L. Parrington's *Main Currents in American Thought* (1927). Parrington's very influential intellectual history sought to reconstruct a usable past that was liberal and progressive, and he aligned Thoreau with such other forward-thinking exponents of these allegedly "main currents" as Roger Williams, Jefferson, Twain, and Whitman. Reversing the trend of previous decades but echoing earlier British criticism, Parrington downplayed Thoreau's interest in nature and, as Scharnhorst says, made *Walden* less a guide to the Concord woods and more a " 'handbook of an economy that endeavors to refute Adam Smith,' 'a book of social criticism' aimed at the principles of laissez-faire capitalism."[21] Although it might be argued that Parrington's focus on *Walden* as social critique replaced one sort of partial reading with another, his interpretation set the tone for the next decade and, as Michael Meyer puts it, constitutes "the first significant American attempt to find Thoreau's politics . . . useful."[22]

Predictably, commentary in the thirties tended to focus on Thoreau's economic critique, but, more important, *Walden*'s stature as a key text in the oppositional canon also continued to increase. Henry Seidel Canby, whose 1939 biography was the first to consider seriously Thoreau's career as a writer, prefigured F. O. Matthiessen's *American Renaissance* in his *Classic Americans* of 1931, by claiming that *Walden, Moby-Dick, Leaves of Grass, The Scarlet Letter,* Emerson's *Essays,* and Poe's *Poems* were "the six most remarkable books of our single century of national existence."[23] Except for Poe's *Poems,* this is almost precisely the same list that Matthiessen was to make the core canon of American Renaissance (Matthiessen included Emerson's *Representative Men* rather than the *Essays,* one suspects, to preserve his neat temporal focus on books that were published between 1850 and 1855).

Perhaps the oddest testament to Thoreau's and *Walden*'s growing popularity in the thirties came at the end of the decade when the *Reader's Digest* first excerpted Van Wyck Brooks's treatment of Thoreau in *The Flowering of New England* in 1937 (titled "Thoreau, Master of Simplicity") and then, three years later, printed a seven-page condensation of *Walden.* The extracts provide a simplified (to say the least) snapshot of the book, chiefly relating to Thoreau's actual life and his activities at the pond, and emphasizing his self-sufficiency and jaunty self-confidence. As one might expect from the editorial bent of the magazine, the *Reader's Digest* Thoreau comes across as a restorative tonic for a nation in the grips of a long depression. The redaction process is pretty brutal; the editor plucked sentences and parts of sentences from different paragraphs in "Economy," for example, making new and mostly simple declarative sentences for a short paragraph that Thoreau never wrote:

> The mass of men lead lives of quiet desperation. Their incessant
> anxiety and strain is a well-nigh incurable form of disease. They
> have no time to be anything but machines. It is a fool's life.[24]

However bowdlerized and distorted, though, such excerpts mark a sort of
"arrival" for *Walden* in a popular medium not associated with either the academy or highbrow culture. Even more noteworthy than the excerpts themselves is the conceptual frame provided by the editor's preface: "*Walden* is the
record of an experiment in serene living, a venture in simplicity and discipline
as timely today as it was nearly 100 years ago. It is a book of which everyone
has heard, but which few now read."[25] Thus, it would seem that by 1940
Walden had surpassed canonical stature and become a classic in Mark
Twain's sense of a book that everyone praises but no one reads. Perhaps it
would be more accurate to say that this preface indicates that the book had
achieved a kind of hypercanonical status, with an autonomous existence in
popular culture independent from the text itself. Thoreau at Walden, like Rip
Van Winkle, Uncle Tom, Captain Ahab, and Tom Sawyer's whitewashed
fence, had become one of those American images or characters that everyone
knew, whether they had read the book they came from or not.

III

While critics of the thirties debated Thoreau's relevance for contemporary
social and economic problems, especially clashing over the usefulness of
his individualistic approach in an age of collective programs, the rise of American literature as an academic discipline and the growth of New Criticism
and close textual analysis set the stage for *Walden*'s emergence as one of
a small group of acknowledged classics of American literature. Above all,
F. O. Matthiessen's *American Renaissance* (1941) claimed for *Walden* a place
in the front rank of essential American books and set the pattern for two in-
terrelated and yet somewhat contradictory approaches that would dominate
the first period of post-World War II criticism and promotion of the book
within the academy. In keeping with the biblical associations of canonization,
Matthiesen's story of the creation of American literature constructed a Penta-
teuch of five texts published between 1850 and 1855 that formed the core
of the canon: *Moby-Dick, The Scarlet Letter, Representative Men, Leaves of
Grass,* and *Walden.* He made the case for *Walden* by scrutinizing it, like the

other works mentioned, "in accordance with the enduring requirements for great art," universal and essential qualities that didn't need explanation.[26] In *Walden*'s case, the particular marks of its greatness lay in its formal characteristics—language, structure, organic form—which surpassed the achievement of Thoreau's mentor Emerson, and its subject matter, especially the symbolic and mythic dimensions of what Matthiessen phrased as the artist's duty "to renew the primitive experience of the race."[27] Matthiessen gestured toward Thoreau's importance as a social critic and political thinker, but he gave this thrust of the book short shrift, summarizing Thoreau somewhat oxymoronically as tending toward "a left-wing individualism."[28] Tellingly, his discussion of *Walden*'s organic structure mostly leaves out "Economy" and "Where I Lived, and What I Lived For," the first third of the book and that portion containing the bulk of Thoreau's critique of contemporary cultural, social, and economic issues.

Nevertheless, it would be nearly impossible to exaggerate the importance of *American Renaissance* in promoting *Walden* to the "A" list of American books and setting the agenda for the next three decades of criticism. Although the distinguishing feature of all the writers Matthiessen treated was a Parringtonian commitment to the possibilities of democracy, Matthiessen's *Walden* was the work of a writer, not a naturalist or a social critic. Scholars following Matthiessen tended to extend his close readings of *Walden* along formalist, New Critical lines, as well as to probe the mythic and symbolic dimensions of the text and its heroic fables along lines mapped out in such works as Henry Nash Smith's *Virgin Land* (1950), R. W. B. Lewis's *The American Adam* (1955), and Charles Feidelson Jr.'s *Symbolism and American Literature* (1953). Close readings of the text were also supported by evidence from the *Walden* manuscripts, which survived in surprising completeness and were available to scholars at the Huntington Library. The evidence of at least eight extensive drafts of the book, with much revision evident within each draft, reinforced critical readings that stressed the verbal intricacy, careful craftsmanship, and highly self-conscious literariness of the book. The first critical book devoted exclusively to *Walden*, J. Lyndon Shanley's study of the manuscript and recreation of the first draft, *The Making of "Walden"* (1957), also established an important strain of inquiry that sought to understand the book by tracing its development from journal and lecture versions of the 1840s to a much longer and more complex book manuscript that Thoreau was revising as late as 1854.[29]

Both the myth/symbol approach and the close reading, which often worked in tandem and supported one another, operated under the still larger rubric of Cold War ideology, in which Thoreau was reconstructed as positive avatar of American values of freedom and rugged individualism, and Matthiessen's "left-wing" qualifier quietly disappeared. As Michael Meyer tersely summarized this trend, "The postwar tendency to minimize Thoreau's politics in favor of formalistic and mythic readings of his prose is related to the predominant politics of the period."[30] One of the underlying leaders of this movement not often given appropriate credit (or blame) was Perry Miller, whose influential anthologies of and writing about the Transcendentalists valorized the individualists Emerson and Thoreau over the associationist and socialist leanings of other Transcendentalists, especially those associated with utopian communities such as Brook Farm. To be sure, Miller didn't really much care for Thoreau—as his condescending introduction and notes to his edition of a "lost" volume of Thoreau's journal, *Consciousness in Concord* (1958), make clear; one suspects he found him lacking in the sterner masculine stuff of the Puritan forebears—but if Miller suspected Thoreau of homoerotic feelings, at least he wasn't a pinko.

The apogee of these approaches to *Walden* was reached in the late fifties and sixties with Sherman Paul's *The Shores of America: Thoreau's Inward Exploration* (1958) and Charles R. Anderson's *The Magic Circle of Walden* (1968). Paul's superb study might be said to have fulfilled the promise of Matthiessen's exploratory sketch by a rich New Critical reading of *Walden* as what he termed "A Fable of the Renewal of Life," and Anderson's book, a decade later, brought the trend to its perhaps inevitable culmination by reading *Walden* as if it were a poem, a self-contained verbal artifact, along lines sketched out long previously in *The Well-Wrought Urn*.

These studies, combined with the bountiful evidence of its lapidary construction, succeeded admirably in enshrining *Walden* as perhaps the Verbal Icon *par excellence* of American literature. Unfortunately, though, what these books, as well as many other studies of the period, tended to do in the process was to empty *Walden* of its literal content in favor of a concentration on its narrator's "inward exploration" (in Paul's phrase) and its dazzling surface of wit, imagery, metaphor, allusiveness, myth, rhetoric, structural patterns, and the like. Perhaps predictably, *Walden* had become a modernist text. The narrator's proclamation in the opening that he wished to say something to his contemporaries in New England concerning their "condition, especially [their] outward condition or circumstances in this world" was largely disregarded as a cue that this was a book intensely implicated in and about its own cultural moment. The other negative repercussion of the canonization of *Walden* on these terms is that the critical focus on this text tended to reconceive Thoreau as a one-book writer, and to create an unbridgeable gap between *Walden* and his other works, which came to be regarded, generally, as warm-up exercises for or fallings off from the achievement of *Walden,* a view which constituted the underlying narrative of Paul's book and probably still underpins much writing on Thoreau.

There was a major exception to this pattern, of course, for the sixties also saw the rise of Thoreau's reputation as a radical political thinker whose dissenting voice was claimed as a model and antecedent for a variety of causes, especially the Civil Rights movement and opposition to the Vietnam War. This shift codified an interesting change in the canonization of *Walden,* one that in effect appended "Civil Disobedience," or, as the textually reconstructed know it, "Resistance to Civil Government," as a kind of coda to it. As early as the 1960 Signet edition, Perry Miller's "Afterword" announces, "The short piece now known as 'Civil Disobedience' has through the years come to be thought of as an adjunct to *Walden,* so much so that a reprint of the book seems incomplete unless the essay accompanies it."[31] Most text editions, including the widely used Norton Critical Edition, continue this practice. In any event, the brushfire of interest in Thoreau as a radical political thinker at this time, epitomized by the popularity of the play *The Night Thoreau Spent in Jail,* rarely led to looking at *Walden* in the context of political thought and reform movements in the 1840s and 1850s; rather, it was all about Thoreau's relevance (or lack of it) for contemporary issues.

The most important book on *Walden* during the seventies was undoubtedly Stanley Cavell's *The Senses of Walden* (1972), a treatise by a philosopher that takes Thoreau's book to be a scripture directed at teaching its readers how to live and capable of sustaining and rewarding a kind of biblical exegesis. Despite its often abstruse philosophical language and argument, *The Senses of Walden* is also a culmination of the close-reading school, with the important difference that it directs our attention not to the persona of *Walden* or the formal characteristics of the text, but to ourselves, enjoining the reader to live deep and suck out all the marrow of life, with the text as a guide. Again, setting aside Cavell's particular philosophical vocabulary, one suspects that this kind of reading is indeed what readers privately at least have always done, and his book had the effect of legitimizing and providing a philosophical framework for such reading, as well as contributing to the enshrinement of *Walden* as even more than an icon of high literary culture.

The sixties and seventies, of course, following Rachel Carson's *Silent Spring*, also saw an exponential growth in environmental awareness and activism, an aspect of modern American culture in which Thoreau plays an important role as Buell's "environmental saint." But I mention this important theme only briefly, for two reasons. The more obvious is that Buell has already covered this subject admirably. The other is that this is an issue more bound up with Thoreau once again as a kind of hypercanonical figure of popular culture than with the book *Walden;* and, besides, *Walden* is not the text containing the most important of Thoreau's ecological and environmental observations. Buell summarizes these last points cogently: "Thoreau's importance as an environmental saint lies in being remembered, in the affectionate simplicity of public mythmaking, as helping to make the space of nature ethically resonant. He went a certain distance in *Walden;* he went farther thereafter."[32] Walden Pond itself, as a cultural shrine, is probably more important to the environmental movement than *Walden* the book.

IV

I now rush in where the sensible would fear to tread, and consider the arc of the last twenty years, following the demise of the traditional schools of criticism and the end of the Cold War, the rise (and sometimes fall) of such movements as deconstruction, structuralism and poststructuralism, the new historicism, cultural studies, feminist criticism, ecocriticism, and queer theory, along with dramatic enlargements in the American canon. It is obviously impossible to locate *Walden* precisely amid either the heteroglossia of contemporary criticism or the diverse and fragmented field of Thoreau studies itself, but here follow a couple of provisional groupings and a tentative assessment. One of the marked trends in recent decades, I think, has been to see *Walden* as clearly a less triumphant and less optimistic book with regard to the self-fashionings of its narrator. Walter Benn Michaels's 1977 article "*Walden's* False Bottoms" inaugurates the tendency I have in mind by demonstrating how the optimistic rhetoric of *Walden* continually undercuts and contradicts itself, and thereby frustrates the kind of scriptural reading that Cavell advocates.[33] And there is the trend in more recent studies, responding to the troubled Thoreau of Richard Lebeaux's psychoanalytic biographies, to focus on the darker, more pessimistic, and conflicted sides of the character who narrates *Walden:* Richard Bridgman's *Dark Thoreau* (1982) and Robert Milder's *Reimagining Thoreau* (1995) come to mind; more positive recent studies of *Walden,* like H. Daniel Peck's *Thoreau's Morning Work* (1990), which might in some ways be said to extend and deepen Sherman Paul's work, still focus also on the trope of loss as an underlying theme of the book.

Another prominent trend in recent decades has been toward studies focusing on the rhetoric and the language of the book, both on contemporary influences on Thoreau's language and language theory such as those by Gordon Boudreau, William C. Johnson Jr., Michael West, and Philip Gura; and from more contemporary theoretical perspectives, such as those by Frederick Garber and Henry Golemba in the nineties.[34]

If I were to attempt a sweeping generalization about the status of *Walden* as a canonical text on its 150th birthday, it seems to me that while it remains firmly ensconced in the canon, its status has been made somewhat problematic by virtue of what I might call its overcanonization—that is, the tendency mentioned earlier to situate it far above Thoreau's other writings, which tends in turn to render it more anomalous than it actually is and to diminish the overall coherence of Thoreau's work in its engagement with crucial social and intellectual issues of his day. The shrinking space available in anthologies as neglected texts are recovered exacerbates this problem, making it unlikely that students will be exposed to anything beyond selections from *Walden* and "Resistance to Civil Government," if that. There is, to be sure, work being done at present that resists this isolation and monumentalizing of the book by exploring Thoreau's developing interest in science, his journal and the relations of his published texts to it, and the late natural history writings recently edited by Brad Dean, for example; and there is a hopeful uptick in recent years in articles and books that treat different aspects of the contemporary cultural milieu of *Walden,* and thus bring us closer to what Thoreau had in mind when he said *Walden* was a book addressed to the outward conditions of those who were said to live in New England. In some ways the canonical status of *Walden* a hundred years ago was more favorable to balanced appreciation and understanding than its hypercanonical status today—when the sales of *Walden, Cape Cod,* and *The Maine Woods* were comparable, and it was typical for commentators to treat *Walden* as part of a larger canvas. One of the unfortunate consequences of canonization, of course, is that it tends to remove the canonized text from time and its historical circumstances and to place it on the shelf of supposedly timeless monuments. I trust that will not be the case with *Walden*, for it may be that it still has several more lives to live.

Notes

1. Lawrence Buell, *The Environmental Imagination: Thoreau, Nature Writing, and the Formation of American Culture* (Cambridge: Harvard University Press, 1995); see especially Part III, "Environmental Sainthood," 311–423.

2. See Wendell Glick, *The Recognition of Henry David Thoreau: Selected Criticism since 1848* (Ann Arbor: University of Michigan Press, 1969); Michael Meyer, *Several More Lives to Live: Thoreau's Political Reputation in America* (Westport, CT: Greenwood Press, 1977); Walter Harding and Michael Meyer, *The New Thoreau Handbook* (New York: New York University Press, 1980); Raymond R. Borst, *Henry David Thoreau: A Reference Guide, 1835–1899* (Boston: G. K. Hall, 1987); and Gary Scharnhorst, *Henry David Thoreau: A Case Study in Canonization* (Columbia, SC: Camden House, 1993); for Buell, see note 1.

3. *The Correspondence of Henry David Thoreau*, ed. Walter Harding and Carl Bode (1958; rpt. Westport, CT: Greenwood Press, 1974), 343.

4. Borst, *Thoreau: A Reference Guide*, 6–7; Scharnhorst, *Thoreau: A Case Study*, 10.

5. Borst, *Thoreau: A Reference Guide*, 14.

6. Walter Harding, *The Days of Henry Thoreau* (New York: Alfred A. Knopf, 1965), 340.

7. Scharnhorst, *Thoreau: A Case Study*, 11.

8. Harding, *Days*, 340–41.

9. Buell, *Environmental Imagination*, 348.

10. *Correspondence*, 515–16.

11. Ibid.

12. Buell, *Environmental Imagination*, 346.

13. Ibid., 357.

14. Harding and Meyer, *New Thoreau Handbook*, 219.

15. H. S. Salt, *Life of Henry David Thoreau* (1890; rpt. Hamden, CT: Archon Books, 1968), 176.

16. Scharnhorst, *Thoreau: A Case Study*, 53.

17. Ibid., 53–54.

18. John Macy, *The American Spirit in Literature* (1913; rpt. New York: Johnson Reprint Corporation, 1969), 11, 172, 183.

19. Buell, *Environmental Imagination*, 355.

20. Scharnhorst, *Thoreau: A Case Study*, 57; Harding and Meyer, *New Thoreau Handbook*, 220.

21. Scharnhorst, *Thoreau: A Case Study*, 59.

22. Meyer, *Several More Lives to Live* 42.

23. Scharnhorst, *Thoreau: A Case Study*, 61.

24. *The Reader's Digest* 37 (September 1940), 130.

25. Ibid., 129.

26. F. O. Matthiessen, *American Renaissance: Art and Expression in the Age of Emerson and Whitman* (Oxford: Oxford University Press, 1941), xi.

27. Ibid., 174.

28. Ibid., 77.

29. J. Lyndon Shanley, *The Making of "Walden"* (Chicago: University of Chicago Press, 1957); see also Ronald Earl Clapper, "The Development of *Walden:* A Genetic Text," Diss. in 2 vols., University of California, Los Angeles, 1967; Stephen Adams and Donald A. Ross, *Revising Mythologies: The Composition of Thoreau's Major Works* (Charlottesville: University Press of Virginia, 1988); and Robert Sattelmeyer, "The Remaking of *Walden*," in *Writing the American Classics,* ed. James Barbour and Tom Quirk (Chapel Hill: University of North Carolina Press, 1990), 53–78.

30. Meyer, *Several More Lives to Live,* 117.

31. Perry Miller, "Afterword," in *Walden and "On the Duty of Civil Disobedience"* (New York: New American Library, 1960), 254.

32. Buell, *Environmental Imagination,* 394.

33. Walter Benn Michaels, *Glyph* 1 (1977): 132–49.

34. Gordon V. Boudreau, *The Roots of Walden and the Tree of Life* (Nashville: Vanderbilt University Press, 1990); William C. Johnson Jr., *What Thoreau Said: "Walden" and the Unsayable* (Moscow: University of Idaho Press, 1991); Michael West, *Transcendental Wordplay: America's Romantic Punsters and the Search for the Language of Nature* (Athens: Ohio University Press, 2000); Philip F. Gura, *The Wisdom of Words: Language, Theology, and Literature in the New England Renaissance* (Middletown, CT: Wesleyan University Press, 1981); Frederick Garber, *Thoreau's Fable of Inscribing* (Princeton: Princeton University Press, 1991); and Henry Golemba, *Thoreau's Wild Rhetoric* (New York: New York University Press, 1990).

Lakes of Light

Modes of Representation in Walden

H. DANIEL PECK

In *Rural Hours* (1850), a work of bioregional literature published in the United States four years before *Walden,* Susan Fenimore Cooper took note of a significant change in American artistic and intellectual culture: "Some foundation for the change [a shift from abstraction to particularity] may doubtless be found in the fact, that all descriptive writing, on natural objects, is now much less vague and general than it was formerly; it has become very much more definite and accurate within the last half century." "[P]eople," she adds, "had grown tired of mere vapid, conventional repetitions, they felt the want of something more positive, more real."[1]

We know that Thoreau read at least part of *Rural Hours* while he was writing *Walden*[2] and, whether or not it directly influenced him, this passage unmistakably anticipates certain aspects of his book. Furthermore, its sentiments are in accord with some contemporary understandings of *Walden,* which have emphasized its relation to natural history. These understandings—influenced by the new ecocriticism—have, to some extent, supplanted older mythic and poetic readings of the work.[3] In this view, *Walden*'s particularity contrasts with the abstracted nature that characterizes much of nineteenth-century American antebellum literature. It thus appears as an antidote to the philosophical idealism of the age, including the Transcendental symbolism of Thoreau's mentor Emerson. A focus on *Walden*'s concreteness is certainly not misdirected, and indeed has sharpened our sense of the very real nature of nature in this work.

But there is a problem here. Defining exactly what constitutes *Walden's* particularity is made complicated by the fact that we have to wait more than 170 pages for an extended description of the actual landscape of the Pond. This description occurs in "The Ponds," a chapter that is often regarded as the book's structural center but which in fact falls somewhat past the book's midpoint. Readers interested in description, as such, may wonder why they have had to wait so long for it.

By making this observation, I do not mean to suggest that *Walden,* prior to "The Ponds" chapter, is lacking in concrete descriptions of nature. At every stage of the book's development, we find a mixture of fact and truth, to employ Thoreau's own terms.[4] Even a predominantly ideological chapter like "Economy" has its share of descriptive moments. Yet it is striking to consider how little we learn about the landscape of Walden and its neighborhood prior to "The Ponds."

That Thoreau is aware of this deferral is consistent with what we know about the composition of the book. Very little of "The Ponds" was written during his two-year stay (1845–47) at Walden. In fact, most of the chapter appears to have been composed during and after 1852, in the final two years of the book's eight-year composition. At one point in the chapter, Thoreau, in an unusual gesture, locates the precise moment of his writing—"now, in the summer of '52" (*W* 180).[5] Some parts of "The Ponds" were written even later than 1852—deep into the final phases of composition.[6] That so much of this chapter was composed late suggests that Thoreau withheld the view that it affords, in some sense, even from himself, and that he was able to offer such a view only when the passage of time had enabled his revisioning and remembrance of the Walden experience.

Another way to think about this deferred description is that *Walden* began primarily as a work of social reform in which depictions of landscape were at the service of the larger argument, in something of the way that landscape serves as background and allegory in religious painting of the Middle Ages. Such depictions are necessarily partial (as, for example, in Thoreau's descriptions of the environment of his hut in "Economy"), and insofar as landscape figures as an important mode of representation during the first half of *Walden,* it figures largely in an intermittent and strategic way. But just as landscape, during the Renaissance, emerged to fill the canvas and became a center of meaning in its own right, it emerges halfway through *Walden*—in a kind of Renaissance moment—to fill the pages of this pivotal chapter.

It may also be true that, up to this point in his unconventional book, Thoreau has resisted extended landscape description because such description, at least the kind that Susan Fenimore Cooper calls "vapid" and "conventional," embodied for his generation so many prior understandings. In a work written, in part, to "wake my neighbors up" (W 84), landscape might just put them to sleep by speaking directly to their expectations and inviting their most predictable responses. One of the implicit challenges that Thoreau faced in writing "The Ponds" was to refigure landscape description in such a way as to deepen it to the level of his reformist and utopian purposes.

Thoreau's awareness of all these matters seems clear from the way he begins this chapter. The brief prefatory section concludes with one of *Walden*'s most famous passages, the one describing an experience of "midnight fishing from a boat by moonlight" (W 174):

> It was very queer, especially in dark nights, when your thoughts
> had wandered to vast and cosmogonal themes in other spheres, to
> feel this faint jerk, which came to interrupt your dreams and link
> you to Nature again. It seemed as if I might next cast my line up-
> ward into the air, as well as downward into this element which
> was scarcely more dense. Thus I caught two fishes as it were with
> one hook. (W 175)

In its supreme verticality, this image of fishing the heavens and the depths gets as close as Thoreau ever does in *Walden* to high Romantic symbolism, and the passage reads rather more like the ending of a chapter than a preface to one. Yet, immediately following this passage, and a break on the page, Thoreau moves in a very different direction, one that is less high than "low," less symbolic than descriptive, and less vertical than horizontal—which is to say, representational and analogical.[7] Here, then, is the passage that follows:

> The scenery of Walden is on a humble scale, and, though very
> beautiful, does not approach to grandeur, nor can it much concern
> one who has not long frequented it or lived by its shore; yet this
> pond is so remarkable for its depth and purity as to merit a par-
> ticular description. (W 175)

This "particular description," the passage makes clear, is the unfinished business of *Walden*. Up to this point Thoreau has given us only glimpses of the Pond, and now he is going to present a view of it that is both more comprehensive and more particularized than anything rendered earlier. At the beginning of the passage, the word "scenery," with its associations of panorama and pictorialism, suggests the larger view, and the phrase that closes the passage promises an empirical and focused examination. Both of these views will be rendered in this chapter, which is, all at once, one of the most site-specific and most lyrical chapters in *Walden*. The ways in which it combines these qualities are dependent upon Thoreau's manipulation of descriptive modes. And the fact that this is so substantial a chapter—the second longest, after "Economy"—suggests its importance and its pivotal place in the development of the book.

When Thoreau says that he is now going to provide "a particular description," I think we should take him at his word, and accept that this chapter is going to be very much about description and the activity of describing—that description is the category of thought into which Thoreau is now taking us. And if we are also going to be lifted into the realm of the lyrical or even the miraculous, it will be description that gets us there.

Thoreau's stated intention in "The Ponds" is to examine Walden for its specific features—its dimensions and size, its varying responses to climate ("Walden is blue at one time and green at another" [W 176]), its geography and ecology. But equally important is an unstated intention—to consider Walden *in* the particular, that is, as a thing in itself—a singular phenomenological entity. Walden's singularity is dramatized by a geological parable in which we learn that it has "no visible inlet nor outlet"; while the Concord River may once have flowed through it, now the Pond is "reserved and austere, like a hermit in the woods" (W 194), its remarkable purity thus preserved through isolation.

This is the Walden that stands alone, defined as a thing unto itself by its distinctive qualities. It is self-referring, and, so long as we are working in this descriptive frame of reference, the other ponds can be understood to point up Walden's special status. Flint's Pond, unfortunately named, is the largest of the neighboring ponds, yet, unlike Walden, it is "shallow, and not remarkably pure" (W 194). Fair Haven Pond is merely a widening of the Concord River, which is to say that it is not, like Walden, a "little world" (W 130) unto itself; it is not integral. Goose Pond, "of small extent" (W 197), is barely mentioned, its omission to be understood as a function of its inferiority to Walden. Pictorially, this Walden that stands alone is the "foreground" whose only "background" is the surrounding forest. In such a bipolar landscape, Walden establishes its singular status by distinguishing itself, through comparison and contrast, from the neighboring ponds, and by standing forth from its visual contexts. Bordered, highlighted, by its "stony shore" (*W* 197), it resonates as "a gem" (*W* 179) of the forest.

Yet, for all of Walden's distinctiveness, Thoreau, we recall, begins his description of it with a qualification: "The scenery of Walden is on a humble scale, and, though very beautiful, does not approach to grandeur." This distinction between grandeur and beauty implicitly calls attention to the European sublime (Byron's Alps, for example), as set against New England's more "humble," yet somehow more "beautiful," landscapes. From another perspective, Thoreau's employment of the terms "beautiful" and "grandeur" responds to the landscape aesthetics that he had inherited from English thinkers like William Gilpin, whose works he was actively reading in these final years of *Walden*'s composition. From them he learned to see landscape *as* scenery, and he depends upon their aesthetic categories.

Thoreau's relation to such categories, however, is complex. While his observations show his acceptance of terms such as beauty and grandeur, not to mention "scenery," they also reveal his restlessness with them. In his Journal, on August 6, 1852 (during one of *Walden*'s most formative periods), Thoreau had written as follows: "I wish he [Gilpin] would look at scenery sometimes not with the eye of an artist. It is all side screens & fore screens— and near distances—& broken grounds with him."[8] That is, Gilpin's is but a surface view of nature, and the qualities that most concern Thoreau in *Walden*, "depth and purity," are those that can be ascertained only through lived experience—sentiently, and through close observation. They are literally below the surface, and would not be immediately evident to someone taking the panoramic, distanced view, or the view required to produce a sense of grandeur.

European landscape aesthetics had been built upon the panoramic view, and Walden's "humble scale" thus implicitly becomes a characteristic distinguishing it as a certain kind of American landscape, and, more particularly, as Nina Baym has shown, a quintessentially New England (as opposed to Hudson River Valley) landscape.[9] In a related way, Thoreau's observation about Walden's "humble scale" reinforces the value he places on familiarization and inhabitation. Only when one "frequent[s]" the pond and lives "by its shore"—

experiences that depend on time and memory rather than upon the shock of the sublime—do its remarkable purity and beauty stand forth.

Thus, even as Thoreau uses "scenery" as his embracing term for landscape description, he sets out in this chapter implicitly to undermine the term's European lineage. Quickly, as the chapter proceeds, he identifies what *he* means by scenery. In the sentence following Thoreau's promise of a "particular description," he begins to make good on it, telling us for the first time the Pond's dimensions: "half a mile long and a mile and three quarters in circumference, and contain[ing] about sixty-one and a half acres" (W 175). This is the beginning of one important strain of natural description in the chapter. It includes a report on the seasonal variation of Walden's temperature ("[on] the sixth of March, 1846, the thermometer having been up to 65° or 70°" [W 183]), another on the "rise and fall of Walden at long intervals" (W 181), an inventory of its fish ("at least three different kinds" of pickerel [W 184]) and animals (frogs, tortoises, minks, mud turtles), as well as birds (kingfishers, gulls, and "one annual loon" [W 185]).

In Thoreau's Journal, empirical observations of this kind often continue uninterrupted for pages at a time, but here in *Walden* they appear briefly and intermittently, moving in and out of other, varying modes of representation. As we have seen, these modes include the scenic or pictorial: a description of "the beautifully scolloped southern shore" is followed by a celebration of reflected water as "the best foreground" for a forest "setting" (W 185). Another mode might be called the extravagantly metaphorical: the Pond famously imaged as "earth's eye" (W 186), and the shoreline trees figured as "the lips of the lake on which no beard grows" (W 181). Still another would be that of legendary association—the identification of certain objects like the "old log canoe" (W 190) and the mysterious tree tipped wrong-end-upward in the depths of the Pond—that evoke and elaborate Walden's deeper natural history. And there are, as well, allegorical elements in these descriptions; for example, in describing the "regularly paved" (W 182) appearance of the shoreline, Thoreau calls upon a village fable of an ancient upheaval caused by an Indian tribe's indiscretion, and of a squaw named Walden from whom, it is said, the Pond took its name.

One of the most important modes of representation in "The Ponds" is the lyrical: "I have spent many an hour, when I was younger, floating over [Walden's] surface as the zephyr willed, having paddled my boat to the middle, and lying on my back across the seats, in a summer forenoon, dreaming awake" (*W* 191). Yet, interestingly, this passage describes the past, not the present. It is Thoreau's "younger" self who is being characterized here, and this is the Walden of his youth—the one that, in an earlier chapter, he had called "that fabulous landscape of my infant dreams" (*W* 156). The diminished present weighs heavily on this reverie, which quickly gives way to loss, and the effect is to transform the lyrical into the elegiac: "But since I left those shores the woodchoppers have still further laid them waste. . . . How can you expect the birds to sing when their groves are cut down?" What follows is virtually a litany of loss: "Now the trunks of trees on the bottom, and the old log canoe, and the dark surrounding woods, are gone" (*W* 192).

What is most interesting about this passage, however, is how quickly Thoreau recovers himself. Immediately following his enumeration of Walden's losses we find this: "Nevertheless, of all the characters I have known, perhaps Walden wears best, and best preserves its purity" (*W* 192). "Nevertheless" is a verbal gesture of a distinctively pastoral kind. Rather than directly engaging the realities it displaces, it deflects them, turns them aslant. Its purpose is to smooth the temporarily ruffled surface of the pond, and to restore the idyll that has been interrupted.[10]

Thus, in the course of two pages we have moved from the lyrical to the elegiac to the pastoral, never once losing our balance. We keep our balance, in part, because these modes of representation do not compete with one another, but exist in a relation of relative equality, one receding as another becomes (temporarily) dominant. Sometimes, Thoreau overtly manages their transitions: "I have a faint recollection," he says, "of a little fish some five inches long, with silvery sides and a greenish back, somewhat dace-like in its character, which I mention here chiefly to link my facts to fable" (*W* 184).

All of these modes are interwoven in such a way as to provide the engine of the chapter's development. It might be said that the shifts of descriptive modality in "The Ponds" serve the same developmental function in this chapter as argumentation does in "Economy." These shifting modes of landscape description, and the variance that characterizes them, have both a *modulating* and a *moderating* effect, and they work toward—in Thoreau's phrase—"the equilibrium of the whole lake" (*W* 187); they work to stabilize his presentation.

The *OED* gives four or five meanings for "description," but they boil down to two: 1) representation of a generally pictorial kind, and 2) delineation, as in the activity of mapping. Interestingly, Thoreau holds this chapter centrally within the range of the first meaning, and, for the most part, defers delineation to a later chapter called "The Pond in Winter." There, rather than here, he provides a map of Walden, and it is in that later, more "scientific" chapter as well that Thoreau demonstrates through measurement that, contrary to local legend, Walden is not bottomless.[11]

This apportionment of different modes of description to these two chapters has the effect of reserving for "The Ponds" an essentially pictorial, or "aesthetic," quality; it broadens or dilates pictorial space, and in doing so emphasizes the idea of landscape as such. The chapter essentially creates the landscape of Walden, and the landscape thus created transcends the mere "scenery" that Thoreau attributed to English aestheticians such as Gilpin. In this way "The Ponds" chapter maintains its equilibrium through its commitment to a certain balanced register of description, description itself being generally a stabilizing and grounding mode of literary activity. The chapter is partly *about* keeping one's balance, and dramatizes this process.

Scholarship and criticism surrounding *Walden,* however, have traditionally not seen "The Ponds" this way. Charles Anderson's 1968 reading of *Walden* as a long lyric poem was especially influential in this regard. Anderson understood "The Ponds" chapter as the place where Thoreau, now making explicit his Emersonian legacy, fully identifies Walden as "a symbol of his transcendent self."[12] Commentators from later decades, including textual scholars with an agenda very different from Anderson's, have followed in line, seeing "The Ponds" as "the book's symbolic center," or, with a related emphasis, as "the central mystical chapter" of *Walden.*[13] A still more recent account understands "The Ponds" as "the mythological fulcrum of a new rhetoric of ascent."[14] In such interpretations, the mythical and mystical aspects of *Walden,* as they surface in "The Ponds," owe much to Thoreau's reimmersion in Romantic thought—especially the writings of Coleridge—during the late 1840s and early 1850s.[15]

Without denying that "The Ponds" reflects this influence, I think that such readings move to the level of the mythic faster and more decisively than Thoreau himself does.[16] Still, as we saw in the midnight fishing passage, there are moments in "The Ponds" that unmistakably evoke the Transcendental or symbolic mode, and another one occurs prominently as the climax of the chapter's first major movement. This is the passage in which Thoreau recognizes Walden as "the same woodland lake that I discovered so many years ago," and, looking into its waters, its "face," finds "that it is visited by the same reflection; and I can almost say, Walden, is it you?" (*W* 193).

The reflection of this landscape "unchanged" (*W* 193) since Thoreau's childhood—the Romantic myth of childhood imagination is powerfully at work here—prompts in him a profound moment of address and recognition. And surely this "face" is also Thoreau's own. Looking into these waters, he has, for a moment, found himself. Such a reading of this passage is consistent with the familiar Transcendental trope of reflection as the sign and medium of Reason. What Thoreau glimpses in this moment is not his inadequate temporal personality (the Coleridgean Understanding) but the unchanging ideal and eternal self reflected through time and nature.[17]

In this moment Thoreau can "almost" say, "Walden, is it you?", but not quite. One might understand this reservation as a form of modesty or humility; Thoreau knows he can never attain the purity of Walden. But there is, I believe, another reason for his hesitation. For Walden to become "you" in this sense would make it into me; it would involve the collapse, in Emersonian terms, of the NOT ME into the ME, and in the end this was not a viable position for Thoreau.[18] If it were, the chapter would end right here, with this moment of near epiphany. And the various modes of description that Thoreau had deployed up this point could be understood, retrospectively, as contributing to this key moment of recognition (re-cognition), which transcends all the chapter's earlier rendered landscape views. Here would be the picture of all pictures, that of the human soul.

But the chapter does not end here. It pauses and moves on. It may be that this moment of "almost saying" is as far as Thoreau can go in representing Walden as a thing unto itself, a form of representation that I would argue is implicitly related to Transcendental symbolism. Interestingly, the two paragraphs that immediately follow Thoreau's powerful question, "Walden, is it you?" work to intensify our sense of Walden's uniqueness. This is where we learn that it "has no visible inlet nor outlet"; though "in some other geologic period" it may, Thoreau speculates, have been connected to the Concord River (the river of time, of temporality), it now stands isolated, "like a hermit in the woods." "God forbid," he writes, that some "digging" should erode this privileged isolation and the purity it guarantees. Needless to say, Walden the hermit symbolizes Thoreau the hermit; its purity is the condition he seeks to attain for himself through isolation from the human community. Like the Pond as described in this chapter's famous pun, he is *"Walled-in"* (*W* 183).

But in the end neither Walden nor Thoreau can go it alone. In another context, I have written about certain underground currents in *Walden,* particularly in the haunting subchapter "Former Inhabitants," that express the writer's acknowledgment of his necessary connection to the human world, to his neighbors living and dead.[19] Walden too needs neighbors. It cannot, all by itself, carry the range of meanings and values that Thoreau needs it to carry, and in the final movement of the chapter he turns—more authentically than before—to a description of the other ponds in the neighborhood. In short, he turns away from defining Walden as a thing unto itself, and turns instead to defining Walden in its relations. The chapter, we should remember, is titled "The Ponds," not "The Pond."

As we look back upon Thoreau's moment of symbolic recognition— "Walden, is it you?"—from this subsequent perspective, it appears as just that, a moment, a gesture toward the symbolic mode, followed by a return to what now can be seen as the predominant descriptive mode of the chapter. Earlier, in a hydrologic context, Thoreau had spoken of how the other ponds "sympathize with Walden" (*W* 181). Now, in the closing paragraph of the chapter, he dramatizes this sympathetic relation by foregrounding what he calls his "Lakes of Light" (*W* 199), a phrase that refers to Walden and White Pond as co-equal landscapes of desire. The thing to notice about this passage from the closing paragraph of "The Ponds" is its insistent plurality, its conjunctive emphasis, its repetition of the pronoun "they":

> White Pond and Walden are great crystals on the surface of the earth, Lakes of Light. If they were permanently congealed, and small enough to be clutched, they would, perchance, be carried off by slaves, like precious stones, to adorn the heads of emperors; but being liquid, and ample, and secured to us and our successors forever, we disregard them, and run after the diamond of Kohinoor. They are too pure to have a market value; they contain no muck. How much more beautiful than our lives, how much more transparent than our characters, are they! (*W* 199)

While Thoreau had earlier referred to White Pond as Walden's "lesser twin" (*W* 197), making a curious, unexplained distinction between White Pond's attractiveness and Walden's beauty, he never indicates what is "lesser" about it. The key aspect of White Pond, in relation to Walden, is the fact that it *is* a twin. The chapter gains the lyric intensity of its closing moments not through transcendence but through the process of twinning, or what we might call aggregation: Lakes of Light. Essentially, Thoreau doubles the real, rather than pointing beyond it, as the means by which he valorizes Walden and the experience that it represents for him.

This method of aggregation is appropriate to what, in the chapter's penultimate sentence, Thoreau calls "the wild luxuriant beauty of Nature" (*W* 200). This luxuriant beauty is a very different kind of beauty from that of Gilpin's "scenery," on the one hand, and from the beauty of the Coleridgean Ideal, on the other. Thoreau has chosen another, middle way, which we might call Wordsworthian: "This is my lake country," he exclaims; "These, with Concord River, are my water privileges" (*W* 197). This "country," this assemblage, of lakes, which now interestingly embraces a river as well, is a spacious and comprehensive geography that radiates its reflected light back and forth across its elements rather than to a world beyond. On this point let us allow Thoreau the last word, which is indeed the closing sentence of "The Ponds": "Talk of heaven! ye disgrace earth" (*W* 200).

Notes

This essay is excerpted from a longer version published in *Midwest Studies in Philosophy* 28.1 (2004): 85–101 and appears here with the permission of that journal. The longer version, titled "Thoreau's Lakes of Light: Modes of Representation and the Enactment of Philosophy in *Walden*," includes a discussion of philosophical approaches to Thoreau, with special emphasis on Stanley Cavell's *The Senses of Walden*.

1. Susan Fenimore Cooper, *Rural Hours* (1850), ed. Rochelle Johnson and Daniel Patterson (Athens: University of Georgia Press, 1998), 208.
2. In a journal entry of October 8, 1852, Thoreau mentions reading a newspaper report about a fisherman catching a loon eighty feet below the surface of Seneca Lake in New York State, and comments, "Miss Cooper had said the same," as indeed she does on the first page of the opening section of *Rural Hours* (4). For the relevant journal entry, see *Journal 5: 1852–1853, The Writings of Henry D. Thoreau*, ed. Patrick F. O'Connell (Princeton: Princeton University Press, 1997), 368. I am indebted to Robert Sattelmeyer, author of *Thoreau's Reading: A Study in Intellectual History with Bibliographical Catalogue* (Princeton: Princeton University Press, 1988), for alerting me to this passage. For a comparison of *Walden* and *Rural Hours* around environmental issues, see Rochelle Johnson, "*Walden, Rural Hours,* and the Dilemma of Representation," in *Thoreau's Sense of Place: Essays in American Environmental Writing*, ed. Richard J. Schneider (Iowa City: University of Iowa Press, 2000), 179–93.

3. The most comprehensive ecocritical study of Thoreau is Lawrence Buell's *The Environmental Imagination: Thoreau, Nature Writing, and the Formation of American Culture* (Cambridge: Harvard University Press, 1995).

4. An early instance of this distinction, central to *Walden,* appears in Thoreau's essay "The Natural History of Massachusetts," where he writes, "Let us not underrate the value of a fact; it will one day flower in a truth," in *Excursions and Poems,* vol. 5 of *The Writings of Henry David Thoreau,* ed. Bradford Torrey and Francis H. Allen (Boston: Houghton Mifflin, 1906), 130. The essay first appeared in *The Dial* 3 (July 1842).

5. Henry David Thoreau, *Walden,* ed. J. Lyndon Shanley (Princeton: Princeton University Press, 1971), 180. All subsequent citations of *Walden* are from this edition, and follow quotations in parentheses.

6. For the composition of *Walden,* see J. Lyndon Shanley, *The Making of Walden with the Text of the First Version* (Chicago: University of Chicago Press, 1957); Steven Adams and Donald Ross Jr., *Revising Mythologies: The Composition of Thoreau's Major Works* (Charlottesville: University Press of Virginia, 1988); and Ronald Earl Clapper, "The Development of *Walden*: A Genetic Text," Diss. in 2 vols., University of California, Los Angeles, 1967.

7. For the "horizontal" and associative vision of nature in Thoreau's Journal, see my *Thoreau's Morning Work: Memory and Perception in "A Week on the Concord and Merrimack Rivers," the Journal, and "Walden"* (New Haven: Yale University Press, 1990), especially chap. 3.

8. For the journal passage that contains Thoreau's comments on Gilpin, see 283–84 of the Princeton edition *Journal* 5, cited in note 2. For Thoreau's equally dissatisfied response to the nature aesthetics of John Ruskin, see a journal entry of October 6, 1857, in which he reflects on his reading of Ruskin's *Modern Painters*: "I am disappointed in not finding it a more out-of-door book. . . . He does not describe Nature as Nature, but as Turner painted her, and though the work betrays that he has given a close attention to Nature, it appears to have been with an artist's and critic's design" (*The Journal of Henry David Thoreau,* ed. Bradford Torrey and Francis H. Allen, vol. 10 [Boston: Houghton Mifflin, 1906], 69).

9. Nina Baym, "English Nature, New York Nature, and *Walden's* New England Nature," in *Transient and Permanent: The Transcendentalist Movement and Its Contexts,* ed. Charles Capper and Conrad Edick Wright (Boston: Massachusetts Historical Society, 1999), 168–89.

10. For an extended treatment of the pastoral dimension of this passage, see my essay "The Crosscurrents of *Walden's* Pastoral," in *New Essays on Walden,* ed. Robert F. Sayre (Cambridge: Cambridge University Press, 1992), 73–94.

11. For an interesting discussion of Thoreau's measuring the depth of the Pond, and of measurement generally in his work, see Laura Dassow Walls, *Seeing New Worlds: Henry David Thoreau and Nineteenth-Century Natural Science* (Madison: University of Wisconsin Press, 1995), 109–12.

12. Charles R. Anderson, *The Magic Circle of Walden* (New York: Holt, Rinehart, and Winston, 1968), 225.

13. Adams and Ross, *Revising Mythologies*, 183, 171.

14. Robert Milder, *Reimagining Thoreau* (Cambridge: Cambridge University Press, 1995), 121.

15. Thoreau's reading of Coleridge's *Aids to Reflection* in the early 1840s must have powerfully reinforced for him the idea of nature as a transcendent symbol of spirit that he had encountered in Emerson's *Nature* in the 1830s. But the work by Coleridge that Thoreau seems to have read closest to the final phase of *Walden*'s composition is *Hints toward the Formation of a More Comprehensive Theory of Life*, which would have emphasized for him the importance of nature's particularity as well as its symbolic meanings. See Robert Sattelmeyer and Richard A. Hocks, "Thoreau and Coleridge's *Theory of Life*," in *Studies in the American Renaissance*, ed. Joel Myerson (Charlottesville: University Press of Virginia, 1985), 269–84; cf. William Rossi, " 'The Limits of an Afternoon Walk': Coleridgean Polarity in Thoreau's 'Walking,'" *ESQ: A Journal of the American Renaissance* 33 (2nd Quarter 1987): 94–109. Russell B. Goodman discusses the "Romantic empiricism" of Coleridge in his *American Philosophy and the Romantic Tradition* (Cambridge: Cambridge University Press, 1990), 20ff.

16. An implicit corrective to such readings is an insightful essay by Barry Tharaud, "Being and Transcendence in Thoreau and Heidegger," *Journal of American Culture and Literature* (1995–1996): 37–56. Focusing on "The Ponds" chapter of *Walden*, Tharaud writes, "While we often think of Thoreau's style as highly concentrated, convoluted, and metaphorical, it actually has a range of modulations that are appropriate to the mode of consciousness that it momentarily embodies" (38).

17. I am indebted to William Rossi for helping me articulate the Coleridgean, symbolic meanings of reflection in this passage, and for alerting me to the following related passage in Thoreau's *A Week on the Concord and Merrimack Rivers* (Princeton: Princeton University Press, 1980): "We noticed that it required a separate intention of the eye, a more free and abstracted vision, to see the reflected trees and the sky, than to see the river bottom merely" (48).

18. Emerson introduces the term "NOT ME" to signify everything outside the soul in his "Introduction" to *Nature* (1836): *The Collected Works of Ralph Waldo Emerson*, vol. 1: *Nature, Addresses, and Lectures*, Introductions and Notes by Robert E. Spiller; text established by Alfred R. Ferguson (Cambridge: Harvard University Press, 1971), 8.

19. See *Thoreau's Morning Work*, chap. 6.

Thoreau and Idealism

"Face to Face to a Fact"

DAVID M. ROBINSON

IN LIGHT of the recent critical emphasis on Thoreau's engagement with empirical studies of plant and animal life, it is crucial to see his increasing attention to the detail of the material world as one part of a larger project of categorization and explanatory theorizing about the unifying laws and structures of the universe. *Walden* and the Journal are permeated with moments of observational intensity, moments that are not "mystical" or "transcendent" in any ordinary sense, but which certainly do not strike us as ordinary moments of perception, even in the context of close scientific observation. These interpretive encounters are legion, and include some of the most memorable moments of *Walden,* such as the description and symbolic personification of Walden in "The Ponds" and its measurement in "The Pond in Winter," the account of animal life in "Brute Neighbors," and the sand foliage passage in "Spring." These moments are marked by Thoreau's keen observational eye and his usually vivid account of the process by which he comes into fuller recognition of the world around him, a world to which, he implies, we should all be more attentive. But they display not only an arresting sense of detail, but a concomitant desire to reach for a more comprehensive category of explanation for the particular phenomenon. Thoreau consistently tries to see a particular fact or event not as a random or unique occurrence but as indicative of a more comprehensive idea or law. "Men esteem truth remote," he writes, "in the outskirts of the system, behind the farthest star, before Adam and after the last man. In eternity there is indeed something true and sublime. But all these times and places and occasions are now and here. God himself culminates in the present moment, and will never be more divine in the lapse of all the ages" (*W* 96–97).[1]

Such a conception neither denigrates nor subordinates "facts" and their study, nor does it refuse the intellectual task of categorization, generalization, and system-building. The intellectual ferment of *Walden,* the element that so vividly communicates a sense of philosophical breakthrough, is Thoreau's growing recognition that "fact" and "theory" are inextricably fused, that the observation or close reading of detail is the entry point of comprehensive and ordered knowledge. A "fact" is always a bundle of relations, the product of a convergence of many entities and events. To "know" a particular fact, he saw with increasing clarity and excitement, is to be given a glimpse into a much wider array of processes and circumstances, an event that is revelatory in every sense.

"If you stand right fronting and face to face to a fact, you will see the sun glimmer on both its surfaces, as if it were a cimeter, and feel its sweet edge dividing you through the heart and marrow, so you will happily conclude your mortal career" (*W* 98). Thoreau's strange celebration of death by fact suggests the dual quality of such moments of insight. The "fact" is the dividing edge, on either side of which we see the sun, here the representation of both illumination and power. Those two surfaces, coordinate aspects of the same fact or object, are the particular detail and the inclusive law that constitute such revelations. We are indeed "divided" by this edge, asked to look in two directions simultaneously, toward the unique specificity of things and to the larger frames of reference that make them discernible. We are permitted to achieve this seemingly impossible feat in that single moment when fact opens itself to us, or as Thoreau would have it, opens *us* in its presence.

Thoreau of course wants passionately to be so divided. The passage captures his desire to find a way to hold fact and law in a correlative unity, to perceive always with a fruitfully dual posture that never abandons the particular or dismisses its inclusive and defining category. He struggled to keep his empirical studies within a larger purposive framework that included philosophical speculation and the search for a unifying theory of the nature and structure of the universe. "Facts should only be as the frame to my pictures," he wrote in 1851. "They should be material to the mythology which I am writing" (JP 4:170).

Thoreau's skill and dedication in empirical study, signaled by his closely

observed field notes and his collecting of botanical and even zoological specimens, set him apart from Emerson temperamentally, and most readers of
Emerson and Thoreau have recognized Thoreau as a more "physical" or embodied thinker, closer in a practical way to the natural world than Emerson,
and somewhat less ethereal in his imagination and forms of expression. The
year after Thoreau's death, Emerson praised, with a touch of envy, his gift for
concrete metaphor and vivid description, attributing it to "the vigor of his
constitution."

> That oaken strength which I noted whenever he walked or
> worked or surveyed wood lots, the same unhesitating hand with
> which a field-laborer accosts a piece of work which I should shun
> as a waste of strength, Henry shows in his literary task. He has
> muscle, & ventures on & performs feats which I am forced to de-
> cline. In reading him, I find the same thought, the same spirit that
> is in me, but he takes a step beyond, & illustrates by excellent
> images that which I should have conveyed in a sleepy generality.[2]

Robert Kuhn McGregor has described this difference as much more than
a question of temperament or style, finding in Emerson's philosophical idealism a major point of distinction between them and a significant obstruction
to Thoreau's intellectual development.[3] In developing a portrait of Thoreau as
one of the first ecologists, McGregor depicts Emerson's idealism as a subordination of the material world, a theory that reduced "Nature to the point of
possible nonexistence" and also devalued Thoreau's real scientific expertise.
"By devaluing the importance of the facts of natural history, Emerson reduced
to a mere symbol a portion of the world where Henry possessed some real
knowledge." For McGregor, Thoreau's development was a struggle to throw
off Emersonian idealism in order to become a naturalist.[4]

At issue here is the complex question of Emerson's influence (and
Thoreau's "originality"), an influence that is unquestionably significant but
very hard to measure and assess. There was a deep bond between the two
men and a shared vision and sense of purpose, but also, as we have come
to see more clearly, a tension and a growing sense of betrayal and failed intimacy in their relationship. But McGregor also raises a question that is vital
to our understanding of the motives and methods with which Thoreau perceived the natural world. In what ways, and with what impact, did Emerson's

idealistic theorizing affect the impressionable and intellectually hungry Thoreau? Did an idealism that seems to subordinate the material world philosophically become a cumbersome hindrance to Thoreau's perceptual engagement with nature?

Emerson's "noble doubt . . . whether nature outwardly exists" (CW 1:29) is one of the more striking and controversial aspects of *Nature*. But his vivid account of idealism was not a novel or unique philosophical theory for Thoreau, but one articulation among several of the problem of reconciling the singularity of things with their equally compelling similarities and relations. Emerson's seemingly ethereal dismissal of nature seems strange and even somewhat sinister to many present-day twenty-first-century readers, who react to it as a dismissal of the reality of bodily experience. Those same readers are likely to feel an ardent sense of kinship with Thoreau because of his compelling descriptions of his experience in the natural world and his implicit advocacy of the preservation of the wild. Emerson's idealism thus strikes the modern reader as alien to Thoreau's central message and purpose.

Thoreau, however, found in *Nature* less a denial of the reality and specificity of the material world than a theory that gave facts significance because of their interrelations. He brought to his reading of *Nature* an already well-developed sense of the Platonic tradition and of eighteenth-century idealism. As he was formulating his own sense of an intellectual mission, idealism suggested to him that the task of philosophy is both to observe and to speculate, to collect facts and to synthesize them into larger categories and explanatory systems. Thoreau's interest in idealism was thus more than a deferential imitation of Emerson. He shared Emerson's concern with a set of questions that idealist philosophy was attempting to answer: How can we understand the many particulars of experience as constituting coherent patterns or categories, or of providing discernible similarities among themselves? How can we think of the things of the world as related, or of our own relation to the world? How can the mind comprehend matter? These are among the oldest of philosophical questions, but they posed a fresh challenge to Thoreau, who was introspective, inclined to philosophical speculation, and keenly observant of the natural world.

In the last issue of the *Dial* in 1844, James Elliot Cabot wrote an essay that emphasized how idealism had framed the epistemological basis of modern thought: "Modern speculation, therefore, has returned to the fundamental problem of human science; and asks, first of all, 'Can we know anything?'"[5]

Nature had been Emerson's attempt to address this question, and his conclusion, that a particular fact can be known completely only as one part of a much larger web of relations and interconnections, proved to be a dynamic and energizing principle for Thoreau. Idealism remained at the center of the continuing discourse among the Transcendentalists, who kept these issues alive for him through the 1840s and 1850s as he was becoming more committed to his field studies in natural history.

A close examination of Emerson's discussion of idealism in *Nature,* moreover, suggests another reason for its appeal to Thoreau, one that continued well into his Walden experiment and beyond. Emerson was not proposing an idealism that made nature disappear, but an idealism that made nature dynamic. He presented idealism as a theory that undermined the common view of matter as inert, and of nature as fixed or static. Idealism was for Emerson, as it was for Thoreau, a way to confirm the ever-mutating energy of the material world. Thoreau was an attentive reader who would not have missed Emerson's nuanced discussion of the paradox of disappearing nature.

To begin with, Emerson rejected the naïve idea that idealism should alter our behavior in relation to material things. Most telling is the ironic humor of Emerson's guilty confession that there is "something ungrateful" about his theorizing, and his resulting declaration of his innocent devotion to nature. "I have no hostility to nature, but a child's love to it. I expand and live in the warm day like corn and melons. Let us speak her fair. I do not wish to fling stones at my beautiful mother, nor soil my gentle nest" (CW 1:35–36). This disarming rhetoric responds to our instinctive mistrust of idealism by allowing Emerson to explain how idealism is both misperceived and unacknowledged in daily life, a part of the fabric of our ordinary experience even while we reject it on the grounds of common sense. Our capacity to interact with and use the material world, and our obligation to respect its laws and operations, are not open to question or alteration. "Whether nature enjoy a substantial existence without, or is only in the apocalypse of the mind," he argued, "it is alike useful and alike venerable to me" (CW 1:29). The "permanence of laws" remained inviolable whatever the ontological constitution of nature, and only "the frivolous make themselves merry with the Ideal theory, as if its consequences were burlesque" (CW 1:29).

This quality of permanence did not mean that the material world was dead or inert, or that there was no essential relation between it and our consciousness. One of Emerson's most amusing illustrations of the theory of idealism is his recommendation that we view the world through our legs, one of several examples of optical distortions that serve to undermine the settled familiarity and solidity of the world. "Turn the eyes upside down, by looking at the landscape through your legs, and how agreeable is the picture, though you have seen it any time these twenty years!" (*CW* 1:31). The appeal is that the familiar is made new, the fixed is made indeterminate. Our sense of the variety and richness of things is reconfirmed, and the possibilities of experience are vastly expanded.[6]

The fundamental perceptual shift that he describes as idealism replaces a static world with a dynamic one, a detached or isolated world with one that shares with us a fundamental identity. Thus even when he refers to nature as "an accident and an effect," his actual purpose is to reinvest it with a significance that will pull us into closer relation. "It is the uniform effect of culture on the human mind, not to shake our faith in the stability of particular phenomena, as of heat, water, azote; but to lead us to regard nature as a phenomenon, not a substance; to attribute necessary existence to spirit; to esteem nature as an accident and an effect" (*CW* 1:30). The distinction between "substance" and "phenomenon" is critical, the first indicating a fixed and inert entity, and the second a convergence of energies or forces. A phenomenon is both in process and in relation, and represents nature's openness and mutability, and the affinity of all its constituent parts. As H. Daniel Peck has observed, "the term that Thoreau most often uses to reconcile the power of the creative eye with the independent status of the world is 'phenomenon.' "[7]

Emerson speaks of idealism less in terms of its absolute truth than of its relative advantage, its pragmatic effect on the human ability to respond to and reshape experience. "It is essential to a true theory of nature and of man, that it should contain somewhat progressive" (*CW* 1:36), he argued. The phenomenal quality of nature implies its mobile and pliant quality as well, and suggests a progressive dynamism that mirrors human nature. "Nature is not fixed but fluid. Spirit alters, moulds, makes it" (*CW* 1:44). To understand the fluidity of nature is to recognize a correspondent energy within that is the basis of constructive and purposive action. "Know then, that the world exists for you. For you is the phenomenon perfect" (*CW* 1:44). This is less a justification for the subordination of nature, as many modern readers might at first suspect, than a declaration of the unperceived harmony between nature and the soul, making men and women an essential component of the "phenomenon" of nature that Emerson has been describing. This recognition begins "when the fact is seen under the light of an idea," making us understand that "a fact is true poetry, and the most beautiful of fables" (*CW* 1:44).

The recognition of nature as a changing, multifarious "phenomenon" of manifold relations takes us more deeply and securely into the world of facts rather than divorcing us from that world. "The invariable mark of wisdom is to see the miraculous in the common," Emerson wrote. "What is a day? What is a year? What is summer? What is woman? What is a child? What is sleep?" (*CW* 1:44). These questions about the nature of ordinary experience are the most profound, and open the interconnected fabric of phenomena that we call nature. To face a fact, then, is to face the world, to see the particular thing or event clearly and directly, but not in isolation. The most crucial lessons of *Walden* are Thoreau's repeated enactments of the intimate connection between observation and synthesis. The larger identities and relationships of things, their ideal qualities, yield the specific, factual identities to Thoreau, just as their specific identities inevitably suggest their relationships and their partaking of larger categories of identity.

Thoreau's celebration of "fact" and his demonstration of the fruits of detailed observation in *Walden,* however insightful and philosophically significant, betray a growing self-doubt about the course of his intellectual development and the state of his philosophical and speculative powers. At times he felt himself to be drying up intellectually, and though drawn temperamentally toward more intensive projects of field observation and data collection, he distrusted his own tendency to become a collector of information. In August 1851, after his stay at Walden but before he had finally revised and reshaped his manuscript, he confessed his struggle to rein in the increasingly dominant empirical side of his personality.

> I fear that the character of my knowledge is from year to year becoming more distinct & scientific—That in exchange for views as wide as heaven's cope I am being narrowed down to the field of the microscope—I see details not wholes nor the shadow of the whole. I count some parts, & say 'I know'. The cricket's chirp now fills the air in dry fields near pine woods. (JP 3:380)

Thoreau senses a certain dishonesty in claiming to "know" when that knowledge excludes the larger frame of reference that invests details with their significance. But this worried self-analysis leads to an observation of the "cricket's chirp," the kind of detail that he has just labeled as problematic. While Thoreau's fascination with the details of the natural world grows, he continues to doubt that such details can in themselves be fulfilling. He fears that he is gaining the particulars of the world, but losing his soul.

This tension between the close observation of the particular and the more expansive pursuit of the whole sharpened for Thoreau in the late 1840s and early 1850s, as he was drawn more directly into the growth of scientific study at Harvard. In 1847 Louis Agassiz began a major effort to build Harvard's presence in science. Committed to a theory of the "special creation" of particular species, as opposed to a developmental theory that would later be articulated by Darwin, Agassiz began an extensive effort to gather and preserve large numbers of animal specimens and developed a network of field naturalists to collect them. Thoreau was one of his cooperating colleagues in this endeavor, enlisted by James Elliot Cabot, who was Agassiz's assistant and a *Dial* contributor. Laura Dassow Walls has noted that Thoreau devoted a month or more to such hunting and capturing in 1847, his first spring at Walden, a detail that he does not include in his narrative of his life at the pond. "What are we to make," Walls asks, "of a Thoreau who so cheerfully trapped, packed, and shipped so many of his Walden 'friends' and neighbors to Harvard's halls of science?" While he "seems to have lost interest quickly" in such collection, and returned to his more literary projects while at the pond, the experience had a definite impact on him. Even though Agassiz's scientific theories had at best a limited appeal to Thoreau, participating in such collecting provided him with the opportunity to observe and participate in the systematic fieldwork of scientific observation and collection. Though his misgivings about the activity surfaced quickly, the work had, as Walls argues, reinforced his penchant for vigilant alertness and observational acuity in the field, and reinforced what he felt were his growing tendencies to move "away from a grand and abstract transcendentalism toward a detailed observation of the specifics of nature, in all its unaccountable diversity."[8]

That Thoreau excelled in this work of field observation, data collection and recording, and specimen gathering, is unquestionable, but his continuing uneasiness about the ends of such work is suggested in his reaction to a questionnaire sent him by the American Association for the Advancement of Science asking him "to fill the blanks against certain questions—among which the most important one was—what branch of science I was specially interested in." Unable to answer the questions as he felt he should—"I felt that it would be to make myself the laughing stock of the scientific community"—he was "obliged to speak to their condition and describe to them that poor part of me which alone they can understand." The questionnaire could not get at the vital truth about him: "The fact is I am a mystic—a transcendentalist—& a natural philosopher to boot. Now I think—of it—I should have told them at once I was a transcendentalist—that would have been the shortest way of telling them that they would not understand my explanations" (JP 5:469–70). Thoreau's insistence on his dual identity as a "transcendentalist" and a "natural philosopher" and his derisive discomfort with the narrow categories that the fields of "science" offered him are important reminders of a tension that sharpened for him through the 1850s, years which were marked by his struggle to balance, and finally to reconcile, this seemingly dual identity.

Even as his interest in gathering the facts that now dominated the study of "natural history" was growing, it is perhaps somewhat surprising to find that his interest in Hinduism was rekindled by an 1848 article by James Elliot Cabot, an essay that, as Robert D. Richardson Jr. argues, "gave Thoreau an added impetus to explore Hinduism as a powerful independent corroboration of the central concept of Idealism" and initiated an extensive reading project on Hinduism. The impact of Thoreau's immersion in Hinduism can be seen in *Walden,* with its extensive network of allusions to Hindu texts.[9]

Cabot's article was less an essay than a compilation of passages from recent translations of the *Vishnu Purana,* the *Bhagavat Gita,* and other Hindu texts, providing a brief anthology of Hindu wisdom and philosophical precepts. Cabot explained that he had gathered "fragments of a speculative character" from "the theogonies and myths of the Hindoos." These fragments did not "properly [amount] to a system," but they did represent "an attempt to theorize on the Universe." While Cabot kept his own explication and theorizing to a minimum, the selection and arrangement of his compilation did have a controlling thesis, one of particular relevance to Thoreau's own philosophical concerns in the late 1840s and early 1850s. Cabot describes the development of "three very distinct epochs" in Hindu literature, beginning with "the age of the Vedas," which shows "little trace of reflection, or of intense religious consciousness." The succeeding era, "the age of the Puranas and the *Bhagavat Gita,* is a meditative, mystical period, during which speculation

among the Hindoos reached its highest point." That high point has been followed by a long "age of commentators, of subtile distinctions, and of polemics," a "Scholastic Age" secondary to the creative age that preceded it.[10] Cabot
argued that the meditative and mystical era of the *Bhagavat Gita,* "the essence of the Hindoo metaphysics," could be expressed in one fundamental
precept: "the reduction of all Reality to pure, abstract Thought." Though this
idea cannot be illustrated by "a methodical arrangement of propositions," it is
nevertheless a "constant theme," expressed metaphorically in "often sublime
imagery." "The main principle of Hindoo Idealism—that Reality is equivalent
to pure abstract Soul or Thought, unexistent, and thus simple and unformed;
in a word, pure Negation,—is presented especially under the aspect of the
unity and identity of all things in the Deity."[11]

Thoreau read Cabot's essay with care, copying out a number of quotations,
including the following passage from the *Vishnu Purana:*

> Liberation, which is the object to be effected, being accom-
> plished, discriminative knowledge ceases. When endowed with
> the apprehension of the nature of the object of inquiry, then there
> is no difference between it and supreme spirit; difference is the
> consequence of the absence of true knowledge. When that igno-
> rance which is the cause of the difference between individual and
> universal spirit is destroyed, finally and for ever, who shall make
> that distinction between them which does not exist?[12]

Perception is described here as a process of unification, in which the isolated part is reunited with its original whole through the act of perception.
"Difference," the result of an initial act of discriminating perception, is the
condition that complete knowledge hopes eventually to overcome.

The idea that "difference is the consequence of the absence of true knowledge" had important implications for Thoreau's conception of his work as
a naturalist, especially as he took up the more detailed activities of data
and specimen collection. The empirical accumulation of facts could be justified only as one stage of a process that ultimately aimed at an explanation of
the inclusive whole of nature. Thoreau's immersion in the world of "fact"
in the late 1840s and early 1850s was accompanied then by a continuing, indeed renewed, interest in idealism, significantly reinforced by his interest in
Hinduism.

It seems clear from this seemingly incongruent pattern of study and reading that the intensity with which Thoreau engaged in empirical science in the late 1840s and early 1850s did not undermine his interest in and broad adherence to idealism, if we give that term the comprehensive characterization that Thoreau did. One view of Thoreau's intellectual development, based largely on the increasingly factual character of his Journal entries through the 1850s, is that for better or worse he increasingly surrendered to his passion for fact and detail, and became progressively distanced from the kind of philosophical speculation that Emerson had shown him. But Thoreau's persistent efforts in *Walden* and beyond to push specific observations toward more encompassing theories were a response to his fear of losing his capacity to see "wholes." This fear is also related to a worried sense of personal declension and inadequacy that haunted him in the early 1850s as he revised and augmented the *Walden* manuscript.[13]

Thoreau's struggle to reconcile the particularized empiricism of Agassiz and others with the quest for unified wholes that were represented by the traditions of both Western idealism and Hindu mythology was intensified by a more personal crisis of confidence in his own perceptual capabilities. On July 16, 1851, Thoreau confessed, "Methinks my present experience is nothing my past experience is all in all." He fears the fading of his perceptual power, of a present whose intensity is dwarfed by a remembered past. "I think that no experience which I have today comes up to or is comparable with the experiences of my boyhood—And not only this is true—but as far back as I can remember I have unconsciously referred to the experience of a previous state of existence. 'Our life is a forgetting' &c" (JP 3:305). Underlying this Wordsworthian lament is a wish for a liminal experience in which the boundaries of self and nature evaporate, and we experience an unusual sense of both harmony and elevation. "Formerly methought nature developed as I developed and grew up with me. My life was extacy. In youth before I lost any of my senses—I can remember that I was all alive—and inhabited my body with inexpressible satisfaction, both its weariness & its refreshment were sweet to me. This earth was the most glorious musical instrument, and I was audience to its strains" (JP 3:305–6). Thoreau associates the health and vigor of youth with a bond with the natural world, and expresses some alarm at the progressive diminishment of that bond.[14]

But what of Thoreau's project both to live and to describe the "natural life" under these conditions? The "simple and sincere account of his own life"

(W 3) that he had set out to provide had become deeply problematic. Thoreau's ultimate completion of *Walden*, made possible around 1852 by a breakthrough in his sense of the work's structure and a corresponding recovery of purpose and vision, was in part a response to this sense of intellectual and experiential slippage. Shaping an account of his experience in *Walden* thus became one part of Thoreau's answer to a disappearing capacity to envision enlarged and unifying categories. The *Walden* manuscript, beginning with his Journal entries and lectures while living at the pond, and evolving through its seven stages of composition in the late 1840s and early 1850s, became the repository of his struggle to maintain his capacity for philosophical reflection on the natural world and the place of the self within it.[15]

Thoreau's chapter "The Ponds," which includes his intricate analysis of the richly symbolic identity of Walden Pond, is indicative of his strategy of portraying perception as factual and sensuous, yet also productive of ever-enlarging frames of reference.[16] Walden is a character who is absolutely pure and "perennially young" (W 193). Thoreau attributes such human characteristics as eyelids and lips to Walden, and dramatizes his relationship with the pond as that of friendship. Such tactics infuse an imaginative life into material nature and contribute to Thoreau's attempt to re-mythologize the natural world. The humanization of the pond helps to quicken and vitalize it and stands as the culmination of a series of depictions of an animated natural world that include the besotted, "aldermanic" bullfrogs who "tr-r-r-oonk" (W 126) at the pond shore in the evening in "Sounds," and the visits from the "old settler and original proprietor, who is reported to have dug Walden Pond" and the "ruddy and lusty old dame, who delights in all weathers and seasons" (W 137–38).

Personification is the most easily recognizable strategy through which Thoreau attempts to use the pond and its landscape to enlarge our commonplace perception. It is supplemented by the more extensive passages of description in which Thoreau strives to produce a mental image of the scenery of Walden, which, though "on a humble scale" (W 175), becomes impressive through his careful verbal reconstructions. His close observations of the pond's shoreline and the shifting color of its water help us to locate ourselves and begin to see the world with him. But perhaps the most subtle and telling of these passages, rich not only in descriptive power but resonant with suggestiveness about the pond's integrative qualities, is his observation of the revelatory qualities of the pond's still surface, the very blankness of which is shown to be its secret of association.

Thoreau describes the unusual optical impression of the pond surface on "a calm September afternoon, when a slight haze makes the opposite shore-line indistinct." In a comment that recalls Emerson's looking through his legs at the world in "Idealism," Thoreau writes, "when you invert your head, it looks like a thread of finest gossamer stretched across the valley, separating one stratum of the atmosphere from another." Whereas Emerson altered his usual perspective to make the solid world seem unfixed and malleable, Thoreau likes to think of the surface of the pond as solid, a perfectly integrated extension of the shoreline. "You would think that you could walk dry under it to the opposite hills, and that the swallows which skim over might perch on it" (W 186). This shift in perspective discloses the pond as the point of union among the disparate elements of nature, connecting land, water, and sky to suggest that each of these is a version of all the others, and that each part or aspect of nature contains all nature if seen completely.

Thoreau's descriptive argument extends to his portrait of the remarkable power of the pond's surface to record all the life and energy around it, its even, smooth plane a medium that can disclose the smallest presence and the finest movements above and below it.

> It is literally as smooth as glass, except where the skater insects, at equal intervals scattered over its whole extent, by their motions in the sun produce the finest imaginable sparkle on it, or, perchance, a duck plumes itself, or, as I have said, a swallow skims so low as to touch it. It may be that in the distance a fish describes an arc of three or four feet in the air, and there is one bright flash where it emerges, and another where it strikes the water; sometimes the whole silvery arc is revealed; or here and there, perhaps, is a thistle-down floating on its surface, which the fishes dart at and so dimple it again. (W 186–87)

This closely observed and poetically expressive prose is of course one of Thoreau's great achievements in *Walden,* but aside from the compelling visual image that he creates, the description recreates the pond surface as a medium of cognition, an ideal analogue for the completely perceptive mind.

The line of demarcation between two different realms, water and sky, the surface is also the place at which these realms meet and merge, recording and thus comprehending each such event. Perception, as represented by Thoreau through the perfectly impressionable pond surface, is thus a process of merger or unification.

Thoreau confirms the metaphoric reach of his description of the pond's surface by concluding that "a field of water betrays the spirit that is in the air. It is continually receiving new life and motion from above" (W 188). The spirit above the lake's surface is of course the wind, but Thoreau's choice of words here is significant. "*Spirit* primarily means *wind*," Emerson had written in *Nature*, using this etymological connection as one of his illustrations of how language reveals the connection between the ideal and material realms. "Every word which is used to express a moral or intellectual fact, if traced to its root, is found to be borrowed from some material appearance" (CW 1:18). Thoreau uses "spirit" with this same sense of the identity of the material and the ideal, suggesting that the act of perception unifies the material and the ideal, that the physical discernment of a phenomenon in nature suggests more intangible "moral or intellectual" facts.

Thoreau's account of his return to the frozen surface of the pond in "The Pond in Winter" adds new emphasis on the pond as an embodiment of an enlarged perception that encompasses both material and ideal, fact and law.[17] His morning work of cutting through the ice to obtain fresh water, one of the most memorable lyric moments in the narrative, confirms the eternal presence and inevitable return of the pond's natural life, and also represents the importance and availability of the inner life, perhaps buried or not immediately apparent, but always available. He cuts through the ice and looks down "into the quiet parlor of the fishes, pervaded by a softened light as through a window of ground glass, with its bright sanded floor the same as in summer." The "perennial waveless serenity" of the scene, the inner possession of the pond and of every individual who can delve deeply enough within, leads Thoreau to declare that "heaven is under our feet as well as over our heads" (W 283). The pond reveals a further lesson when Thoreau sets about measuring it, intending both to satisfy his curiosity and to dispel the lore that it is bottomless. He finds and records its depth, using measurable fact to counter superstition, but also concludes that fact will open into law if fully examined.

Discovering "that the line of greatest length intersected the line of greatest breadth *exactly* at the point of greatest depth" (*W* 289), Thoreau believed that he might have discovered a law for determining the deepest point in any lake.[18] While such is not, in fact, the case, the immediacy of Thoreau's reach for the larger implications of his experiment, his eagerness to make Walden a representative entity, is indicative of his need to see his work of observation as a search for more inclusive categories. In this sense, detail can become transformative insight. "If we knew all the laws of Nature, we should need only one fact, or the description of one actual phenomenon, to infer all the particular results at that point" (*W* 290). This is an assertion about the nature of knowledge, but, perhaps more important, about the unity of what the mind perceives:

> Our notions of law and harmony are commonly confined to those instances which we detect; but the harmony which results from a far greater number of seemingly conflicting, but really concurring, laws, which we have not detected, is still more wonderful. The particular laws are as our points of view, as, to the traveller, a mountain outline varies with every step, and it has an infinite number of profiles, though absolutely but one form. (*W* 290–91)

This faith that no matter how various it may seem, nature was "absolutely but one form" was Thoreau's justification for his attention to the particulars of nature, an assurance that no act of observation or recognition ended in itself.

The most dramatic and far-reaching of these incidents of observation is the well-known description of the "sand foliage," in which Thoreau recognizes that the forms of melting sand and clay manifest the workings of the laws that control and shape all natural processes of growth and change, including those of the body. One small and seemingly insignificant occurrence becomes revelatory of the entire system of nature. Generally recognized as the climactic scene of *Walden,* the passage has been accorded both intense scrutiny and illuminating explication in recent criticism. Gordon V. Boudreau has shown in impressive detail that the sand foliage passage was a culminating statement of a "resurrection myth" toward which Thoreau had striven in *A Week* and his Journal, in which the thawing of the earth becomes an act of both birth and utterance. Thoreau's observation and description of it links mental perception and linguistic expression to this archetypal moment in the

creative process. Robert D. Richardson Jr. calls attention to Thoreau's excla-
mation that "there is nothing inorganic" (W 308) as the recognition that the
unifying processes of law invigorate and explain all physical phenomena.
Noting that the expansion of the sand foliage description was the most important revision in the final drafts of the *Walden* manuscript, Richardson connects this late expansion with Thoreau's sighting of the thawing sand flow on
February 2, 1854, a signal to him of the end of winter. This climactic insight of
the triumph of life is part of Thoreau's own emergence from a period of disorientation and despondency in the early 1850s in which his emotional resiliency
was keyed to seasonal change. The completion of the *Walden* manuscript,
after its long postponement and repeated revision, thus seems to have represented a personal and spiritual achievement as well as a literary one. As
Richardson explains, "The 'Spring' chapter of *Walden,* with its exhilarating
description of the flowing clay bank at its center, is finally an affirmation of
foliage over fossil, natural fact over historical relic, life over death."[19]

Thoreau's detailed and intricate description of the sand foliage phenomenon, coupled with the reach of his interpretive insight, make this one of the
most telling examples of the "reading" that was the cornerstone of his natural
life at Walden. Confessing the "delight" (W 304) that the sand foliage gave
him, the loving detail with which he unfolds his description and interpretation dramatizes his enraptured witness to life's origin. The earth's "living
poetry" (W 309) was a vivid expression of the merging of fact with law, a process that required language as an essential element. The earth itself became
a poem, and Thoreau its reader. His toil over Homer and his devotion to his
Journal were thus as natural and necessary as the seasonal cycle, and a part of
that larger process. "You find thus in the very sands an anticipation of the
vegetable leaf. No wonder that the earth expresses itself outwardly in leaves,
it so labors with the idea inwardly. The atoms have already learned this law,
and are pregnant by it" (W 306). Thoreau thus recognized his own efforts to
understand and express, the work of thinking and writing, as consonant with
the very process of creation itself. The natural life around him corresponded
to the natural life within.

Notes

This article is reprinted from David M. Robinson, *Natural Life: Thoreau's Worldly Transcendentalism.* Copyright © 2004 by Cornell University. Used by permission, Cornell University Press.

1. For parenthetical documentation, I have used the following abbreviations: *CW:* Ralph Waldo Emerson, *The Collected Works of Ralph Waldo Emerson,* ed. Alfred R. Ferguson et al. (6 volumes to date; Cambridge: Harvard University Press, 1971–); *JP:* Henry David Thoreau, *Journal,* ed. John C. Broderick, Robert Sattelmeyer, Elizabeth Hall Witherell, et al. (7 volumes to date; Princeton: Princeton University Press, 1981–); *W:* Henry David Thoreau, *Walden,* ed. J. Lyndon Shanley (Princeton: Princeton University Press, 1971).

2. Ralph Waldo Emerson, *The Journals and Miscellaneous Notebooks of Ralph Waldo Emerson,* vol. 15, *1860–1866,* ed. Linda Allardt, David W. Hill, and Ruth H. Bennett (Cambridge: Belknap Press of Harvard University Press, 1982), 352–53.

3. Robert Kuhn McGregor, *A Wider View of the Universe: Henry Thoreau's Study of Nature* (Champaign: University of Illinois Press, 1997), 33–86. McGregor also notes, however, the importance of Emerson's influence in encouraging Thoreau to begin his career as a writer. More subtle readings of the complexities of Thoreau's reception of idealism are offered by Charles R. Anderson (*The Magic Circle of Walden* [New York: Holt, Rinehart, and Winston, 1968], 93–130), H. Daniel Peck, and Laura Dassow Walls. Peck (*Thoreau's Morning Work: Memory and Perception in "A Week on the Concord and Merrimack Rivers," the Journal, and "Walden"* [New Haven: Yale University Press, 1990), 66–78) has depicted Thoreau's early work, including *Walden,* as a test of idealism, a theory that Thoreau eventually rejected for a conception of experience that much more closely resembles the phenomenology of Heidegger. "Philosophical idealism was inevitably his legacy," Peck writes. "But what makes him so interesting to us is that he inherited idealism not as a faith but as a problem" (73). Walls (*Seeing New Worlds: Henry David Thoreau and Nineteenth-Century Natural Science* [Madison: University of Wisconsin Press, 1995], 53–93) describes Thoreau's principal direction of intellectual development as a rejection of "rational holism," one form of idealism that she terms the "dominant paradigm of romanticism" (54) propounded by Coleridge and Emerson, and a movement toward a more fact-oriented "empirical holism" characteristic of the scientific method of Humboldt.

4. McGregor, *A Wider View of the Universe,* 40, 44. Recent critical discourse on two related issues, the history of science and "ecocriticism," has helped to frame this issue. Both seek to present Thoreau as a "naturalist" as opposed to a literary or philosophical figure, and concentrate on his later Journal, and the natural history projects of his later career. In addition to the work of Peck, Walls, and McGregor, see also Nina Baym, "Thoreau's View of Science," *Journal of the History of Ideas* 26 (April-June 1965): 221–34; William Howarth, *The Book of Concord: Thoreau's Life as a Writer* (New York: Viking, 1982); Lawrence Buell, *The Environmental Imagination: Thoreau, Nature Writing, and*

the *Formation of American Culture* (Cambridge: Harvard University Press, 1995); William Rossi, "Education in the Field: Recent Thoreau Criticism and Environment," *ESQ: A Journal of the American Renaissance* 42 (2nd Quarter 1996): 125–51, and "Thoreau's Transcendental Ecocentrism," in *Thoreau's Sense of Place: Essays in American Environmental Writing,* ed. Richard J. Schneider (Iowa City: University of Iowa Press, 2000), 28–43); and Michael Benjamin Berger, *Thoreau's Late Career and "The Dispersion of Seeds": The Saunterer's Synoptic Vision* (Rochester, NY: Camden House, 2000). Also of importance is the recent editorial work on late Thoreau manuscripts by Bradley P. Dean: Henry David Thoreau, *Faith in a Seed: The Dispersion of Seeds and Other Late Natural History Writings* (Washington, DC: Island Press, 1993), and Henry David Thoreau, *Wild Fruits: Thoreau's Rediscovered Last Manuscript* (New York: Norton, 1999).

5. James Elliot Cabot, "Immanuel Kant," *Dial* 4 (April 1844): 409–15, 409.

6. See Anderson, *The Magic Circle of Walden,* 112–30, for further discussion of Emerson's and Thoreau's experiments with the eye and its perspective.

7. Peck, *Thoreau's Morning Work,* 67–68.

8. Walls, *Seeing New Worlds,* 113–16, quote from 115. As Robert Sattelmeyer (*Thoreau's Reading: A Study in Intellectual History with Bibliographical Catalogue* [Princeton: Princeton University Press, 1988], 82–86), and Robert D. Richardson Jr. (*Henry Thoreau: A Life of the Mind* [Berkeley: University of California Press, 1986], 362–68), have shown, Thoreau also read Agassiz and A. A. Gould's *Principles of Zoology* (1848; rev. ed. 1851) and Agassiz's "Essay on Classification" (1857), learning much from them even as he moved away from Agassiz's larger conception of special creation of each species. Thoreau's struggles with the emerging science of his day have been recounted by Nina Baym in "Thoreau's View of Science." For an informative reading of Thoreau's developing reaction to pre-Darwinian ideas of evolution, see William Rossi, "Thoreau's Transcendental Ecocentrism," cited in note 3.

9. Richardson, *Henry Thoreau,* 205. On the impact of Hindu writings on Thoreau, see Alan D. Hodder, " 'Ex Oriente Lux': Thoreau's Ecstasies and the Hindu Texts," *Harvard Theological Review* 86 (1993): 403–38, and *Thoreau's Ecstatic Witness* (New Haven: Yale University Press, 2001), 139–59.

10. James Elliot Cabot, "The Philosophy of the Ancient Hindoos," *Massachusetts Quarterly Review* 4 (September 1848): 401–22; reprinted in Kenneth Walter Cameron, *Transcendental Apprenticeship: Notes on Young Henry Thoreau's Reading* [Hartford, CT: Transcendental Books, 1976]), 400–401.

11. Cabot, "The Philosophy of the Ancient Hindoos," 403.

12. Ibid., 417; Richardson, *Henry Thoreau,* 206–7; Cameron, *Transcendental Apprentice,* 222.

13. Stanley Cavell has remarked on the problematic quality of "the depth of the book's [*Walden's*] depressions and the height of its elevations" and "the absence of reconciliation between them" (*Senses of Walden: An Expanded Edition* [San Francisco: North Point, 1981], 110). These gaps can be taken as the signs of Thoreau's attempt to use his literary task in *Walden* to address his inner conflicts and fears of slippage and deteriora-

tion. Of pertinence on this issue is Robert D. Richardson Jr.'s discussion of *Walden* as "the earned affirmation of a man who had to struggle almost constantly against a sense of loss, desolation, and decline that grew on him with age" (*Henry Thoreau*, 256).

14. See John Hildebidle's comments on this passage, which he reads in the context of Thoreau's struggle with the emerging new discourse of science (*Thoreau: A Naturalist's Liberty* [Cambridge: Harvard University Press, 1983], 102–11).

15. See Robert Sattelmeyer, "The Remaking of *Walden*," in *Writing the American Classics*, ed. James Barbour and Tom Quirk (Chapel Hill: University of North Carolina Press, 1990), 53–78. For detailed information on the *Walden* manuscript, see Ronald Earl Clapper, "The Development of Walden: A Genetic Text," Diss. in 2 vols., University of California, Los Angeles, 1967.

16. For perceptive analyses of the profusion of symbolic associations of the pond, see Sherman Paul, *The Shores of America: Thoreau's Inward Exploration* (Champaign: University of Illinois Press, 1958), 332–45; and Melvin E. Lyon, "Walden Pond as Symbol," *PMLA* 82 (May 1967): 289–300.

17. Robert Milder has provided an informative discussion of the evolution of this chapter in Thoreau's development of the *Walden* manuscript in *Reimagining Thoreau* (Cambridge: Cambridge University Press, 1995), 144–51.

18. Paul, *The Shores of America*, 343–45.

19. Gordon V. Boudreau, *The Roots of Walden and the Tree of Life* (Nashville: Vanderbilt University Press, 1990), 117; Richardson, *Henry Thoreau*, 310–13, quotation from 312. Other important readings of the sand foliage passage include Charles R. Anderson's emphasis on the centrality of the "leaf metaphor" (*Magic Circle of Walden*, 243) and its connection to Thoreau's reading of Goethe; and Milder, *Reimagining Thoreau*, 151–60. The particular linguistic context of the passage has been helpfully worked out by Philip F. Gura (*The Wisdom of Words: Language, Theology, and Literature in the New England Renaissance* [Middletown, CT: Wesleyan University Press, 1981], 124–41) and Michael West (*Transcendental Wordplay: America's Romantic Punsters and the Search for the Language of Nature* [Columbus: Ohio University Press, 2000], 183–96).

The Cimeter's "Sweet" Edge

Thoreau, Contemplation, and Violence

LARRY J. REYNOLDS

ENRY DAVID THOREAU'S most revered sacred text, the *Bhagavad Gita*, dramatizes the problem of how to live in a world on the edge of violence and warfare. It was a problem Thoreau faced and we still face 150 years after the publication of *Walden* (1854). The *Gita* begins with the warrior hero Arjoon on the battlefield of Kooroo in the open space between two warring armies made up of his kinsmen. As he surveys the scene, he is filled with doubt and despair because he wishes to remain virtuous and nonviolent. He even declares himself more ready to be killed than to kill. His charioteer, the supreme Hindu god Kreeshna incarnate, urges him to do his duty and fight: "Death is certain to all things which are subject to birth, and regeneration to all things which are mortal."[1] In the climactic eleventh section of the poem, Kreeshna reveals his overwhelming multiform divinity to Arjoon, providing him with even stronger arguments about why he must slay his kinsmen and thus become the agent of divine principle:

> I am Time, the destroyer of mankind, matured, come hither to seize at once all these who stand before us. Except thyself not one of all these warriors, destined against us in these numerous ranks, shall live. Wherefore, arise! Seek honor and renown! Defeat the foe, and enjoy the full-grown kingdom! They are already, as it were, destroyed by me. Be thou alone the immediate agent. (*BG* 93)

As readers of *Walden* know, the *Gita* held incomparable inspiration for Thoreau: "The reader is nowhere raised into and sustained in a higher, purer, or *rarer* region of thought than in the Bhagvat-Geeta" (*Wk* 137).[2] And much of its appeal came from its focus on the tension between contemplation and action, a tension that disquieted Thoreau throughout his life. As he phrased it in a journal entry made while living at the pond, "The struggle in me is between a love of contemplation and a love of action—the life of a philosopher & of a hero."[3] Time and again he chose the former, but he remained sensitive to the call of the latter, which came from the *Gita* and other martial sites, including ancient Troy and contemporary Concord. In "The Bean-Field" chapter of *Walden*, Thoreau tells of music he hears coming from the village: "sometimes it was a really noble and inspiring strain that reached these woods, and the trumpet that sings of fame, and I felt as if I could spit a Mexican with a good relish,—for why should we always stand for trifles?" (*W* 160–61).[4] His statement is a satirical joke, of course, directed at supporters of the Mexican War, but the "different drummer" (*W* 326) he stepped to indeed often played to a martial strain. In a journal entry of May 14, 1840, he declared, "Every man is a warrior when he aspires. He marches on his post. The soldier is the practical idealist—he has no sympathy with matter, he revels in the annihilation of it. So do we all at times."[5]

Despite these militant (and chilling) sentiments, in *A Week on the Concord and Merrimack Rivers*, where Thoreau discusses the *Gita* at length, he explicitly rejects Kreeshna's arguments on behalf of violent action, declaring that "no sufficient reason is given why Arjoon should fight. Arjoon may be convinced, but the reader is not. . . . The duty of which he speaks is an arbitrary one" (*Wk* 140). Similarly, in "Civil Disobedience," Thoreau seems to argue for nonviolent resistance as the best means to combat injustice. Recently Wai Chee Dimock has traced the political philosophy of "Civil Disobedience" to the radical pacifism of William Lloyd Garrison and to the *Gita* as well, not Kreeshna's exhortation to fight, but "Arjuna's protest against it."[6] Dimock explains that Thoreau came "to think of action, not as a feat of the body, proven on the battle field, but as a feat of the soul, proven by the will to disarm and to suffer the bodily consequences of disarming."[7] Dimock acknowledges, however, that pacifism "only had a tenuous and rescindable sway on Thoreau. If anything, militancy was temperamentally more congenial to him."[8] As I plan to argue in this essay, Thoreau's militancy accounts in large part for the attraction the *Gita* exerted upon him, and he responded to

Kreeshna's arguments just as strongly as he did to Arjoon's. They provided a religious rationale for the deep-seated violent impulses he periodically felt.

Throughout his career, Thoreau revealed glimpses of his imaginary participation in warrior culture and his receptivity to the idea that to engage in violent warfare could bring honor to the warrior and justice to the land. In his early *Dial* essay "The Service," which he incorporated into *A Week,* he asserts, "Let not our Peace be proclaimed by the rust on our swords, or our inability to draw them from their scabbards, but let her at least have so much work on her hands, as to keep those swords bright and sharp" (*RP* 13).[9] In "Slavery in Massachusetts" and "The Last Days of John Brown," he likewise argues for the purifying benefits of righteous violence. "It is not an era of repose," Thoreau declares in "Slavery in Massachusetts." "We have used up all our inherited freedom. If we would save our lives, we must fight for them" (*RP* 108). In "A Plea for Captain John Brown" he argues on behalf of Brown's raid on the federal arsenal at Harpers Ferry, describing the United States government as a wounded yet dangerous "monster" that deserves to be slain, "a semi-human tiger or ox, stalking over the earth, with its heart taken out and the top of its brain shot away" (*RP* 129). Like all holy warriors, Thoreau felt compelled to dehumanize the enemy before calling for its annihilation.

Did Thoreau condone terrorism? He never committed a violent act, never tried to intimidate a population or government through violent means, yet his rhetorical support of political violence when linked to the United States' current "War on Terrorism" encourages us to take a fresh look at his struggle with this issue, especially in *Walden,* which draws upon the political context surrounding its composition. In the spring of 1854, as Thoreau was preparing the final copy of *Walden* for the printer, President Franklin Pierce ("the Devil," Thoreau called him), in an attempt, as he saw it, to defend the Constitution of the United States (and appease his Southern base) sent federal troops to Boston to return the fugitive slave Anthony Burns to his owner.[10] Outraged, Thoreau declared in his journal, "Rather than thus consent to establish Hell upon earth—to be a party to this establishment—I would touch a match to blow up earth & hell together. I will not accept life in America or on this planet on such terms."[11] Thoreau engaged in no suicide bombing, of course, but he heaped contempt on the government and its representatives, especially the marines and militia who carried out orders from above. One of these individuals, a 24-year-old Irish-born truckman and volunteer policeman named James Batchelder, was murdered during the failed mob attack on the courthouse where Burns was being held. Thoreau called the attack "bloody & disinterestedly heroic,"[12] and afterward the Transcendentalist minister Theodore Parker condemned Batchelder, writing, "a man has been killed. He was a volunteer in this service. He liked the business of enslaving a man, and has gone to render an account to God for his gratuitous wickedness."[13] Thoreau expressed a similar estimate of the police and marines, for they, he claimed, "were not men of sense nor of principle—in a high moral sense they were not *men* at all."[14] In his most bloodthirsty entry, Thoreau asserts, "I am calculating how many miscreants each honest man can dispose of. I trust that all just men will conspire."[15] Though he did not conspire, his "just" friends Parker, Thomas Wentworth Higginson, and Franklin Sanborn did, joining five years later with three others as John Brown's "Secret Six," who provided Brown with weapons and money for his activities in "Bleeding Kansas" and his raid on Harpers Ferry.[16]

Broadswords, pikes, Sharps repeating rifles—these were Brown's weapons of choice in disposing of "miscreants," and he used them not only to slash, split, and pierce the bodies of his enemies, but also to "shock and awe" their sympathizers. In Kansas, which many considered in a state of war in 1856, Brown reacted to reports of murder, rape, and theft by proslavery ruffians from Missouri and to their sacking and burning of the town of Lawrence. Believing that "without shedding of blood there is no remission of sin" (Hebrews 9:22),[17] he led a party of seven men along the Pottawatomie Creek in Kansas in the middle of the night of May 24–25, 1856, and they used small, heavy broadswords to kill five Southern settlers. The first was James P. Doyle, living with his wife, daughter, and three sons, who was dragged from his cabin, along with his two older sons, and hacked to death by Brown's men. For good measure Brown shot him through the head. Doyle's twenty-year-old son Drury, who tried to run, was found the next morning with his head gashed open and his arms cut off. The two other victims of this raid, Allen Wilkinson, who lived with his wife and two children, and William Sherman, a bachelor, were likewise hacked and dismembered. None was armed; none owned slaves.

Some three years later, when Brown led his raid on Harpers Ferry, he brought 21 men, 950 pikes, 200 revolvers, and 198 Sharps repeating rifles. The pikes, relatively inexpensive weapons, effective for silent and repeated use at a distance of six feet or less, were purchased by Brown to arm the slaves he expected to join him in an insurrection. The Sharps rifles, purchased by donations from the "Secret Six" and others in the North, had more immediate uses, to kill anyone who tried to stop the raiders. Thoreau, who had almost certainly read reports about the Pottawatomie massacre,[18] said of the Harpers Ferry raid: "I know that the mass of my countrymen think that the only righteous use that can be made of Sharps' rifles and revolvers is to fight duels with them, when we are insulted by other nations, or to hunt Indians, or shoot fugitive slaves with them, or the like. I think that for once the Sharps' rifles and the revolvers were employed in a righteous cause. The tools were in the hands of one who could use them" (RP 133).

Ironically, the first person Brown and his men killed at Harpers Ferry was Hayward Shepard, a free black who worked as the porter at the Harpers Ferry train station. He was shot in the back, the bullet "going through his body and coming out the nipple of his left breast," according to the train conductor.[19] He died a lingering and agonizing death after being taken inside the station. By the time Brown was captured, ten of his men were dead, plus three townsmen, two slaves, one slaveholder and one marine.[20]

For Thoreau, Brown's violent behavior in Kansas, and later Virginia, was righteous work, comparable to Christ's driving the money-changers from the temple. "The same indignation that is said to have cleared the temple once will clear it again," he asserted in "A Plea for Captain John Brown": "The question is not about the weapon, but the spirit in which you use it" (RP 133). Given the Western belief in the reality of the body, one can question Thoreau's logic here and prefer Christ's hand to Brown's rifle, yet it is Brown as agent of the divine, as enforcer of a "higher law," that inspires the rhetoric, or "transcendental slang," as Sophia Hawthorne called it.[21] In Thoreau's eyes, Brown was a Puritan warrior, an immortal avatar from the English Civil War, whose weapons and words were in service to his Lord. "It would be in vain to kill him," Thoreau declared, "He died lately in the time of Cromwell, but he reappeared here. Why should he not?" (RP 113). Obviously identifying with Brown, Thoreau calls him "a transcendentalist above all, a man of ideas and principles" (RP 115), ignoring the bodily pain and death Brown inflicts upon others to achieve his ends, the instantiation of his principles. When Thoreau spoke to William Dean Howells about his vision of John Brown, he recalled "a sort of John Brown type, a John Brown ideal, a John Brown principle,"[22] rather than John Brown himself. Emerson, too, quoted with approval what Brown said to him privately about the Golden Rule and the Declaration of Independence: "Better that a whole generation of men, women and children should pass away by a violent death than that one word of either should be violated in this country."[23] In other words, that which is spiritual and ideal renders mortal flesh and blood unimportant. In "The Last Days of John Brown," Thoreau thus asserts that before Brown died, "he had taken up the sword of the spirit—the sword with which he has really won his greatest and most memorable victories. Now he has not laid aside the sword of the spirit, for he is pure spirit himself, and his sword is pure spirit also" (*RP* 152). Brown's family, in gratitude for Thoreau's support, reportedly presented him with "a huge knife that had belonged to Brown,"[24] and one wonders if his idealism faltered when he held it in his hand.

For most readers, *Walden* seems unrelated to Thoreau's antislavery activities and violent impulses. After all, in "Economy," Thoreau ridicules reformers, argues for self-reform as opposed to social reform, including abolitionism, and he makes only passing reference to the issue of slavery, as for example, in "Visitors" when he mentions a runaway slave whom he "helped to forward toward the northstar" (*W* 152). A celebration of the simple pastoral life seems to be the main emphasis of the book. Yet, despite *Walden's* apparent quietude, beauty, and hopefulness, it reveals glimpses of violent forces at work beneath its calm surface. In "Spring," for example, Thoreau recalls the smell of a dead horse in the night air and asserts, "I love to see that Nature is so rife with life that myriads can be afforded to be sacrificed and suffered to prey on one another; that tender organizations can be so serenely squashed out of existence like pulp,—tadpoles which herons gobble up, and tortoises and toads run over in the road; and that sometimes it has rained flesh and blood!" (*W* 318). The expressed "love" of such violence, though jarring, suggests that while the explicit theme of *Walden* is the promise of rebirth and immortality, an additional undertone is the appeal of death and destruction.

From the *Gita,* Thoreau acquired an understanding that the forces of destruction are inseparable from the forces of creation and that the divine encompasses them both. The supreme Hindu being, a form of elemental energy, is creator, preserver, and destroyer. In his recent "Introduction" to the *Gita,* Stephen Mitchell explains why this concept is difficult for most Westerners to grasp or accept: "There is little precedent for it in our own scriptures, which split the universe into good and evil and place God solely on the side of the good. The only exceptions are the Voice from the Whirlwind at the end of the Book of Job and a single, hair-raising verse from Second Isaiah: 'I form the light, and create darkness; I make peace, and create evil: I the Lord do all these things.' " [25] From the *Gita* and other Eastern texts such as *The Laws of Menu*, the *Harivansa*, the *Vishnu Purana*, the *Sankhya Karika*, the *Vedanta*, and the *Upanishads*, Thoreau came to regard even the warfare within nations and between nations not as a matter of good or evil, but rather as a spectacle to rise above and regard with detachment. [26] His poem, "The Spirit of Lodin," which he entered in his journal on May 1, 1851, achieves this perspective:

> I look down from my height on nations,
> And they become ashes before me;
> Calm is my dwelling in the clouds;
> Pleasant are the great fields of my rest. [27]

Thoreau's apparent aloofness here, like that displayed toward the Boston courthouse guard and John Brown's victims, is part of an Eastern spiritual process that transforms bloody actuality into heroic spiritual joy. Just as the intricate patterns of the flowing sand at the deep cut result from Nature "in full blast" within (*W* 308), so, too, *Walden* as a whole owes much to Thoreau's subtle and brilliant control of his inner fire, the violent aggression he attributes to some savage instinct within himself, like that of a "half-starved hound" (*W* 210), as he puts it, ranging the woods seeking prey to devour. At the beginning of "Higher Laws," he thus generalizes, "I found in myself, and still find, an instinct toward a higher, or, as it is named, spiritual life, as do most men, and another toward a primitive rank and savage one, and I reverence them both" (*W* 210). Thoreau's reverence for the savage grew out of his belief that violence can be a means of purification and enlightenment, contributing to an ongoing beneficent and deathless process. This process is addressed in the *Gita* as Kreeshna explains,

> These bodies, which envelope the souls which inhabit them, which are eternal, incorruptible, and surpassing all conception, are declared to be finite beings; wherefore, O Arjoon, resolve to fight. The man who believeth that it is the soul which killeth, and he who thinketh that the soul may be destroyed, are both alike deceived; for it neither killeth, nor is it killed. (*BG* 36)

Emerson, who admired the *Gita* as much as Thoreau, expressed this idea in his poem "Brahma": "If the red slayer think he slays, / Or if the slain think he is slain, / they know not well the subtle ways / I keep, and pass, and turn again."[28] Thoreau, likewise, responded to the idea that unity of the soul with the Supreme Being eliminated the fear of death, by revealing it as a temporal and temporary phenomenon.

In *Walden*, the invisible counterpoints to the motifs of morning and rebirth are the darkness and death that necessarily precede them, and, although John Thoreau's shocking 1842 death by lockjaw never rises to the book's surface, its absence looms as a powerful background to the book's hopefulness. Henry's sublimated reaction to the loss of his brother, I believe, informs not only his Eastern detachment, but also his extravagance—"I do not propose to write an ode to dejection, but to brag as lustily as chanticleer in the morning" (*W* 84)—and his mocking treatment of violence and death—"I felt as if I could spit a Mexican with a good relish" (*W* 161). The personal and political merge in *Walden*, and its final drafts of the early 1850s were written as the country was experiencing growing violence over the slavery issue and as Thoreau was studying Eastern texts once more. (He had read the *Gita* in 1846 and returned to it in 1854.)[29] In *Walden* one thus sees a split consciousness resulting from the contradictory demands of contemplation and action, of monk and warrior that grew in intensity within Thoreau as the slavery controversy struck home.

On the one hand, much of *Walden*'s appeal flows from the Oriental contemplative life it celebrates, those moments when time stands still and the narrator grows "like corn in the night" (*W* 111). In "Sounds," "Spring," and "Conclusion," especially, spiritual enlightenment and rebirth seem the result of the narrator's ability to detach himself from the illusory world of getting and spending, to drench himself in the reality of the natural world, and thereby achieve self-realization. On the other hand, for Thoreau, the peace, serenity, and emancipation one sought by means of the contemplation of nature involved a struggle, often one as ferocious as war; and in one of the most imaginative and striking passages of *Walden*, he uses a particular kind of weapon, the scimitar, a moon-shaped Oriental saber, to suggest the overpowering effect of encountering ultimate Reality. "If you stand right fronting and face to face to a fact," he writes, "you will see the sun glimmer on both its surfaces, as if it were a cimeter, and feel its sweet edge dividing you through the heart and marrow, and so you will happily conclude your mortal career. Be it life or death, we crave only reality" (*W* 98). To a yogi, this would be the process by which the conscious self is annihilated and the essential self emerges. Thoreau's readings in the *Gita* may have inspired this vision, for it resembles the moment when Kreeshna reveals his true nature and becomes a "supreme and heavenly form; of many a mouth and eye; many a wondrous sight; many a heavenly ornament; many an up-raised weapon" (*BG* 90), and the effect is that of the sun rising into the heavens with a thousand times more than usual brightness. The vision stuns and frightens Arjoon, but it represents, as does Thoreau's scimitar metaphor, the experience of enlightenment, which is the goal of the yogi.

As Arthur Christy long ago pointed out, Thoreau's life at Walden Pond, though in some sense a writer's retreat during which he finished *A Week* and wrote the first draft of *Walden,* can also be viewed as a yogi's search for self-realization through renunciation of desires and union with ultimate Reality.[30] In a letter to his admirer H. G. O. Blake on November 20, 1849, Thoreau declared, "Depend upon it that rude and careless as I am, I would fain practice the *yoga* faithfully. 'The yogin, absorbed in contemplation, contributes in his degree to creation: he breathes a divine perfume, he hears wonderful things.'"[31] Similarly, in one of the most serene and affecting passages in *Walden,* Thoreau shows his indebtedness to the yoga of meditation in "Sounds":

> Sometimes, in a summer morning, having taken my accustomed bath, I sat in my sunny doorway from sunrise till noon, rapt in a revery, amidst the pines and hickories and sumachs, in undisturbed solitude and stillness, while the birds sang around or flitted noiseless through the house, until by the sun falling in at my west window, or the noise of some traveller's wagon on the distant highway, I was reminded of the lapse of time. I grew in those seasons like corn in the night, and they were far better than any work of the hands would have been. They were not time subtracted from my life, but so much over and above my usual allowance. I realized what the Orientals mean by contemplation and the forsaking of works. (*W* 111–12)

Those who visited Thoreau at the pond sensed the success of his contemplative habits. In February 1847, Alcott recorded in his journal: "So vivid was my sense of escape from the senses while conversing with Henry today that the men, times, and occupations of coming years gave me a weary wish to be released from this scene and to pass into a state of noble companions and immortal labours."[32] A month later, Alcott reported: "His genius insinuates itself at every pore of us, and eliminates us into the old elements again. A wood-nymph, he abides on the earth and is a sylvan soul."[33] Hawthorne, when he visited, was also impressed, especially by the way Thoreau had tamed the wild birds, who "ceased to be afraid of him, and would come and perch upon his shoulder, and sometimes upon his spade, when he was digging in the little croft that supplied him with potatoes and pumpkins."[34] In his prefaces to *Mosses from an Old Manse* and *The Scarlet Letter,* Hawthorne fondly recalls learning from Thoreau about pond lilies and Indian culture and talking with him "about pine-trees and Indian relics, in his hermitage at Walden."[35]

In *Walden* itself, completed in the eventful spring of 1854, the undercurrent of violence is controlled by the recurrent argument that the contemplative life can not only alter one's consciousness but can indeed change the world. From a Western perspective, of course, the self resides within a Cartesian system of time and space, interacting within a world of objects, including other human beings. A yoga approach to life, however, seeks to dissolve this false conception, as well as the false ego-self associated with it. Through silence, meditation, and detachment from desire, the true Self emerges and becomes one with Reality. At this moment fact is penetrated by a new consciousness, and the world ceases to have an independent existence, becoming instead a fluid and receptive creation of the divine acting through the Self. In "The Pond in Winter," Thoreau dramatizes the dissolution of time and space such a moment involves:

> In the morning I bathe my intellect in the stupendous and cosmogonal philosophy of the Bhagvat Geeta, since whose composition years of the gods have elapsed, and in comparison with which our modern world and its literature seem puny and trivial; and I doubt if that philosophy is not to be referred to a previous state of existence, so remote is its sublimity from our conceptions. I lay down the book and go to my well for water, and lo! There I meet the servant of the Brahmin, priest of Brahma and Vishnu and Indra, who still sits in his temple on the Ganges reading the Vedas, or dwells at the root of a tree with his crust and water jug. I meet his servant come to draw water for his master, and our buckets as

it were grate together in the same well. The pure Walden water is
mingled with the sacred water of the Ganges. (W 298)

Thoreau's poem in the central "Ponds" chapter of *Walden* similarly captures
the moment of spiritual enlightenment, when he and Walden Pond become
one: "I am its stony shore, / And the breeze that passes o'er; / In the hollow of
my hand / Are its water and its sand, / And its deepest resort / Lies high in my
thought" (W 193).

As for the pain and suffering within nature and human society, viewed
from an Eastern religious perspective they become illusions best removed
through self-realization, not by outward action. Because they derive from the
false conception that the body and the senses are the basis of true identity,
their elimination depends upon the liberation of the self from this miscon-
ception. In "Economy," Thoreau makes this point when he asserts, "I sometimes wonder that we can be so frivolous, I may almost say, as to attend to the
gross but somewhat foreign form of servitude called Negro Slavery, there are
so many keen and subtle masters that enslave both north and south. . . . What
a man thinks of himself, that it is which determines, or rather indicates, his
fate. Self-emancipation even in the West Indian provinces of the fancy and
imagination,—what Wilberforce is there to bring that about?" (W 7–8). His
idea here corresponds to one often ridiculed as Emerson expresses it in *Nature*: "As fast as you conform your life to the pure idea in your mind . . . [s]o
fast will disagreeable appearances, swine, spiders, snakes, pests, mad-houses,
prisons, enemies, vanish" (CW 1:45). Only when Thoreau's anger was aroused
by injustice did his belief in the power of the awakened mind waver, to his
regret. His antislavery activities, like Emerson's, were concessions to a materialist conception of reality.

In the "Conclusion" to *Walden,* Thoreau uses the conceptual link between
self reform and social reform to argue disingenuously that the individual
should not willfully oppose the laws of society: "It is not for a man to put
himself in such an attitude to society, but to maintain himself in whatever
attitude he find himself through obedience to the laws of his being, which
will never be one of opposition to a just government, if he should chance to
meet with such" (W 323). This "just" government emerges from the elevated
thought of the individual, for "if one advances confidently in the direction of
his dreams, and endeavors to live the life which he has imagined, he will meet
with a success unexpected in common hours. He will put some things be-

hind, will pass an invisible boundary; new, universal, and more liberal laws will begin to establish themselves around and within him; or the old laws be expanded, and interpreted in his favor in a more liberal sense, and he will live with the license of a higher order of beings" (*W* 323–24). Thoreau's well-known parable of the artist of Kouroo seems intended to illustrate the power of the liberated consciousness, as the artist, striving to create the perfect staff, arrests time and becomes endowed "with perennial youth." Centuries come and go, and when he finishes his work, "it suddenly expanded before the eyes of the astonished artist into the fairest of all the creations of Brahma. He had made a new system in making a staff, a world with full and fair proportions" (*W* 327). This parable of Thoreau's own creation was likely inspired by the *Gita*. As Sherman Paul has pointed out, "Kouroo was clearly Kuru, Kooroo, or Curu, the nation that fought the Pandoos in the *Mahabharata*, the sacred land that Arjuna was assigned to protect in the *Bhagavad-Gita*. . . . The lesson of the *Bhagavad-Gita*—not the lesson of passivity, but of disinterested work and contemplation—was already a part of his thought."[36]

Despite the power Thoreau attributes to the liberated mind, the repressed actual world periodically returns to haunt his thought and writings, evoking his hostility in the process. In *A Week,* one sees little evidence of Thoreau's combative instincts partly because, as Linck Johnson has argued, his main goal was "to depict the brothers' ideal society within a timeless pastoral world."[37] Despite this goal, there are nevertheless moments when an alternative world intrudes. In the "Monday" chapter, for example, after Thoreau's long paean to meditation, to the beauty and serenity of nature, he recalls that into the scene came a canal boat, "like some huge river beast, and changed the scene in an instant; and then another and another glided into sight, and we found ourselves in the current of commerce once more" (*Wk* 144). Such moments are the recurring problem for Thoreau, the intrusion of the beastly and brutal into his serene consciousness, which challenges his sense of control. The slavery issue, more than any other circumstance in Thoreau's life, fell into this category. Yet it was not so much the suffering or oppression of the slaves themselves in the South that seemed to disturb him, though he certainly went out of his way to care for and assist runaway slaves; rather, it was what he perceived as *his* enslavement in Massachusetts caused by the state's compliance with "Webster's Fugitive-Slave Bill" (*W* 232).[38] In 1851 with the arrest of Thomas Sims and again in 1854 with the arrest, trial, and remission of Anthony Burns, Thoreau's savage impulses overpowered his serenity, at least momentarily. Near the end of "Slavery in Massachusetts," he asks, "I walk toward one of our ponds, but what signifies the beauty of nature when men are base? . . . Who can be serene in a country where both the rulers and the ruled are without principle? The remembrance of my country spoils my walk. My thoughts are murder to the State, and involuntarily go plotting against her" (*RP* 108).[39] The anger Thoreau felt at injustice led him both to express it in his journal and reform papers, and to subdue it, which was his preferred method. The latter represented voluntary, rather than involuntary, action.

In *Walden,* Thoreau for the most part represses his grievances against his government as well as his violent impulses. All but the beginning of "Higher Laws" in fact argues on behalf of such repression and sublimation: " 'A command over our passions, and over the external senses of the body, and good acts, are declared by the Ved to be indispensable in the mind's approximation to God' " (*W* 219). Elsewhere he uses humor, the mock heroic, to mask his attraction to the values of warrior culture, so evident in the *Gita* and his other favorite books, Homer's *Iliad* and Carlyle's *Heroes and Hero-Worship.* In "The Bean-Field," the narrator becomes Achilles, the greatest of the Greek warriors and the slayer of Hector, while the Trojan enemy becomes the weeds he battles: "Daily the beans saw me come to their rescue armed with a hoe, and thin the ranks of their enemies, filling up the trenches with weedy dead. Many a lusty crest-waving Hector, that towered a whole foot above his crowding comrades, fell before my weapon and rolled in the dust" (*W* 161–62). In similar humorous fashion, he describes in "Brute Neighbors" one of the ants "whose mother had charged him to return with his shield or upon it" (*W* 229). As he watches the ant battle, he assumes a detached Olympian perspective on the "red republicans" and "black imperialists," mocking their war and its human analogues: "For numbers and for carnage it was an Austerlitz or Dresden. Concord Fight! . . . I have no doubt that it was a principle they fought for, as much as our ancestors, and not to avoid a three-penny tax on their tea" (*W* 230). Yet after this mockery, he describes the fierce combat, as the ants gnaw off each other's legs and feelers, tear open chests, and sever heads from bodies. While Thoreau makes light of this violence, its connection to that which he and a growing number of abolitionists would later applaud gives it a grim resonance. He admits that "I felt for the rest of that day as if I had had my feelings excited and harrowed by witnessing the struggle, the ferocity and carnage, of a human battle before my door" (*W* 231), and he tells the reader the battle was fought "five years before the passage of Webster's Fugitive-Slave Bill," thus politicizing the event and allowing a glimpse of his own fierce political sentiments.

It was while living at Walden Pond during 1845–47 that the issue of slavery intruded upon his life in unavoidable ways. On August 1, 1844, Emerson had delivered his famous "Address on the Emancipation of the Negroes in the British West Indies," sponsored by the Concord Female Anti-slavery Society, of which Thoreau's mother and sisters were active members; and in September 1845, he helped the Society get Emerson's pamphlet published. A year later, on August 1, 1846, he hosted at his cabin the Society's annual meeting to commemorate the freeing of the West Indian slaves, thus marking the overt intersection of the political and the contemplative. His own arrest by Sam Staples, in late July 1846, led to Thoreau's famous "Civil Disobedience" lecture and essay, published in Elizabeth Peabody's *Aesthetic Papers* (1849). Although "Civil Disobedience" argues for the active power of inaction (the refusal to pay one's poll tax to avoid contributing to the harm of others), the potential for more fierce action, for violence against the state, emerges at least once when he responds to the fear of bloodshed by declaring that "even suppose blood should flow. Is there not a sort of blood shed when the conscience is wounded? Through this wound a man's real manhood and immortality flow out, and he bleeds to an everlasting death" (*RP* 77). Thus, the essay differentiates Thoreau's antislavery ethic from those such as William Lloyd Garrison and his followers, who advocated only nonviolent resistance.

During the late 1840s and early 1850s, the antislavery movement turned sharply toward violence as a means to rid the country of slavery. The annexation of Texas, the War with Mexico, the Compromise of 1850, and especially the hated Fugitive Slave Law spurred more and more New England abolitionists to accept the belief, put forward by Frederick Douglass and his followers, that the murder of oppressors was justified.[40] Encouraged by the European revolutions of 1848–49, they came to believe, as Theodore Parker asserted, that "All the great charters of humanity have been *writ in blood,* and must continue to be so for some centuries."[41] Prominent abolitionists Cassius Clay, Angelina Grimké Weld, Samuel May, Wendell Phillips, Henry Wright, and Parker Pillsbury all abandoned their "peace principles" in the 1850s. Clay asserted that "Moral power must always be backed with cold steel and the flashing blade,"[42] and Weld argued that "slavery is more abhorrent . . . to Christianity than murder. . . . We are compelled to choose between two evils, and all we can do is to take the least, and baptize liberty in blood, if it must be so."[43] Pillsbury even told the Massachusetts Anti-Slavery Society that "he longed to see the time come when Boston should run with blood from Beacon Hill to the foot of Broad Street."[44]

As Thoreau absorbed the discourse of the abolitionists and even joined them at the famous July 4, 1854, meeting in Framingham Grove, he maintained his belief that Reality was to be found apart from the tangible world of the senses.[45] In *A Week,* he had asserted that "to one who habitually endeavors to contemplate the true state of things, the political state can hardly be said to have any existence whatever. It is unreal, incredible, and insignificant to him" (*Wk* 129). He returned to this position in his journals, especially after becoming politically engaged, and in *Walden* he dismisses current events as "shams and delusions" (*W* 95), adding "we inhabitants of New England live this mean life that we do because our vision does not penetrate the surface of things. We think that that *is* which *appears* to be" (*W* 96). In Hindu thought such illusion is *maya,* the mistaking of matter for reality, and it is through the practice of virtue, that is, knowing right as opposed to doing right, that the self achieves understanding that spirit is the essential reality of the universe.[46]

After his participation in the Framingham meeting, Thoreau in a journal entry of August 1, 1854, revealed his preference for this Eastern vision, writing, "I feel the necessity of deepening the stream of my life—I must cultivate privacy. It is dissipating to be with people too much."[47] A week later, he wrote H. G. O. Blake, "Methinks I have spent a rather unprofitable summer thus far. I have been too much with the world, as the poet might say. . . . I find it, as ever, very unprofitable to have much to do with men" (*Corr* 330). Thoreau's turn to the white water lily at the end of "Slavery in Massachusetts," which has been interpreted as escapist in Western terms,[48] can thus be viewed as his turn back toward Reality in Eastern terms. He calls the water lily "the emblem of purity . . . extracted from the slime and muck of earth," and asserts, "What a confirmation of our hopes is in the fragrance of this flower! I shall not so soon despair of the world for it, notwithstanding slavery, and the cowardice and want of principle of Northern men" (*RP* 109). He made a comparable move three years later, when, as Robert Richardson has observed, "Thoreau's absorption in John Brown ceased almost as suddenly as it began."[49] By the summer of 1860, when asked about giving a lecture, he declared that his subjects were "Transcendentalist & aesthetic. I devote myself to the absorption of nature generally" (*Corr* 583), and in April 1861, he wrote Parker Pillsbury, "As for my prospective reader, I hope that he *ignores* Fort Sumpter & Old Abe, & all that, for that is just the most fatal and indeed the only fatal, weapon you can direct against evil ever; for as long as you *know of* it, you are *particeps criminis*. . . . I do not so much regret the present condition of things in this country (provided I regret it at all) as I do that I ever heard of it. . . . Blessed are they who never read a newspaper, for they shall see Nature, and through her, God" (*Corr* 611). In the struggle between contemplation and action, the former attained dominance as Thoreau's life and his nation approached dissolution.

Perhaps the one contemporary of Thoreau's who best understood the struggle he waged within himself and the toll it took upon him was Nathaniel Hawthorne, who returned to Concord from abroad in 1860 and found himself marginalized due to his unwillingness to align himself with Northern abolitionists. As the insightful Emerson disciple Moncure Conway observed, "He had not the flexibility of principle displayed by so many in those days. He thus had no party,—then nearly equivalent to having no country."[50] Hawthorne and Thoreau had known each other for some twenty years when Thoreau died in 1862. During this time, Hawthorne had studied his friend closely, visiting him at Walden, reading his works, promoting his career, and using him as a model for a number of his characters, including the guide in "The Hall of Fantasy," Owen Warland in "The Artist of the Beautiful" (1844), Donatello in *The Marble Faun,* and, finally, I believe, the title character of his unfinished romance "Septimius Felton."[51] In fashioning these characters, Hawthorne captured the ambivalence of Thoreau's personality, the contradictory attractions of the wild and savage on the one hand and the detached and contemplative on the other.

In his notebooks and letters, Hawthorne invariably uses the term "Indian-like" to describe Thoreau, yet he also associates him with the classical world of Greece and Rome. In April 1843, Hawthorne identified Thoreau as "being one of the few persons, I think, with whom to hold intercourse is like hearing the wind among the boughs of a forest-tree; and with all this wild freedom, there is high and classic cultivation in him too."[52] Hawthorne was fascinated, if not obsessed, by the ways in which apparently noble individuals could fall under the sway of their passions and become burdened with sin, and he apparently saw Thoreau as capable of such a transformation. It is quite likely he read Thoreau's "Slavery in Massachusetts" while living in England,[53] and thus encountered clear evidence of Thoreau's violent impulses, but even as early as "The Artist of the Beautiful" (1844), the protagonist Owen Warland, creator of ideal beauty, experiences a metaphorical war-land within himself when he lashes out at Annie, who represents the threat of the worldly to the spiritual.

In *The Marble Faun* (1860), published in England under the title *Transformation,* the title character Donatello also shares traits Hawthorne attributed to Thoreau, and he is transformed from a simple, sylvan innocent, resembling the Faun of Praxiteles, into a guilt-ridden murderer. In a moment of rage he throws Miriam's persecutor, the model, over a cliff, and thus loses his innocence and his connection to the natural world. Perhaps even closer to home—Concord, that is—Hawthorne creates in "Septimius Felton," one of the manuscripts he left unfinished at his death in 1864, a protagonist even more closely linked to Thoreau. Septimius is a hermit-like scholar, with Indian blood in his veins, who kills a foe during the warfever developing in Concord at the beginning of the American Revolution. Begun in 1862, the romance grew out of a story Thoreau told Hawthorne about a former inhabitant of the Wayside who resolved never to die. As Hawthorne put it in his first memorandum to himself, this inhabitant "would sit there while oaks grew up and decayed; he would be always here. This was all that Thoreau communicated; and that was many years ago, when I first came to live at the old cottage. . . . I staid here but a little while; but often times, afar off, this singular idea occurred to me, in foreign lands, when my thoughts returned to this place which seemed to be the point by which I was attached to my native land."[54]

Like Thoreau, Septimius is a native of Concord who has studied at Harvard and returned home, there becoming "possibly a student of theology with the clergyman." His habits are meditative, and he studies nature closely: "Let him alone a moment or two, and then you would see him, with his head bent down, brooding, brooding, with his eyes fixed on some chip, some stone, some common plant, and commonest thing, as if it were the clue and index to some mystery; and when, by chance startled out of these meditations, he lifted his eyes, there would be a kind of perplexity, a dissatisfied, wild look in them, as if, of his speculations, he found no end" (*SF* 6). Septimius, like Thoreau, prefers to remain detached from political events, yet finds himself drawn to them. When the farmers and neighbors start assembling for battle, he

went into his house, and sat there, in his study, for some hours, in
that unpleasant state of feeling, which a man of brooding thought
is apt to experience when the world around him is in a state of
intense motion, which he finds it impossible to chord with. There
seemed to be a stream rushing past him, which, even if he plunged
into the midst of it, he could not be wet by it. He felt himself
strangely ajar with the human race, and would have given much,
either to be in full accord with it, or to be separated from it forever.
(*SF* 22–23)

Despite his isolation, Septimius ends up shooting and killing a British soldier in a face-to-face confrontation on the hillside behind his house, and
Hawthorne attributes this act to Septimius's Indian blood, which represents
a repressed savagery in his behavior: "This mixture of bloods had given him a
strange and exceptional nature; and he had brooded upon the legends that
clung around his race, following his ancestry, not only to the English univer-
sities, but into the wild forest, and hell itself" (*SF* 512). The sense of guilt
Hawthorne projects upon Septimius, Thoreau himself never felt, of course,
especially with regard to the "primitive rank and savage" instinct he confesses
to in *Walden* and claims to reverence. To fight, and even to kill, the *Gita* had
taught him, was not sinful during wartime, but rather one's duty to perform.

In gratitude to Thoreau for giving him the idea of "Septimius Felton,"
Hawthorne planned to include as his preface a short biography of Thoreau, "a
little sketch," as he put it, because "it seems the duty of a live literary man to
perpetuate the memory of a dead one, where there is such fair opportunity as
in this case;—but how Thoreau would scorn me for thinking that *I* could
perpetuate *him*!"[55] Hawthorne displays his habitual modesty here, of course,
but indeed Thoreau's wild, contradictory, paradoxical personality is almost
beyond capture. Those who do not think that destruction is creation, death is
life, inaction action, and detachment compassion, cannot know well the
subtle ways that Thoreau keeps. His example, which may seem escapist and
irresponsible to many, holds the key to rising above a world of opposition by
seeking truth and reality on another conceptual plane. Only heightened spiritual consciousness, not knives, guns, or bombs, can change the world in ways
that matter beyond the present. In his journal for 1845, Thoreau asserted,
"One emancipated heart & intellect—It would knock off the fetters from a
million slaves."[56] His friend Hawthorne in "Earth's Holocaust" made the

same point: "The Heart, the Heart. . . . Purify that inward sphere; and the many shapes of evil that haunt the outward, and which now seem almost our only realities, will turn to shadowy phantoms and vanish of their own accord."[57] The world has yet to comprehend the truth of what these two friends perceived, yet even they could not hold onto this truth at times when their anger was aroused.

Notes

1. *The Bhagvat-Gita,* tr. Charles Wilkins (1785; rpt. Gainesville, FL: Scholars' Facsimiles & Reprints, 1959), 37. Hereafter cited parenthetically in the text as *BG.*

2. *A Week on the Concord and Merrimack Rivers,* ed. Carl F. Hovde, William L. Howarth, and Elizabeth Hall Witherell (Princeton: Princeton University Press, 1980), 137. Hereafter cited parenthetically in the text as *WK.* For informative discussions of the influence of the *Gita* on Thoreau, see Arthur Christy, *The Orient in American Transcendentalism: A Study of Emerson, Thoreau, and Alcott* (1932; rpt. New York: Octagon Books, 1963), 185–234; and Arthur Versluis, *Transcendentalism and Asian Religions* (Oxford: Oxford University Press, 1993), 79–104. Christy makes the important point that the *Gita* "is a merging of the Yoga and Sankhya philosophies; and it advocates ways of life that are inherently incompatible" (25).

3. *Journal 2: 1842–1848,* ed. Robert Sattelmeyer (Princeton: Princeton University Press, 1984), 240.

4. *Walden,* ed. J. Lyndon Shanley (Princeton: Princeton University Press, 1971), 161. Hereafter cited parenthetically in the text as *W.*

5. *Journal 1: 1837–1844,* ed. Elizabeth Hall Witherell et al. (Princeton: Princeton University Press, 1981), 124.

6. Wai Chee Dimock, "Planetary Time and Global Translation: 'Context' in Literary Studies," *Common Knowledge* 9.3 (2003): 503.

7. Ibid., 505.

8. Ibid., 504.

9. *Reform Papers,* ed. Wendell Glick (Princeton: Princeton University Press, 1973), 13. Hereafter cited parenthetically in the text as *RP.*

10. For a full account of this event and its relation to the New England Transcendentalists, see Albert von Frank, *The Trials of Anthony Burns: Freedom and Slavery in Emerson's Boston* (Cambridge: Harvard University Press, 1998).

11. *Journal 8: 1854,* ed. Sandra Harbert Petrulionis (Princeton: Princeton University Press, 2002), 165–66.

12. Ibid., 175.

13. Quoted in von Frank, *Trials of Anthony Burns,* 111.

14. *Journal 8,* 185.

15. *Ibid.,* 501, 200. As Sandra Harbert Petrulionis has shown, many of Thoreau's more furi-

ous journal entries (including those I have quoted here) did not make it into his "Slavery in Massachusetts" speech. She argues that he thus worked to cultivate the potential audience for *Walden,* which was soon to appear. See "Editorial Savoir Faire: Thoreau Transforms His Journal into 'Slavery in Massachusetts,' " *Resources for American Literary Study* 25 (1999): 206–31.

16. See Jeffery Rossbach, *Ambivalent Conspirators: John Brown, the Secret Six, and a Theory of Slave Violence* (Philadelphia: University of Pennsylvania Press, 1982); and Edward J. Renehan Jr., *The Secret Six: The True Tale of the Men Who Conspired with John Brown* (New York: Crown, 1995).

17. See James M. McPherson, *Battle Cry of Freedom: The Civil War Era* (Oxford: Oxford University Press, 1988), 203.

18. See Michael Meyer, "Thoreau's Rescue of John Brown from History," in *Studies in the American Renaissance 1980,* ed. Joel Myerson (Charlottesville: University of Virginia Press, 1980), 301–16. Details about Brown's activities are taken from *John Brown: The Making of a Revolutionary,* ed. Louis Ruchames (New York: Grosset & Dunlap, 1969); Benjamin Quarles, *Allies for Freedom: Blacks on John Brown* (Oxford: Oxford University Press, 1974); and Stephen B. Oates, *To Purge This Land with Blood: A Biography of John Brown* (Amherst: University of Massachusetts Press, 1984).

19. See Quarles, *Allies for Freedom,* 94, and 212, n. 3.

20. Oates, *To Purge This Land,* 302.

21. Sophia Hawthorne, speaking for her husband and herself, told her sister Elizabeth, "When you get so far out of my idea of right as to talk of its being proper to violate laws sometimes, because we 'can obey higher laws than we break'—this, dear Elizabeth, U used to hear in days past and I consider it a very dangerous and demoralizing doctrine and have always called it 'transcendental slang.'. . . I am just on the point of declaring that I hate transcendentalism because it is full of such immoderate dicta" (quoted in Louise Hall Tharp, *The Peabody Sisters of Salem* [Boston: Little, Brown, 1950], 288–89).

22. Quoted in Walter Harding, *The Days of Henry Thoreau* (New York: Knopf, 1970), 434.

23. Ralph Waldo Emerson, "Remarks at a Meeting for the Relief of the Family of John Brown," in *Complete Works,* vol. 11, *Miscellanies* (1904; rpt. New York: AMS Press, 1968), 268.

24. Harding, *Days of Henry Thoreau,* 423.

25. Stephen Mitchell, "Introduction," *Bhagavad Gita: A New Translation* (New York City: Three Rivers Press, 2000), 28.

26. For the most thorough study of Thoreau's readings in and use of Hindu texts, see Miriam Alice Jeswine, "Henry David Thoreau: Apprentice to the Hindu Sages," Diss., University of Oregon, 1971. See also Alan D. Hodder, "Concord, Orientalism, Thoreauvian Autobiography, and the Artist of Kouroo," in *Transient and Permanent: The Transcendentalist Movement and Its Contexts,* ed. Charles Capper and Conrad Edick Wright (Boston: Massachusetts Historical Society, 1999), 190–226.

27. *Journal 3: 1848–1851,* ed. Robert Sattelmeyer et al. (Princeton: Princeton University Press, 1990), 213–14.

28. Ralph Waldo Emerson, *Collected Poems and Translations* (New York: Library of America, 1994), 159.

29. See Robert Sattelmeyer, *Thoreau's Reading: A Study in Intellectual History* (Princeton: Princeton University Press, 1988), 68.

30. See Christy, *Orient*, 220–21. For detailed analysis of the influence of yoga discipline and the *Gita* on Thoreau's Walden experience, see Frank MacShane, "*Walden* and Yoga," *New England Quarterly* 37 (1964): 322–42; and William Bysshe Stein, "Thoreau's *Walden* and the *Bagavad Gita*," *Topic* 3 (1963): 38–55.

31. *The Correspondence of Henry David Thoreau*, ed. Walter Harding and Carl Bode (New York: New York University Press, 1958), 251. Hereafter cited parenthetically as *Corr.*

32. Bronson Alcott, *The Journals of Bronson Alcott*, ed. Odell Shepard (Boston: Little, Brown, 1938), 190–91.

33. Ibid., 192–94.

34. Charles MacKay, *Forty Years' Recollections of Life, Literature, and Public Affairs, from 1830 to 1870* (London: Chapman & Hall, 1877), quoted in Edward Cronin Peple Jr., "Hawthorne on Thoreau, 1853–1857," *Thoreau Society Bulletin* 119 (Spring 1972): 2–3.

35. *The Scarlet Letter*, ed. William Charvat et al. (Columbus: Ohio State University Press, 1962), 25.

36. Sherman Paul, *The Shores of America: Thoreau's Inward Exploration* (Champaign: University of Illinois Press, 1958), 353.

37. Linck C. Johnson, *Thoreau's Complex Weave: The Writing of "A Week on the Concord and Merrimack Rivers"* (Charlottesville: University Press of Virginia, 1986), 96.

38. For a detailed discussion of Thoreau's views of slavery, see Michael Meyer, "Thoreau and Black Emigration," *American Literature* 53 (1981): 380–96.

39. For a thorough discussion of the context of this essay, see Robert C. Albrecht, "Conflict and Resolution: 'Slavery in Massachusetts,'" *ESQ* 19 (1973): 179–88.

40. For a discussion of Thoreau's movement toward Douglass's position, see Lawrence A. Rosenwald, "The Theory, Practice, and Influence of Thoreau's Civil Disobedience," in *A Historical Guide to Henry David Thoreau*, ed. William E. Cain (Oxford: Oxford University Press, 2000), 153–79.

41. Quoted in John Demos, "The Antislavery Movement and the Problem of Violent 'Means,'" *New England Quarterly* 37 (December 1964): 519.

42. Quoted ibid., 520.

43. Quoted ibid., 522.

44. Quoted ibid., 523. Two years earlier, in January 1857, Pillsbury warned his fellow abolitionists, "I think we had better familiarize our minds to the possibility, at least, that the streets of Boston may yet run with blood." See *National Anti-Slavery Standard*, January 17, 1857, quoted in Jane H. Pease and William H. Pease, "Confrontation and Abolition in the 1850s," *Journal of American History* 58 (March 1972): 928.

45. For a summary of Thoreau's relations to social reformers, see Len Gougeon, "Thoreau and Reform," in *The Cambridge Companion to Henry David Thoreau* (Cambridge: Cambridge University Press, 1995), 194–214.

46. See Jeswine, "Thoreau: Apprentice to the Hindu Sages," 142–43.

47. *Journal 8*, 247.

48. See Lawrence Buell, who calls the image "disturbing" in "the insouciance with which the persona turns away from social confrontation for the sake of immersion in a simplified green world" (*The Environmental Imagination: Thoreau, Nature Writing, and the Formation of American Culture* [Cambridge: Harvard University Press, 1995], 38).

49. Robert D. Richardson Jr., *Henry David Thoreau: A Life of the Mind* (Berkeley: University of California Press, 1986), 372.

50. Moncure Daniel Conway, *Life of Nathaniel Hawthorne* (1890; rpt. New York: Haskell House, 1968), 206.

51. See Buford Jones, " 'The Hall of Fantasy' and the Early Hawthorne-Thoreau Relationship," *PMLA* 83 (1968): 1429–38; Richard Predmore, "Thoreau's Influence in Hawthorne's 'The Artist of the Beautiful,' " *ATQ* 40 (1978): 329–34; and Edward Cronin Peple, "The Personal and Literary Relationship of Hawthorne and Thoreau," Diss., University of Virginia, 1970, 94–127.

52. Nathaniel Hawthorne, *The American Notebooks*, ed. Claude M. Simpson (Columbus: Ohio State University Press, 1972), 369.

53. On July 3, 1854, Sophia Hawthorne wrote to Mary Mann, "We receive hundreds of newspapers—whig, democrat, free soil & all kinds, from Washington, New York, Boston & Salem, giving us every one of the speeches in Congress, and all the comments, criticisms, abuse, vituperation, and every thing else going on in those great United States," quoted in Nathaniel Hawthorne, *The Letters, 1853–1856*, ed. Thomas Woodson et al. (Columbus: Ohio State University Press, 1987), 238, n. 1.

54. Nathaniel Hawthorne, *The Elixir of Life Manuscripts: Septimius Felton, Septimius Norton, The Dolliver Romance*, ed. Edward H. Davidson et al. (Columbus: Ohio State University Press, 1977), 499. Hereafter cited parenthetically in the text as *SF*.

55. Nathaniel Hawthorne, *The Letters, 1857–1864*, ed. Thomas Woodson et al. (Columbus: Ohio State University Press, 1987), 605.

56. *Journal 2*, 156.

57. Nathaniel Hawthorne, *Mosses from an Old Manse*, ed. Fredson Bowers et al. (Columbus: Ohio State University Press, 1974), 403–4.

Following Thoreau's Instincts

WILLIAM ROSSI

N OT MANY PEOPLE today would dispute *Walden's* status as an environmental classic. Yet on the central environmental question of human-
animal kinship versus the superiority and privileged separation of human
from nonhuman nature, Thoreau's classic must appear extremely limited.
Animals are interesting to Thoreau as they "carry some portion of our
thoughts" (*W* 225).[1] But in themselves, let alone in the coevolutionary history
of our relations with them, they appear hardly to exist at all. This historical
limitation arises in large part, of course, from Thoreau's having written *Walden*
almost a decade before Darwin published his theory of evolution by natural
selection in *On the Origin of Species* (1859), and two decades before Darwin
developed the implications of human-animal kinship in *The Descent of Man*
(1871). These are watershed documents, to which contemporary environmentalism and ecology trace their own intellectual origins, and without which
they would be literally inconceivable. But they shaped a watershed Thoreau
did not live in.

Yet our own historical horizon is limited as well. To adapt Emerson, the
ruin or blank we see when we look at *Walden* in this respect is in our own eye,
too. As far as evolutionary theory is concerned, our vision has been shaped
both by earlier positivist historians of science and by the ongoing power of
neo-Darwinian explanations. Consequently, when literary historians look for
evolution before 1859, they tend to see only the proto-Darwinian "anticipa-
tions." But as the science historian Evelleen Richards has shown, the path
Darwin took to evolution, "along the route that led to natural selection," was
not the only one. Rather, "there were a number of paths that ran alongside

and sometimes intersected with Darwinism."[2] According to this more recent history of science, the blazing of several such paths was stimulated by a fifteen-year-long controversy over the "development hypothesis" that began in 1844 with the publication of *Vestiges of the Natural History of Creation*, anonymously authored by Robert Chambers, an Edinburgh publisher and geologist. While long recognized as having played a role in delaying publication of Darwin's theory, until recently the *Vestiges* controversy has been considered merely a period curiosity in the history of biology, much like the sentimental novel in literary history and for similar reasons.[3] But as James A. Secord's exhaustive study demonstrates, not only did the *Vestiges* debates acquaint a broad Victorian public on both sides of the Atlantic with competing theoretical paradigms of natural order and the stakes involved in them, they also stimulated the curiosity of naturalists and working researchers in botany, comparative anatomy, and in such new disciplines as embryology and ornithology, leading them down those paths referred to by Richards.[4]

Given Emerson's and Thoreau's keen interest in science, as Laura Dassow Walls and Eric Wilson most recently and most thoroughly have demonstrated, and given that the eruption of the *Vestiges* controversy in the spring and summer of 1845 coincided exactly with Thoreau's move to Walden Pond, perhaps it was inevitable that some of Chambers's ideas would find their way into Thoreau's own story of "development."[5] Had *Walden* been published as expected, Thoreau might not have engaged some of the real evolutionary questions raised by *Vestiges* any more profoundly than he does in *A Week*. But the continuation of the controversy throughout the entire nine-year gestation of *Walden*, Thoreau's deepening interest in natural science and in fathoming his relation to his native place, and not least the permeable membrane that existed between literary and scientific discourses at this relatively early stage of scientific professionalization in the United States—especially on a topic not yet defined as a technical issue best treated by experts—all contributed toward making Thoreau's "experiment," among much else, a meditation on contemporary evolutionary thought, and particularly on human-animal kinship as reflected through his own experience.

A more complete treatment of the subject than I will attempt would consider the animal as other and companion, as metaphor and presence, not neglecting to assess the animalistic and racialist associations of savagery in *Walden*. Although I hope to provide a starting point for future studies, mine will be more limited. Because I am interested in how conflicting notions of

human-nonhuman relations were embedded in the Transcendentalist discourse Thoreau received and reworked, as he wrote and rewrote his experience at Walden, I focus here on Thoreau's representation of instinct through
his book's composition. Traditionally designating a species of intelligence or
awareness proper to animal life, instinct turns out to be a particularly rich site
for my purposes. For while in Darwin's theory, according to Robert Richards,
instinct would come to form "the evolutionary hinge linking the minds of
lower animals with that of man," for Transcendentalists the term also desig-
nated, metaphorically, a privileged mode of intuitive access to a higher human
nature: that is to say, to everything "the animal" was not.[6]

A Brief Genealogy of Thoreau's Instincts

Early nineteenth-century discussions of animal instinct were mostly divided
along predictable lines. On the one hand, many natural theologians followed
Descartes's understanding of instinctive animal behavior as the result of
"blind innate urges instilled by the Creator for the welfare of his creatures."[7]
Natural philosophers in the sensationalist tradition, on the other hand (with
whom Robert Richards associates Lamarck, Erasmus Darwin, and his grand-
son Charles), denied the existence of immutable innate urges, arguing that
instincts represented adaptive behavior that had become habitual and then
was somehow passed down to successive generations as a kind of material
memory. Richards claims, however, that nineteenth-century natural theologians were far from monolithic in "defend[ing] a position inimical to evolution," and that whereas most of them assumed a great chasm between human
reason and brute instinct, a few sought to trace "the continuity of mental
faculties between men and animals."[8] Foremost among the latter were the
entomologists William Kirby and William Spence, whose work would feed
Darwin's theorizing as well as two chapters in *Walden*: Thoreau's allegory of
carnivorism in "Higher Laws" and his depiction of ant warfare in "Brute
Neighbors." Judging from extensive studies of insect behavior, Kirby and
Spence concluded in their *Introduction to Entomology* that although "instinct
is the chief guide of insects, they are also endowed with no inconsiderable
portion of reason."[9]

Chambers's intervention in this debate, in the penultimate chapter of *Vestiges*, illustrates how he capitalized on one of the book's primary rhetorical
strategies: rewriting the then-familiar progressionist narrative as a transmuta-

tionist one. Progressionism and the evidence that supported it were as widely publicized then as genetic engineering is today. While progressionism and transmutationism were often conflated as "development" or, later in the century, as "evolution," Victorians on both sides of the Atlantic remained keenly sensitive to the essential difference between these radically opposed interpretations of natural history. Where progressionists argued that the increasing complexity of organisms evident in the fossil sequence reveals a goal-directed ascent (or "progress") toward humankind and the unfolding of a divine plan, transmutationists interpreted the history of life as a material history of genealogical descent down to humankind. Transmutationism therefore involved nothing less than naturalizing the relation between the human, "moral," or spiritual sphere of creation, on the one hand, and the physical or "brute" sphere, on the other, to use the nineteenth-century categories. And for this Chambers's many detractors readily associated his "beastly book," as Cambridge geologist Adam Sedgwick called it, with atheistic materialism.[10]

Aware that his book would be vulnerable to such a reading, the anonymous author framed his hypothesis within the confines of a progressionist natural theology. The first half of *Vestiges* unfolds like a cosmic panorama, as the genteel narrator conducts his reader through deep time "up" to the present: from the formation of the solar system according to the nebular hypothesis through the emergence of innumerable series of geological, botanical, zoological, and finally human racial orders. As he reads the book of nature, so the spectator reader "passes out of" one era into another, and with each move, we "advance to a new chapter in this marvellous history."[11] Gazing upon the "stages" of this "natural history of creation," the reader is thus constructed as the comfortable witness of the teleological process whereby the earth was "prepared" for "man." Only midway through the book does Chambers introduce "the general likelihood of an organic creation by [natural] law," before turning to a vigorous defense of this hypothesis, by which time it becomes clear that the reader has been materially implicated in a natural history that includes humankind.[12] Arriving at the subject of the "Mental Constitution of Animals," Chambers relentlessly presses the argument for human-nonhuman continuity, while striking directly at the root of traditional resistance to it. If, as progressionists assumed, the gradations "of mind, like the forms of being, are mere stages of development" in an ascending scale, all that prevents our recognizing "the actual progression of species" is stubborn adherence to a false distinction between human mind (itself a "synonyme [for] soul, the immortal part of man") and "the mental manifestations . . . of the lower animals," collectively "term[ed] instinct."[13] Once we accept "that mental phenomena flow directly from the brain," and that "the lower animals manifested mental phenomena long before man existed," then the transmutationist "nature of the distinction between what are called instincts and reason" becomes immediately apparent. With this, the "old metaphysical character" of mind "vanishes in a moment" and the chasm which for progressionists had separated human from animal nature becomes a bridge, as "the distinction usually taken between physical and moral is annulled."[14]

Among those who shaped the terms of Transcendentalist discourse in the decades before *Vestiges* appeared, none had inflected "instinct" with more ambivalent figurative power than Coleridge. On one hand, in *Aids to Reflection* Coleridge elaborated his central distinction between Reason and Understanding precisely to preserve what Chambers termed the "old metaphysical character" of mind, opposing what he saw as "the inadequacy of positivism and empiricism in science" in an age "dominated by the understanding" and "mechanical philosophy."[15] Coleridge agreed with Kirby and Spence (and with François Huber, whom he also cited) that the instinctive behavior of insects showed a level of sentience approaching the human insofar as in maintaining a honeycomb or building a nest, insects exhibit "a power of selecting and adapting means to proximate ends" not blindly but *according to circumstances.*" However, in failing to distinguish this "power" from "Reason," naturalists perpetuated a grave confusion. In Coleridge's scheme of "the ascent of powers of mind," human understanding differs only in degree from the "instinctive intelligence" in lower creatures that prefigures it. But it differs in kind from "Reason."[16] As the God-given faculty of intuitively beholding absolute truth, Reason is "the Power distinctive of Humanity."[17]

But whereas in *Aids to Reflection* Coleridge was careful thus to keep the sphere of instinct separate from that of intuition (the mode by which Reason operates), in writings published a decade earlier, particularly in key passages in the *Biographia Literaria, The Friend,* and the posthumously published "Theory of Life," he conflates them. During this time, when more fully under the influence of F. W. J. von Schelling and Henrik Steffens, Coleridge gradually became aware of the conflict between his religious convictions and the system of *Naturphilosophie,* in which "human consciousness was the end of a continuous evolution in nature," as nature strove instinctively to know itself in humankind.[18] At one point in the "Theory of Life" he seems to have mas-

tered his ambivalence, declaring it heretical to deny "that wide chasm between man and the noblest animals of the brute creation, which no perceivable
or conceivable difference of organization is sufficient to *overbridge.*"[19] Yet
that ambivalence is nonetheless abundantly evident in his writings of this
period, where "instinct" figures as a powerful metaphor for intuitive insight,
represented not as a dispensation from above but as the progressive unfolding
of nature from within. Depending heavily on Schelling while describing in
the *Biographia* the elite "domain of pure philosophy . . . properly entitled
transcendental," Coleridge writes,

> They and they only can acquire the philosophic imagination, the
> sacred power of self-intuition, who within themselves can inter-
> pret and understand the symbol, that the wings of the air-sylph
> are forming within the skin of the caterpillar; those only, who feel
> in their own spirits the same instinct, which impels the chrysalis
> of the horned fly to leave room in its involucrum for antænnae yet
> to come. They know and feel, that the *potential* works *in* them,
> even as the *actual* works on them![20]

Had he been content with presenting caterpillar metamorphosis as but
"the symbol" of emergent self-intuition, that "wide chasm between man
and . . . the brute creation" mentioned in the "Theory of Life" would have remained intact. But when he goes on with Schelling to identify "self-intuition"
with "the same instinct," the chasm collapses. Certainly even here Coleridge's
intention is wholly progressionist. Yet, as he realized in composing the "Theory
of Life," and as he intended the Reason/Understanding distinction to prevent, a transmutationist interpretation of progressionist ascendance was all
too easy to see. For those reading Coleridge in the midst of the *Vestiges* controversy, it must have been easier still. In any event, notwithstanding its
author's fervent progressionism, as a bold, irresistible metaphor for intuition,
Coleridgean "instinct" carried into Transcendentalist discourse, as it were
in larval form, a radically material sense of human relation to nonhuman
nature.

As is well known, when he discovered it in the early 1830s Emerson prized
Coleridge's distinction as "a philosophy itself."[21] But while equally progressionist in his thinking, Emerson was either far less fussy about theology or too
enraptured by the *Naturphilosophie* mediated by Coleridge to care much

about policing "the chasm." As a result, in much of his writing during the 1830s and early 1840s, Emerson uses "Reason" (or "Intuition") and "Instinct" as virtual synonyms.[22] Thus at the end of *Nature* the "Orphic poet" sings of those moments when "man," awakened from his "slumber," "perceives that" his "elemental power . . . is not conscious power," but something "superior to his will. It is 'Instinct.' " In "Self-Reliance" he grandly designates "Spontaneity or Instinct" as "that source, at once the essence of genius, of virtue, and of life," before identifying "this primary wisdom" more conventionally as "Intuition, whilst all later teachings are tuitions." In "The Transcendentalist," Emerson recalls Coleridge's use of Kirby and Spence (significantly attributing to animal instinct a higher power than Coleridge did himself) when describing the "harbingers" of "[the] purely spiritual life" his young seekers aspire to: "Only in the instinct of the lower animals, [do] we find the suggestion of the methods of it, and something higher than our understanding. The squirrel hoards nuts, and the bee gathers honey, without knowing what they do, and they are thus provided for without selfishness or disgrace." Finally, the homocentric progressionism implicit in these passages is made explicit in a lecture (appropriately enough on "The Head") delivered in the later 1830s as part of the Human Culture series, where "The instinct of the Intellect" is translated quite simply as "progress evermore."[23]

The Worship of Aurora

In Transcendentalist parlance, then, to follow one's instincts became equivalent to following one's "genius," a phrase that could well sum up the vocation Thoreau assumed upon moving to Walden Pond. Confident that "No man ever followed his genius till it misled him," he seems to have determined to expand his mentor's program by following his own genius not only heavenward but earthward. From the first, that is, he was intent on grounding his vision in a deeper and finer experience both of nature and of history, obeying an "instinct" (as he wrote in the first version of what became the book's second chapter) "that my head is an organ for burrowing, as some creatures use their snout and fore-paws."[24]

Yet, just as for Emerson, in *A Week* and in material drafted concurrently for the first version of *Walden,* this exploration was still performed within an essentially progressionist paradigm, exhibiting a near complete lack of interest in animals unhitched to the emblematic, excepting perhaps a few fish. This is

evident in Thoreau's early speculations about instinct in what eventually became the central paragraph of "The Village," in which he feels his way home
in the dark with his hands and feet. The germ of this evocative incident appears in a passage from the Walden Journal written that first fall or winter. "I
have thought sometimes when going home through the woods at night," he
writes, "star-gazing all the way—till I was aroused from my reflections by
finding my door before me—that perhaps my body would find its way home if
its master should have forsaken it." This does not lead him to consider that
the body might carry some intelligence apart from its "master," however. Instead, he concludes that "the body is so perfectly subjugated by the mind that
it prophecies the sovereignty of the [mind] over the whole of nature," specu-
lating further that "the instincts are to a certain extent a sort of independent
nobility—of equal date with the crown. They are perhaps the mind of our
ancestors subsided in us. The experience of the race."[25] Needless to say, the
"ancestors" Thoreau has on his mind are not animal ancestors. By punning on
"the crown" as both physical location and Transcendentalist symbol of the
imperial superiority of intuitive human mind over its rightful dominion,
he indicates that the mind of these ancestors more closely approximates "the
one mind common to all individual men" that Emerson evokes in "History": a
unitary and universal human mind containing "the experience of the race."
And following a logic identical to that of the Orphic dictates of "Instinct" at
the end of *Nature*, the very fact that one can access this mind "prophesies" its
complete "subjugation" of the body, and, by extension, its "sovereignty . . . over
the whole of nature."

To be sure, before he finished revising this paragraph in the manuscript's
F version (late 1853–54), its narrative would move in a very different direction,
one whose distinctive resonance we will return to later. Already in the B version (1849), Thoreau deleted the hard-edged progressionist fantasy of sover-
eign mind over nature, while shifting the mode of his woodland navigation:
now guided by his feet and by hands stretched between two pines "not more
than eighteen inches apart," rather than by the stars (*W* 169).[26] Complement-
ing this instinctual reorientation, in B he also developed the powerfully synthetic and synesthetic figure of "morning" experience. From the standpoint of
the published version, this figure—in which the diurnal rejuvenation of the
body following sleep signifies psychic, moral, and even historical renewal
("Morning brings back the heroic ages" [*W* 88])—represents the germ of what
would become the book's famous dawn motif: the dawning inward sense of

Emersonian self-reliance suffused with environmental awareness to which Thoreau wishes "to wake [his] neighbors up" (W 84).[27]

Strangely, however, it was not at this time but after 1852, when Thoreau was simultaneously exploring animal kinship, that this imagery acquired its progressionist uplift. In B the author's morning experience serves chiefly the chapter's theme of living fully in the present, alive to "the overflowing joy of the universe."[28] But later additions to this chapter represent this experience as potentially equivalent to an ontological upgrade, awakening "to a higher life than we fell asleep from" (W 89).[29] This upward trajectory is continued in "Higher Laws," as the narrator struggles to keep himself awake to "our higher nature" (W 219), and is then further magnified in "Spring" by the microcosmic association with that season when he perceives the day as "an epitome of the year" (W 301)—all of which serves to imbue the message of Chanticleer with distinctly progressionist overtones. Consequently, among the associations accumulated by the time we reach the final paragraph's lyrical reprise of dawn images is the reflection that, could the reader only realize it, "these may be but the spring months in the life of the race" (W 331–32).

While this may indeed seem strange for an author believed to have "mov[ed]" during the nine-year course of Walden's composition "pretty clearly . . . along a path from homocentricism toward biocentricism," in fact, Thoreau was hardly alone in struggling to conceive evolutionary process within the dominant progressionist model.[30] Historians and philosophers of science still debate the question of how much Darwin's theorizing assumes teleology, directed change, and even absolute progress.[31] In Chambers, the same process understood to link humankind genealogically to animals, and even thereby to place us "in new moral relations towards them," promises to eventuate, as Emerson put it in his journal, in "a better species of the genus Homo."[32] Indeed, Chambers's peculiar notion of "the operation of the law of development" through the saltatory intervention of a "higher generative law" may well be reflected in Walden's "Higher Laws," all but a few paragraphs of which date from 1852 and after.[33] There, obedient to "the faintest but constant suggestions of his genius," and straining to articulate a vision of sensual and moral purity reminiscent of "Friday" in A Week, the narrator describes how "the generative energy, which, when we are loose, dissipates and makes us unclean, when we are continent invigorates and inspires us" (W 219).

In the process, however, Thoreau's language makes dramatically and painfully clear progressionism's fundamental incompatibility with anything like an acceptance of human natural history in the transmutationist sense, as animal nature is consistently figured as "the inferior and brutish nature to which [humankind] is allied." "He is blessed," Thoreau writes, "who is assured that the animal is dying out in him day by day, and the divine being established" (*W* 220). So much does the logic of progressionism define the terms of his meditation at this point in the chapter that even the argument for vegetarianism—ostensibly a means of reverencing animal life—gets framed as purification and ultimately progressionist, even imperialist, ascendance: "I have no doubt that it is part of the destiny of the human race, in its gradual improvement, to leave off eating animals, as surely as the savage tribes have left off eating each other when they came in contact with the more civilized" (*W* 216), leading inexorably to the conclusion that "Nature is hard to be overcome, but she must be overcome" (*W* 221). Thoreau may well have been trying to fashion a "homemade asceticism," meant not to "leave the body behind" but to reform "bodily life," or a religious asceticism of the body inspired by Hindu scripture, as Lawrence Buell and Alan Hodder argue persuasively.[34] Still, the insistent reification of "the animal" over against the human and the divine links the progressionist voice that rises to dominate this chapter unmistakably with a discourse of species, lately examined by Cary Wolfe, that "relies on the tacit agreement that the full transcendence of the human requires the sacrifice of the animal and the animalistic."[35]

Minding the Other Ancestors

If, like his contemporaries, Thoreau had difficulty thinking evolution from within progressionism, by the time of *Walden's* extensive "remaking," beginning "sometime in 1852," he had also become deeply interested in the transmutationist account of a natural history that included humankind.[36] As the *Vestiges* controversy continued, Thoreau became increasingly curious about human affiliation with animal life and therefore more disposed to ponder wilder instincts than progressionist ones. Fuming in the Journal about the commercialization of a Boston menagerie he visited in summer 1851, where the main attraction was "Master Jack & the poney," though the "proprietors had taken wonderful pains to collect rare and interesting animals from all parts of the world," he exclaimed, "I go not there to see a man hug a lion— or fondle a tiger—but to learn how he is related to the wild beast." During another visit a month earlier, he had gazed into "the gem-like changeable greenish reflections from the eyes of the grizzley bear—So glassy that you never saw the surface of the eye," and concluded it "unavoidable [that] the idea of transmigration [is] not merely a fancy of the poets—but an instinct of the race." That is to say, a faint but actual memory mythologized, or what a popular science writer whose work he had extracted in February called "a faint & shadowy knowledge of a previous state of organic existence."[37]

In this context, Thoreau's tensive presentation of the two instincts at the beginning of "Higher Laws," the way his treatment of the "lower instinct" is subsequently "*dis*placed" (as Frederick Garber first described it) by preoccupation with the "higher," and the chapter's deliberate pairing with "Brute Neighbors" all begin to look more rhetorical than confessional.[38] No doubt Thoreau presented his instincts as opposites out of a long-held conviction that "Truth is always paradoxical."[39] Yet the terms of this paradox also accurately reflected how his Anglo-American contemporaries conceived these relations as mutually exclusive, as indeed the progressionist take-over of "Higher Laws" demonstrates. In constructing the pair of chapters around the Janus-faced question of the animal, Thoreau faced first his own and his humanist culture's instinctive repugnance, then turned to meet his actual animal neighbors on their own ground.

Although its trail is much less clearly marked, in other words, Thoreau's curiosity about his "lower" instinct resurfaces in the excursions recounted in "Brute Neighbors," as he turns from the metaphysics of progressionism to the empirical inspection of local animal lives. This chapter is still often regarded as "lacking structural unity, depth of vision," and "a clear sense of the questions it is asking of the natural world."[40] But, as Daniel Peck points out, structurally the sketches clearly move from the familiar creatures that live with or near him to increasingly wilder inhabitants, while Thoreau's manner of shifting modes of apprehension also heightens our sense of the observer's presence.[41] In that self-conscious presence, which Buell also notes, we witness what Alfred Tauber has called Thoreau's "split-screen self"—detached while communing with the world as an aspect of the self—in full operation.[42] Significantly, the underlying question that informs many of the narrator's descriptions of animal behavior concerns the role instinct has played in their adaptations to the micro-environments in which he finds them: the perfect survival instinct of partridge chicks, the slave raid conducted by one species of ant on another, and the readaptation to woodland life of domestic cats gone feral as contrasted with the comic efforts of "many a village dog" who, through domestication, has become so ill-adapted to that life as to be "fit [now] only to course a mud turtle in a victualling cellar" (*W* 232). One of the cats, the "winged cat," provides Thoreau with tantalizing, if possibly spurious, evidence of species transmutation, since "according to naturalists prolific hybrids have been produced by the union of the marten and domestic cat." But just at this controversial point, the naturalist observer himself conveniently mutates into a "poet," noting whimsically (or so it seems) that "this would have been the right kind of cat for me to keep . . . for why should not a poet's cat be winged as well as his horse?" (*W* 233).

In finally juxtaposing the loon's superior agility and instinctive movement with that of the hopeless but doggedly persistent narrator, the last sketch recalls indeed not the feral cats so much as that domesticated village dog. Thoreau casts the scene as "a pretty game . . . a man against a loon"; and so it is (*W* 235). But in contrast with the hierarchy of human intelligence over and above that of the "lower creation" generally assumed in Thoreau's day and explicitly invoked in "Higher Laws," this game, played as it were on a level field, images a reversal of the standing order. In his 1836 lecture "Humanity of Science," Emerson claimed that "Reason finds itself at home in nature [where] everything fits man and is intelligible to him. My mind is not only an inlet into the human mind," he wrote, "but into the inferior intelligences that surround us in the field and the stall."[43] Against this, Thoreau's description emphasizes the loon's adaptive intelligence as much as his physical ability. Rather than simply reacting, the bird responds to the narrator's maneuvers, underscoring the extent to which his pursuer is outmatched not only by superior adaptation but by *wit*: "It was surprising how quickly he made up his mind and put his resolve into execution." The narrator's failure is made to appear even more arrogantly comic as he tries to access precisely the "inlet" presumed by Emerson—instinct as idealist intuition—noting that "While he was thinking one thing in his brain, I was endeavoring to divine his thought in mine" (*W* 234–35).

In these encounters, then, where Thoreau appears to be humanizing animal behavior he is at the same time questioning and naturalizing his own. Not unlike Kirby and Spence, who ponder the sophisticated communication networks that evidence "the language of ants" and the acts of insectival reconnaissance necessary to carry out successful raids such as the one Thoreau describes, "Brute Neighbors" effectively blurs the very boundary between the human and the "lower creation" that the preceding chapter's progressionist voice seemed so obsessively concerned to maintain.[44]

One last encounter, in "Winter Visitors," suggests that Thoreau's comic failure to achieve intersubjectivity with the loon did not end his self-reflexive explorations. Dutifully trudging out into the deep winter snow to "keep an appointment with . . . an old acquaintance among the pines" (W 265), he is rewarded when observing a barred owl asleep, fifteen feet away on a white pine limb, "in broad daylight." After provoking the owl with noise, disturbing his sleep, Thoreau comments:

> I too felt a slumberous influence after watching him half an hour, as he sat thus with his eyes half open, like a cat, winged brother of the cat. There was only a narrow slit left between their lids, by which he preserved a peninsular relation to me; thus, with half-shut eyes, looking out from the land of dreams, and endeavoring to realize me, vague object or mote that interrupted his visions.

Finally, grown impatient, the owl

> launched himself off and flapped through the pines, spreading his wings to unexpected breadth, [and] I could not hear the slightest sound from them. Thus, guided amid the pine boughs rather by a delicate sense of their neighborhood than by sight, feeling his twilight way as it were with his sensitive pinions, he found a new perch, where he might in peace await the dawning of his day. (W 266)

This incident reawakens the issue of instinct, animal affiliation, and "old acquaintance," while allowing the evocative encounter to speak for itself. As the account merges the identities of observer and observed in ways that recall the animal sketches of "Brute Neighbors," it crosses the threshold into animal subjectivity as they do not. Unexpectedly, too, the situation in "The Village" where Thoreau tactilely navigates the dark woods at night is precisely mirrored here: the owl feels his twilight way between the pines "with his sensitive pinions," steers by the same metaphors around peninsula and through his own "land of dreams." Recall, too, that the same naturalist-poet who wanted to "keep" a winged cat—the totem of transmutation and inspiration—is now face to face with that fabled species' wild brother, suggesting perhaps his own brotherhood. More remarkably, Thoreau subtly assumes the owl's point of view, thus granting this creature a mysterious subjectivity as he finds a new perch and "awaits the dawning of his day." In short, the whole conflicted question of two instincts—one higher and spiritual, the other low and brutish—is reframed in this encounter with a creature who is both brother and other, no less the barred owl (*Strix nebulosa*) than an ancient figure of an even more ancient wisdom: an old acquaintance indeed.

Following Thoreau's instincts leads to three conclusions. First, the "savage delight" and desire to internalize the "wildness" represented by the woodchuck "stealing across my path," described at the beginning of "Higher Laws," introduces a transmutationist narrative that runs counter to the more visible progressionist one (*W* 210).[45] Woven into the manuscript after 1851, this counter-narrative thus comprises another in "the sum of [Thoreau's] histories" at Walden that, as Sattelmeyer has shown, lie "simultaneously present in a text at once fabular, mythic, scientific, and even scriptural in its dimensions."[46] Second, if, as I have argued, the obscurity of Thoreau's depiction of his transmutationist instinct points to the difficulty of thinking evolutionary relations within the dominant progressionist model, it no doubt also registers the highly charged atmosphere of the controversy in the United States, where vigorous opposition to Chambers's theory was led not only by clerics but also by scientists such as Asa Gray, whom Thoreau respected. If the evolutionary debates helped awaken his affiliation for the wild, the ferocity of those debates, at a time when the commercial failure of *A Week* had appeared to maroon his literary career, might well have contributed to driving that exploration, textually speaking, underground. Finally, while the co-presence of two opposed narratives of development complicates Buell's picture of the author's intellectual formation during the composition of *Walden* as following "a path from homocentricism toward biocentricism," the continuation of that trajectory is evident enough after *Walden*. In light of that later career, the tension between the two narratives seems as much an indication of Thoreau's struggle to let go of the progressionist origins of the Walden project as of a difficulty coming to terms with "the animal."[47] For, judging by the comparative absence of progressionism in post-*Walden* writings, he did let it go.

Notes

1. Henry D. Thoreau, *Walden*, ed. J. Lyndon Shanley (Princeton: Princeton University Press, 1971). All references are to this edition and will hereafter be noted in the text.

2. Evelleen Richards, "A Question of Property Rights: Richard Owen's Evolutionism Reassessed," *British Journal for the History of Science* 20 (June 1987): 168.

3. Milton Millhauser, *Just before Darwin: Robert Chambers and "Vestiges"* (Middletown, CT: Wesleyan University Press, 1959).

4. James A. Secord, *Victorian Sensation: The Extraordinary Publication, Reception, and Secret Authorship of "Vestiges of the Natural History of Creation"* (Chicago: University of Chicago Press, 2000).

5. Laura Dassow Walls, *Seeing New Worlds: Henry David Thoreau and Nineteenth-Century Natural Science* (Madison: University of Wisconsin Press, 1995) and *Emerson's Life in Science: The Culture of Truth* (Ithaca, NY: Cornell University Press, 2003); and Eric Wilson, *Emerson's Sublime Science* (New York: St. Martin's Press, 1999).

6. Robert J. Richards, *Darwin and the Emergence of Evolutionary Theories of Mind and Behavior* (Chicago: University of Chicago Press, 1987), 8.

7. Ibid., 35.

8. Ibid., 127.

9. Quoted in ibid., 141.

10. Quoted in Adrian Desmond, *Archetypes and Ancestors: Palaeontology in Victorian London, 1850–1875* (Chicago: University of Chicago Press, 1982), 29. On the distinction between progressionism and transmutationism, see Evelleen Richards, " 'Metaphorical Mystifications': The Romantic Gestation of Nature in British Biology," in *Romanticism and the Sciences*, ed. Andrew Cunningham and Nicholas Jardine (Cambridge: Cambridge University Press, 1990), 130–43.

11. [Robert Chambers], *Vestiges of the Natural History of Creation*, 2nd ed. (New York: Wiley and Putnam, 1845), 47. Unless otherwise noted, all citations are to this edition, the one Emerson owned and, I assume, Thoreau borrowed.

12. Ibid., 124.

13. Ibid., 243, 227. The phrase "actual progression of species" appears in *Explanations: A Sequel*, reprinted in *Vestiges of the Natural History of Creation and Other Evolutionary Writings*, ed. James A. Secord (Chicago: University of Chicago Press, 1994), 109–10.

14. [Chambers], *Vestiges*, 232, 237, 240, 232.

15. Trevor Levere, *Poetry Realized in Nature: Samuel Taylor Coleridge and Early Nineteenth-Century Science* (Cambridge: Cambridge University Press, 1981), 207, 57.

16. Ibid., 213; Samuel Taylor Coleridge, *Aids to Reflection*, ed. John Beer (Princeton: Princeton University Press, 1993), 247.

17. Coleridge, *Aids to Reflection*, 235.

18. Samuel Taylor Coleridge, *Shorter Works and Fragments*, ed. H. J. Jackson and J. R. de J. Jackson, 2 vols. (Princeton: Princeton University Press, 1995), 1:483 [editors' note]. On Coleridge's use of and divergence from Schelling and Steffens in the "Theory of Life," see Levere, *Poetry Realized in Nature*, 205–19.

19. Coleridge, *Shorter Works*, 1:501. The editors argue that because of Coleridge's religious convictions, "the degree of concordance between his views and [the *Naturphiloso-phen*], which is reflected in the "Theory of Life" was probably gone by the end of 1817" (483). For documentation and analysis of Thoreau's reading of the "Theory of Life" in late 1848, see Robert Sattelmeyer and Richard A. Hocks, "Thoreau and Coleridge's *Theory of Life*," *Studies in the American Renaissance* (Charlottesville: University Press of Virginia, 1985), 269–84.

20. Samuel Taylor Coleridge, *Biographia Literaria: or, Biographical Sketches of My Literary Life and Opinions*, ed. James Engell and W. Jackson Bate, 2 vols. (Princeton: Princeton University Press, 1983), 1:237, 241–42.

21. Letter to Edward Bliss Emerson, May 31, 1834, *The Letters of Ralph Waldo Emerson*, ed. Ralph L. Rusk, 6 vols. (New York: Columbia University Press, 1939), 1:412. Paraphrasing Coleridge, Emerson describes it as "the distinction of Milton Coleridge & the Germans."

22. Similarly, Emerson's junior American Scholar, the "schoolboy under the bending dome of day," closely resembles Coleridge's philosophical chemist in *The Friend*, who "labours instinctively to extract . . . the unity of principle through all the diversity of forms," a "principle of connection given by the mind, and sanctioned by the correspondency of nature" (*The Friend*, ed. Barbara E. Rooke [Princeton: Princeton University Press, 1969], 1:470–71).

23. *The Collected Works of Ralph Waldo Emerson*, ed. Alfred R. Ferguson, Joseph Slater, and Douglas Emory Wilson, 6 vols. to date (Cambridge: Harvard University Press, 1971–), 1:42; 2:37; 1:206–7; *The Early Lectures of Ralph Waldo Emerson*, ed. Stephen E. Whicher and Robert Spiller, 3 vols. (Cambridge: Harvard University Press, 1966), 2:254.

24. J. Lyndon Shanley, *The Making of Walden, with the Text of the First Version* (Chicago: University of Chicago Press, 1957), 191, 143.

25. Henry D. Thoreau, *Journal 2: 1844–1848*, ed. Robert Sattelmeyer (Princeton: Princeton University Press, 1984), 146.

26. Ronald Earl Clapper, "The Development of *Walden*: A Genetic Text," Diss. in 2 vols., University of California, Los Angeles, 1967, 2:475, n. 1, 2:476, n. 1. Guidance by the stars presumably indicates obedience to the higher self. As Thoreau glosses them in *A Week*, the stars "chiefly answer to the ideal in man" (*A Week on the Concord and Merrimack Rivers*, ed. Carl F. Hovde, William L. Howarth, and Elizabeth Hall Witherell [Princeton: Princeton University Press, 1983], 391).

27. Clapper, "Development," 1:276.

28. Ibid., 1:277–78, n. 8.

29. According to Clapper, this section of the paragraph ("Little is to be expected . . . darkening way.") was added in F (1:278–79).

30. Lawrence Buell, *The Environmental Imagination: Thoreau, Nature Writing, and the Formation of American Culture* (Cambridge: Harvard University Press, 1995), 125, 138.

31. See the essays by Robert J. Richards, Michael Ruse, Daniel W. McShea, and Stephen J. Gould in *The Philosophy of Biology*, ed. David L. Hull and Michael Ruse (Oxford:

Oxford University Press, 1998). For a comprehensive study, see Ruse's *Monad to Man: The Concept of Progress in Evolutionary Biology* (Cambridge: Harvard University Press, 1996).

32. Chambers, *Explanations: A Sequel*; Emerson, *Journals and Miscellaneous Notebooks of Ralph Waldo Emerson*, ed. Ralph H. Orth and Alfred R. Ferguson, 16 vols. (Cambridge: Harvard University Press, 1971), 9:232. Chambers argues further in *Explanations* that because of this "essential connect[ion]," we "are bound to respect the rights of animals as of our human associates. We are bound to respect even their feelings" (184–85).

33. *Vestiges*, 164, 177.

34. Buell, *Environmental Imagination*, 392, 393; Alan D. Hodder, *Thoreau's Ecstatic Witness* (New Haven: Yale University Press, 2001), 188–90.

35. Cary Wolfe, *Animal Rites: American Culture, the Discourse of Species, and Posthumanist Theory* (Chicago: University of Chicago Press, 2003), 6. Wolfe argues further that this "in turn makes possible a symbolic economy" that legitimates the destruction of "other *humans* as well by marking *them* as animal," a symbolic economy arguably at work in the way Thoreau represents vegetarianism as the next step in the same unilinear civilizing process that earlier had displaced cannibalism.

36. Robert Sattelmeyer, "The Remaking of *Walden*," in *Writing the American Classics*, ed. James Barbour and Tom Quirk (Chapel Hill: University of North Carolina Press, 1990), 58.

37. Henry D. Thoreau, *Journal 3: 1848–1851*, ed. Robert Sattelmeyer, Mark R. Patterson, and William Rossi (Princeton: Princeton University Press, 1990), 350, 351, 277, 199. The popular writer was Robert Hunt, from *The Poetry of Science* (Boston: Gould, Kendall, & Lincoln, 1850).

38. Frederick Garber, *Thoreau's Redemptive Imagination* (New York: New York University Press, 1977), 120.

39. Henry D. Thoreau, *Journal 1: 1837–1844*, ed. Elizabeth Witherell et al. (Princeton: Princeton University Press, 1981), 143.

40. Robert Milder, *Reimagining Thoreau* (Cambridge: Cambridge University Press, 1995), 140, 139.

41. H. Daniel Peck, *Thoreau's Morning Work: Memory and Perception in "A Week on the Concord and Merrimack Rivers," the Journal and "Walden"* (New Haven: Yale University Press, 1990), 117–22.

42. Buell, *Environmental Imagination*, 258; Alfred I. Tauber, *Henry David Thoreau and the Moral Agency of Knowing* (Berkeley: University of California Press, 2001), 162.

43. *Early Lectures of Ralph Waldo Emerson*, 2:34.

44. William Kirby and William Spence, *An Introduction to Entomology: or Elements of the Natural History of Insects*, 3rd ed. (London: Longman, Hurst, Rees, Orme, and Brown, 1823), 2:61.

45. I should note that while, according to Clapper, the woodchuck incident does not appear in the manuscript until E (late 1852–53), a version of it was first recorded in the Walden journal during Thoreau's first summer at the pond. There, after identifying "an instinct in me conducting to a mystic spiritual life—and also another—to a primitive

savage life," he describes the scene as though managed by a higher power: "Toward evening—as the world waxes darker I am permitted to see the woodchuck stealing across my path, and tempted to seize and devour it" (Clapper, "Development," 2:565; *Journal 2*, 177).

46. Sattelmeyer, "Remaking of *Walden*," 55.
47. Buell, *Environmental Imagination*, 138.

Thoreau's Materialism

From Walden *to* Wild Fruits

LANCE NEWMAN

"Think of our life in nature—daily to be shown matter, to come in contact with it,—rocks, trees, wind on our cheeks! the *solid* earth! the *actual* world! the *common sense! Contact! Contact! Who* are we? *where* are we?"

THOREAU'S RETROSPECTIVE outburst about climbing Ktaadn is so extravagantly fractured that its argument can get lost. It begins with relaxed contemplation of the central Romantic idea, "our life in nature," and then descends rhythmically from the abstract to the concrete until it grounds that idea in the irreducible facticity, the thingness, of the planet. Having found a *point d'appui*, it rises again, the rhythm more insistent and confident now, opening outward from the actuality of the nonhuman "earth," to the materiality of the complete ecosocial "world," and finally to the patterns of human understanding that bind its communities. The climactic ejaculation— "Contact! Contact!"—occurs only now, with the thought that we live together not only with nature but with each other. We—people and the earth—are in material fact a "we."[1]

The movement of this soliloquy mirrors Thoreau's intellectual growth over the course of his adult life. Beginning in the thin atmosphere of Romantic idealism, with its sharp distinctions between spirit and matter, "man" and nature, Thoreau came over time to see the natural and social worlds as inseparably integrated and concrete. His thinking about natural and human history developed in parallel until, in his final years, he connected issues of environmental and social justice into a synthetic critique of the priorities of capitalism. Moreover, rather than remain satisfied with attempting to reform ideas, he began to experiment with strategies for intervening materially to change the society around him. In other words, he moved gradually away from Transcendental idealism and individualism, becoming not only the scientific ecologist we see in the late natural history manuscripts but increasingly a political radical as well, one who stressed the need to make ideas into tools for collectively transforming the existing ecosocial order.

This essay begins by briefly surveying competing theories of Thoreau's ideas on the relations between mind and matter, and then turns to the critique of capitalism framed in the first chapter of *Walden,* showing that the recently published *Wild Fruits* proposes a second answer to the question of "Economy." Emerson famously scolded Thoreau for his habit of contradiction. And readers frequently encounter, as James McIntosh argues, "opposed attitudes vibrating against each other in the crucible of an essay, a poem, or a day's journal." Thoreau's writings are structured by a "programmed inconsistency" that reflects his constantly "shifting stance toward nature."[2] It has usually been thought that the axis along which this shifting occurs had Mind and Nature as its poles, so that the metaphysical question Thoreau faced was this: Which of these two forces dominates as they interact to create human experience of the world? *Walden,* the text on which most of our knowledge of its author has been built, suggests that he placed his final faith in the power of the imagination to make a new day dawn. However, recent readers describe Thoreau's dilemma as a complex choice between idealist and materialist accounts of the world and between intuitive and empiricist modes of knowing it. Thoreau died just as his later ways of thinking about mind and matter, about people and nature, had begun to reach maturity, and just as he was beginning to articulate a new way of thinking. He continued to deplore the alienation from both labor and nature produced by life under capitalism, but in his late natural history essays, and especially in the guidebook he left in manuscript, *Wild Fruits,* he had begun to envision a utopian alternative, an organic community living in daily communion with the physical body of the land.

Thoreau's Materialism

After praising Thoreau for having "dedicated his genius with such entire love
to the fields, hills and waters of his native town, that he made them known
and interesting to all reading Americans," Emerson ended his eulogy on a
note of disappointment: "The country knows not yet, or in the least part, how
great a son it has lost." The disappointment was not just that Thoreau had
died young. Emerson saw his protégé as a broken promise: "Instead of engineering for all America, he was the captain of a huckleberry party." Instead of
taking a leading role in the grand political experiment of republicanism, he
had devoted himself to the relative triviality of natural history. Thoreau himself occasionally expressed anxiety along these lines: "I fear that the character
of my knowledge is from year to year becoming more distinct & scientific—
That in exchange for views as wide as heaven's cope I am being narrowed
down to the field of the microscope—."[3] On the strength of this evidence, it
is possible to read the trajectory of his life as a descent from high idealism and
seriousness to a crabbed and narrow materialism, from truth to mere fact.
Thoreau read both John Locke's *Essay Concerning Human Understanding* and
Emerson's *Nature* during his senior year at Harvard. And according to this
way of thinking about them, *Nature* convinced him to reject Locke's empiricism and to see nature as "the present expositor of the divine mind." If nature
is God's thought for America, rightly apprehended through intuition and
sympathy, then the unrelenting facticity of the Journal in the 1850s may be
read as evidence of a failure of Thoreau's imagination.[4]

On the other hand, readers who appreciate the richly detailed passages of
nature description in the Journal often see the same trajectory but make the
reverse evaluation. For instance, William Howarth reads Thoreau's career as
"a continuous ascent, sustained by the Journal, and rising from youthful confusion into a triumphant maturity." Howarth argues that in his apprentice
years as a writer, Thoreau operated according to a "Platonic bias" he had
learned from Emerson, transforming "the particulars of nineteenth-century
New England into universal symbols." But later Thoreau came to believe that
"the mind must absorb facts and adjust to their complexity," so he used his
Journal "as a place to test his powers of seeing and hearing." Gradually, his
"entries on birds and plants became more precise and detailed," and he became "less fanciful in his reading of their metaphysical significance" and
"gravitated in his writing from the ideal of mystery to that of truth."[5]

Perhaps the most important achievement of Howarth's transformative reading will be that it demonstrated the power of reinterpreting Thoreau from the perspective of texts other than *Walden*. This shift in emphasis has made possible, over the last two decades, a series of increasingly sensitive and accurate readings of Thoreau's relationship to the science of his day. These studies, all of which begin from the late natural history manuscripts, have shown that at the same time that he was strongly attracted to the idea of nature as a subject of systematic study, Thoreau rejected narrow forms of empiricism that emphasized objective observation of tightly limited phenomena. Instead, as Laura Dassow Walls has demonstrated, he participated in a proto-ecological "empirical holism" based on "relational knowing," a form of scientific practice typified especially by the work of Alexander von Humboldt, who saw mind, or knowledge, not as supervening the world of particulars, but as an emergent property of their interrelationships. Thoreau saw his "task to be the joining of poetry, philosophy, and science into a harmonized whole that emerged from the interconnected details of natural facts." In order to come to understand such complex systems, Thoreau attempted to perfect what Donald Worster calls "a new, more intense empiricism" rooted in "day-to-day physical intimacy with nature." In other words, for much of his adult life he was actively mediating between idealist and materialist accounts of the world, as well as between intuitional and empiricist modes of investigating it.[6]

Thoreau's interest in science and the philosophy of science is recognizable as early as his first piece of environmental writing, "The Natural History of Massachusetts," which he ends by observing, "we do not learn by inference and deduction and the application of mathematics to philosophy, but by direct intercourse and sympathy." Thoreau is not rejecting empiricism here, but calling for a more wholly engaged mode of observation: "The true man of science will know nature better by his finer organization; he will smell, taste, see, hear, feel, better than other men. His will be a deeper and finer experience."[7] Despite this early manifestation, Thoreau's interest in natural history and science would remain largely undeveloped during the 1840s. After graduating from Harvard, he moved home to Concord where he struggled to shape his writing to Transcendentalist conventions, composing essays on literary and philosophical topics that would suit the needs of the *Dial*. During this time, probably in response to Emerson's encouragement, he thought of himself mainly as a poet. His verse was mostly quite abstract, though he did experiment with ways to make the conventionally idealist genre of Romantic

lyric poetry open itself to the material particulars of Concord.[8] In 1849,
Thoreau's relationship with Emerson cooled, and he turned wholeheartedly
to interests and proclivities that he may formerly have suppressed in defer-
ence to his mentor. His reading shifted sharply, from the classics, philosophy,
comparative religion, and poetry on one hand, to natural history, American
history, ethnography, and travel writing on the other. By this time daily walks
had become a routine, and the Journal had shifted in the direction of systematic observation of natural phenomena.

The 1850s, then, was a decade of renewed and intensified mediation between idealism and materialism for Thoreau. This philosophical conflict was
concretized by the fierce competition between two models of the study of
natural history. On one hand, there was the residual idealist notion of creation, principally defended in the United States by Harvard's Louis Agassiz,
who posited multiple episodes of divine intervention. On the other, there was
the emergent materialist theory of evolution, which would triumph with the
publication of Darwin's *Origin of Species* in 1859, which Thoreau read eagerly
as soon as it arrived in Concord. Over the course of the 1850s, Thoreau was
clearly moving in Darwin's direction, as evidenced by his two essays in scientific ecology, "The Dispersion of Seeds" and "The Succession of Forest Trees."
At the same time, he continued to think of nature as "an externalization of
spirit" and of divine creation as an ongoing process in a continuous material
present. In other words, he remained committed to the idealist notion of an
active supernatural force driving natural processes, while at the same time his
study of those processes, and the language he used to describe them, became
increasingly materialist and empiricist.[9]

Now, to complicate this picture, Robert Sattelmeyer observes that
Thoreau's overall "development . . . was clearly in the direction of increasing
interest in the study of and writing about nature on the one hand, and on the
other the expression of increasingly sharp and outspoken views on sensitive
social and political issues of his day." But after mapping Thoreau's reading in
the sciences and the complexity of his ways of thinking about natural history,
Sattelmeyer observes that Thoreau's "political writing . . . is less susceptible
to analysis in terms of specific intellectual debts than most other areas of
his thought." His political thought, rather than responding directly to the
political economists and philosophers of his day, "developed in a sort of organic way out of certain political pressure points of his age—the extension of
slavery and the question of individual rights versus civil law in particular—

coming into conflict with some of his most fundamental and strongly held convictions about the purposes and conduct of life." His increasing radicalism, that is, was partly a consequence of participating in the abolitionist movement's increasing willingness to go beyond moral suasion to various forms of direct political action. While this kind of historical pressure, the pressure of events, was surely decisive, it is also true that Thoreau's increasing radicalism found a theoretical warrant in his increasingly materialist understanding of ecosocial history.[10]

William Howarth observes that through the 1850s, Thoreau increasingly "moves away from problems of self-definition toward broader issues of history and culture" and that as this process goes on, Thoreau does not differentiate clearly between human and natural history. "By early 1857 Thoreau's studies in Concord had turned from detailed natural facts to the broader subject of community," so that his Journal became "an open history of his people and the land." More and more, he saw natural and human history as parts of an integrated ecosocial process, and he attempted, as Laura Dassow Walls puts it, "to read and tell a history of man and nature together, as and in one single, interconnected act." Howarth maintains that Thoreau draws quite conservative final political conclusions as a result of reasoning by analogy from his studies of natural cycles. Thoreau, he argues, arrived in his Journal at "a new vision of America's destiny: the country was not immortal, moving always onward and upward, but was caught in cycles of birth and death, the law of natural succession." But this conclusion cuts against the evidence of the increasing radicalism of the reform essays. Thoreau's first published political essay is "Paradise (To Be) Regained," a review of J. A. Etzler's technological utopian manifesto, *The Paradise within the Reach of all Men, without Labor, by Powers of Nature and Machinery* (1842). The young Thoreau ridicules what he sees as the mechanical thinking behind Etzler's scheme, with its vision of planned collective transformation of the material basis of human social relations. As an alternative he endorses self-reliance, the idealist political philosophy of individual reform. However, by the end of the 1850s, in his later abolitionist essays, Thoreau has renounced his faith in the power of ideas to spontaneously reform individuals and, through them, to organically transform whole societies. Instead he has recognized that ideas about reform become a force for material change in the world only when they inspire people to take direct action, to intervene in the course of history. The simultaneous changes in Thoreau's political and scientific thought suggest, in other words, that as he moved increasingly toward a materialist understanding of nature, Thoreau applied this same mode of analysis to the capitalist social order, and therefore was driven more and more toward radical political conclusions.[11]

Walden *and Capitalism*

Walden reflects Thoreau's ongoing process of mediation between idealism and materialism, between transcendentalism and science. On one hand, he achieves a new level, vis-à-vis his prior work, of detailed, representational accuracy in his descriptions of the woods around Concord. On the other, he still consistently pushes natural facts to become metaphors and symbols of human experience. On one hand, the book articulates a moral critique of social relations under capitalism based on a materialist analysis of economic relationships. On the other, it offers an idealist and individualist solution to this problem. *Walden's* first sentence frames the book's concerns: "When I wrote the following pages, or rather the bulk of them, I lived alone, in the woods, a mile from any neighbor, in a house which I had built myself, on the shore of Walden Pond, in Concord, Massachusetts, and earned my living by the labor of my hands only" (*W* 3).[12] Rhetorically, the emphasis here is on the last phrase. The cabin is located in an intermediate space, just a short walk into the woods, and the pond is firmly contained in the township. Moreover, the string of miscellaneous descriptors that locates the cabin also foregrounds the definite assertion about who built it, an assertion that is repeated in the alliterative final phrase. This is not a book that is mainly about the woods. It is about earning a living there. Accounts of aesthetic experience of nature in *Walden* are meant mainly to demonstrate what gets lost—along with reading, introspection, and spirituality—when work dominates our lives. The book's introduction, the pages that precede its systematic discussion of the four basic necessities of life, "Food, Shelter, Clothing, and Fuel," mount an analysis of the process whereby these forms of ideal experience have been cheapened (*W* 12).

"Economy" begins by announcing as its topic its audience's "outward condition or circumstances in this world, in this town, what it is, whether it is necessary that it be as bad as it is, whether it cannot be improved as well as not" (*W* 4). From this starting point, Thoreau describes the effects of capitalist property relations, labor relations, and competition on the lives of individual workers and farmers. On the one hand, there are those small farmers "whose misfortune it is to have inherited farms, houses, barns, cattle, and farming tools; for these are more easily acquired than got rid of" (*W* 5). On the other, there are those who "are poor . . . and have come to this page to spend borrowed or stolen time, robbing your creditors of an hour" (*W* 6). Both face the trap of debt and to escape it must "persuade your neighbor to let you make his shoes, or his hat, or his coat, or his carriage, or import his groceries for him" (*W* 7). Thoreau performs a delicate balancing act here, giving clear attention to the hard material reality of economic relationships between individuals, but then showing that these relationships have moral and social content that gets forgotten. The things that get done for money are the kinds of basic human tasks that carry individual lives forward and bind communities together, and they are demeaned, as human interactions, by their intrication in a cash economy.[13] Thoreau generalizes from his observations on the "outward condition" of his readers to an overall assessment of the effect of capitalist social relations on the character of human aesthetic and spiritual experience. Most people work so much that their inner lives are emptied out; they "are so occupied with the factitious cares and superfluously coarse labors of life that its finer fruits cannot be plucked by them." He goes further, emphasizing that the moral character of individual human lives is compromised specifically because those lives occur within a constraining web of competitive economic relationships, a market: "The laboring man has not leisure for a true integrity day by day; he cannot afford to sustain the manliest relations to men; his labor would depreciate in the market" (*W* 6). In other words, material relationships have aggregate moral effects across whole societies.

Much of the rest of "Economy," after this first framing section, sets out to document various forms of moral debility that are produced when basic human needs are transformed by competitive social relations. Thoreau deplores luxury as an accretion, a kind of plaque that comes with civilization, and he focuses especially on the competitive acquisition and ostentatious display of luxury goods as a display of social and economic power: "It is an interesting question how far men would retain their relative rank if they were divested of their clothes. Could you, in such a case, tell surely of any company of civilized men, which belonged to the most respected class?" (*W* 22). Thoreau describes how this kind of competition for cultural power entraps people so that they become "slave-drivers" of themselves. And he observes that this process is set in motion by the ruling class: "It is the luxurious and dissipated who set the fashion which the herd so diligently follow" (W 36). Thus, it is specifically in the context of class societies that "most of the luxuries, and many of the so-called comforts of life [become] positive hinderances [*sic*] to the elevation of mankind" (W 14). Fine clothes, for instance, are hindrances not only because the hard labor required to get them prevents plucking life's finer fruits. But more, they require participation in an economic system based on exploitation, a "factory system" in which "the condition of the operatives is becoming every day more like that of the English" of Manchester and Birmingham (W 26). After all, in this degraded society, "the principal object is, not that mankind may be well and honestly clad, but, unquestionably, that the corporations may be enriched" (W 26–27). In other words, material structures at the level of whole social orders entangle people in moral relationships that must be taken seriously.

Thoreau recognizes most clearly that moral experience is rooted in materiality when he states that people "are so occupied with the factitious cares and superfluously coarse labors of life that its finer fruits cannot be plucked by them." But this crucial sentence also reveals his conviction that "most men, even in this comparatively free country" become entangled in capitalist economic relations "through mere ignorance and mistake" (W 6). After making such a clear assessment of the moral or ideal effects of these material relations, Thoreau, surprisingly, seems to adopt a cavalierly individualist position about how to respond. It is worth remembering that it was far more plausible during his lifetime than now to imagine that it is possible to withdraw from the labor market. Even so, Thoreau is startlingly confident. He is astonished that people "honestly think there is no choice left" (W 8), for after all, "what a man thinks of himself, that it is which determines, or rather indicates, his fate" (W 7). And he sets out to demonstrate just this possibility by renouncing all forms of luxury, choosing not to spend his time "in earning rich carpets or other fine furniture, or delicate cookery, or a house in the Grecian or the Gothic style just yet" (W 70). Moreover, because he acknowledges that the basic necessities must be secured before it is possible "to entertain the true problems of life with freedom" (W 12), he determines to secure them by his own labor outside the nexus of material social relationships.

Thoreau's individualism in *Walden* is part of a confrontational, aggressive persona designed to startle his audience into new ways of thinking. For the book's final goal is to engender wholesale social reform through individual acts of self-reform: "The only coöperation which is commonly possible is exceedingly partial and superficial. . . . If a man has faith he will coöperate with equal faith every where; if he has not faith, he will continue to live like the rest of the world, whatever company he is joined to" (*W* 71–72). This jab at participants in the failed Brook Farm experiment is also a doctrinaire statement of the idealist philosophy of self-reliance. Thoreau carries this polemic through to the end, but he hints at a consciousness that his experiment has failed. Individual withdrawal from the market into the world of ideal beans is not as easy at it might seem, for "wherever a man goes, men will pursue and paw him with their dirty institutions" (*W* 171).[14] *Walden*'s solution, in other words, is incommensurate with the problem as it is laid out in "Economy." Thoreau reveals this disjunction again in a passage that foreshadows the second solution he will propose to this problem: "When formerly I was looking about to see what I could do for a living . . . I thought often and seriously of picking huckleberries." Like hoeing beans, berry picking would have been an attempt to negotiate an individual solution to a social crisis, and Thoreau acknowledges as much: "But I have since learned that trade curses every thing it handles; and though you trade in messages from heaven, the whole curse of trade attaches to the business" (*W* 69–70). In his next major project, *Wild Fruits,* Thoreau would again experiment imaginatively with picking huckleberries, but no longer alone; this time he saw himself doing so together with a community.

Wild Fruits *and Community*

Thoreau spent his final winter putting his literary affairs in order. At the beginning of April 1862, a month before he died, he sent his last essay, "Wild Apples," to the *Atlantic Monthly.* He had excerpted the essay from a longer book-length manuscript that he left wrapped in a large sheet of paper. On this wrapper, he had written a title, *Wild Fruits.* This manuscript passed through several collections for the next century and a half and has only recently been published.[15] On its surface, the book is a botanical guide to the wild plants of New England. But it moves far beyond the work of cataloging and identifying. "Most of us are still related to our native fields as the navigator to undiscovered islands in the sea. We can any afternoon discover a new fruit there which will surprise us by its beauty or sweetness" (*WF* 3). These are the book's first sentences. Most of us, it turns out, are related to Thoreau's writings in the same way. To read *Wild Fruits* is to be surprised by a beauty and sweetness we do not at all associate with the antagonistic hermit of *Walden*. The manuscript is incomplete, fragmentary, and sometimes self-contradictory, so any reading of it necessarily amounts to a speculative construction of a possible book. Even so, *Wild Fruits* clearly confirms the trajectory of Thoreau's traverse from idealism and individualism to materialism and communalism. It is a guidebook, yes, but it is also a visionary portrait of a devotional life on the land. It not only envisions an organic community as an alternative to capitalism, it works to convoke such a community by modeling rituals of natural communion.[16]

Wild Fruits consists of more than a hundred entries, widely variable in length and completeness, each describing a variety of plant that produces recognizable fruits. The product of a decade of systematic natural history observation, the book is rich in botanical information. Some of the less finished entries consist of little more than the dates on which, from year to year, a particular species first produces fruit. Others work up this and other information into treatments of proto-ecological hypotheses. For instance, the entry for "Black Huckleberry," reflecting Thoreau's 1860 reading of Darwin, describes how speciation allows plants, "slightly modified by soil and climate," to exploit a variety of niches: "Corn and potatoes, apples and pears, have comparatively a narrow range, but we can fill our basket with whortleberries on the summit of Mount Washington" (*WF* 45). The various species of huckleberry have evolved for different elevations, so that at least one species occurs in every available New England habitat.

Unlike most guidebooks, though, Thoreau organizes his entries chronologically by date of fruit production, so that *Wild Fruits* is in effect a botanical almanac. Like all almanacs, it contains not undifferentiated scientific information, but information relevant to the ongoing relationship between humans, plants, and the seasons. However, Thoreau focuses not on agriculture, but on the human significance of *un*cultivated plants. The book's first entry is for "Elm," quoted here in its entirety:

> Before the tenth of May (from the seventh to the ninth), the winged seeds or samaræ of the elms give them a leafy appearance, or as if covered with little hops, before the leaf buds are opened. This must be the earliest of our trees and shrubs to go to seed. It is so early that most mistake the fruit before it falls for leaves, and we owe to it the first deepening of the shadows in our streets. (*WF* 6)

The opening sentence here deals in recognizably empirical botanical information, with matters of fact interrupted only briefly by a simile employed only to allow for accurate visualization. The second sentence, though, quietly introduces a plural subject of this knowledge. And the third flowers into truth, but not the kind of transcendental truth we might expect from Thoreau. Instead, he explains a truth about the experiential meaning of elms for the plural subject of which he is a part, his community. Elms are responsible for the sudden and mysterious transition from the hard white daylight of the New England winter to the warm green shade of summer. Similarly, the next entry, for "Dandelion," notes that at the same time that elms fruit, "we begin to see a dandelion gone to seed here and there in the greener grass of some more sheltered and moist bank, perhaps before we had detected its rich yellow disk —that little seedy spherical system which boys are wont to blow to see if their mothers want them" (*WF* 6). This sentence, like the entry as a whole, is structured around the relationship between an implied community and natural phenomena.

This emphasis on collective aesthetic and ritual experience of nature holds true throughout *Wild Fruits,* and it allows Thoreau to introduce a wide range of kinds of material including quotations from old herbariums and narratives by explorers and settlers, as well as anecdotes about both Native American and folk uses of plants. Of the "Black Cherry," for instance, he writes:

> Some, I hear, make a spirituous drink with them, which they disguise under such names as "cherry-bounce." The common way of gathering them is to shake them down upon sheets spread beneath the tree. I remember once shaking a tree in this wise, and when I came to gather up the edges of the cloth, I found an old cent of the last century among the cherries. (*WF* 98–99)

Individual and collective experiences of this kind, collected across time and cultures, cohere to make up the longest entries. And it soon becomes clear that what determines the fullness of an entry is not the amount of botanical information Thoreau wishes to set down, but the relative cultural importance of the plant described. Thus, the names he chooses for many of the plants, especially those which produce edible berries, are not scientific, but common. Thoreau satirizes the irrationality of naming Black Huckleberry, "*Gaylussacia resinosa,* after the celebrated French chemist":

If he had been the first to distill its juices and put them in this globular bag, he would deserve this honor; or if he had been a celebrated picker of huckleberries, perchance paid for his school-ing so, or only notoriously a lover of them, we should not so much object. But it does not appear that he ever saw one. What if a committee of Parisian naturalists had been appointed to break this important news to an Indian maiden who had just filled her basket on the shore of Lake Huron! (*WF* 37)

Thoreau's alternative to Linnean binomials is to differentiate between kinds of berry according to where and when they can be found by pickers: "Early Low Blueberry," "High Blueberry," "Late Low Blueberry," and so on. This pragmatic method of naming emphasizes the relevance of the book's in-formation to those who wish not just to know abstractly about plants, but to live interactively with them.[17]

Interestingly, this interactivity is not only transcultural, but also transspe-cific. For instance, the entry for "Sweet Flag" describes the growth of that species in the spring, notes that it is a favorite food of muskrats, and then relates that the "Indians of British America" use it as a remedy for colic. Thoreau continues: "Who has not when a child had this same remedy admin-istered to him for that complaint—though the medicine came recommended by a lump of sugar, which the Cree boys did not get. . . . Thus, we begin our summer like the musquash. We take our first course at the same table with him. . . . He is so much like us; we are so much like him" (*WF* 8). The basic likeness across cultures and species that Thoreau emphasizes here is one of materiality, of a necessary rootedness in physical nature. This is a common motif throughout the text. Writing of the "Early Low Blueberry," he describes how two species, endemic to different areas, "pass into one another" in one location "by insensible degrees, so that it appears as if the seeds of the downy Canada blueberry carried far enough south would at length produce the smooth Pennsylvania one, and vice versa—just as men wear furs in the north, but linen in the south" (*WF* 26). Similarly, in the entry for "Thistle," Thoreau observes that "what is called the Canada thistle is the earliest, and the gold-finch or thistlebird . . . knows when it is ripe sooner than I. So soon as the heads begin to be dry, I see him pulling them to pieces and scattering the down, for he sets it a-flying regularly every year all over the country, just as I do once in a long while" (*WF* 100). For Thoreau, plants, animals, settlers, natives, all beings with physical bodies, share parallel experiences of accommodation to and interaction with nature, the ground of existence, the material world.

Thoreau consistently represents the collective experience of the material world in devotional terms. In his introduction to *Wild Fruits*, Bradley Dean rightly observes that Thoreau "would have been most interested in our reading the work as a uniquely American scripture," noting that he refers to it in the Journal as *"my* New Testament" (*WF* xiii). Thus the long entry for "Strawberry" describes picking and eating this fruit as an exercise in awareness. The first ripe berries of the season appear in spots well exposed to sunlight, and they "are at first hard to detect in such places amid the red lower leaves, as if Nature meant thus to conceal the fruit, especially if your mind is unprepared for it" (*WF* 11–12). Because they present such a challenge to our powers of concentration, wild strawberries can be found only by the initiated:

> Only one in a hundred know where to look for these early strawberries. It is, as it were, a sort of Indian knowledge acquired by secret tradition. I know well what has called that apprentice, who has just crossed my path, to the hillsides this Sunday morning. In whatever factory or chamber he has his dwelling-place, he is . . . sure to be by the side of the first strawberry when it reddens. . . . It is an instinct with him. (*WF* 13)

Once found, strawberries are a pantheist "manna" (*WF* 12): "They are the first blush of a country, its morning red, a sort of ambrosial food which grows only on Olympian soil" (*WF* 15–16). Similarly, in the entry for "Early Low Blueberry," Thoreau writes, "These berries have a very innocent ambrosial taste, as if made of the ether itself, as they plainly are colored with it" (*WF* 22). New England is "a land flowing with milk and huckleberries" (*WF* 54), and while only a few may now seek wild berries, they remain available to all as a sign of the Earth's covenant with the communities it supports: "They seem offered to us not so much for food as for sociality, inviting us to a picnic with Nature. We pluck and eat in remembrance of her. It is a sort of sacrament, a communion—the *not* forbidden fruits, which no serpent tempts us to eat. Slight and innocent savors which relate us to Nature, make us her guests, and entitle us to her regard and protection" (*WF* 52). The theological language here is no accident; it marks Thoreau's quite serious sense of the millennial importance of the rituals he describes: "It would imply the regeneration of mankind if they were to become elevated enough to truly worship sticks and stones" (WF 168). The sacramental consumption of wild fruits, should it be taken up by the hundred instead of just the one, might well redeem a New England society that has modernized itself into an almost total ignorance of nature.

New England's debilitating ignorance brings with it a whole host of other ills. Berries grow "wild all over the country—wholesome, bountiful, and free, a real ambrosia. And yet men, the foolish demons that they are, devote themselves to the culture of tobacco, inventing slavery and a thousand other curses for that purpose" (WF 51). In *Wild Fruits,* Thoreau develops and makes even more explicit the materialist analysis that he begins to articulate in *Walden* of the way that capitalist social and economic relations have destroyed humankind's immediate collective relationship with nature. He describes much more particularly than in *Walden* the concrete ways in which the specific institutions of private property and competitive commerce prevent the citizens of a no longer classless republic from experiencing wild land either aesthetically or devotionally. First and foremost, there is the simple problem of decreasing access as more and more wild land is brought under private ownership: "But, ah, we have fallen on evil days! I hear of pickers ordered out of the huckleberry fields, and I see stakes set up with written notices forbidding any to pick there" (WF 57). Thoreau emphatically deplores the motive behind this ongoing process of enclosure:

> What sort of a country is that where the huckleberry fields are private property? When I pass such fields on the highway, my heart sinks within me. I see a blight on the land. Nature is under a veil there. I make haste away from the accursed spot. Nothing could deform her fair face more. I cannot think of it ever after but as the place where fair and palatable berries are converted into money, where the huckleberry is desecrated. (WF 57–58)

Importantly, Thoreau does not single out the farmer who has fenced his fields, but immediately places the profit motive in a broader social context: "I do not mean to blame any, but all—to bewail our fates generally," for privatization shows "to what result our civilization and division of labor naturally tend" (WF 57, 58). This is a significant departure from the voluntarism of

Walden, with its insistence that we each freely choose our own way of life. In *Wild Fruits*, Thoreau consistently places himself inside the community damaged by modernization, rather than haranguing it from afar: "It is my own way of living that I complain of as well as yours, and therefore I trust that my remarks will come home to you" (*WF* 235). The logic of this rhetorical shift is clear. For Thoreau, the "division of labor" is not a static fact, but an ongoing process whereby the relatively uniform population of the post-revolutionary agrarian republic has been divided into far more rigid economic classes. That process has produced a society that exerts a constant pressure on its members to make decisions according to the bottom line of profit. The aggregate result of these innumerable decisions is a privatized rural landscape where huckleberries are guarded by fences. Thoreau looks to post-enclosure England and sees a dismal prognosis: "I suspect that the inhabitants of England and the continent of Europe have thus lost in a measure their natural rights with the increase of population and monopolies" (*WF* 57). Thoreau was, in fact as well as in rhetoric, one of those whose access to the land was increasingly being limited by modernization under capitalism.

What is most important about these changes, for Thoreau, is not merely that people have lost access to natural resources formerly held in common. It is true that "in laying claim for the first time to the spontaneous fruit of our pastures, we are inevitably aware of a little meanness, and the merry berry party which we turn away naturally looks down on and despises us" (*WF* 59). But again, Thoreau is not making a moralistic attack on individual humans for participating in the low business of trade. In fact, he reports wryly on sending two and a half bushels of cranberries to Boston, where he got four dollars for them. This success led him to consider taking up the business on a larger scale, by shipping larger quantities to New York, but he was dissuaded by the discovery that they sold cheaper there than at Boston. Thoreau tells this story to illustrate not his own moral lassitude, but the vitiated taste of urbanites by contrast with "country people" (*WF* 104–5). The problem with privatization of the land is that when "we exclude mankind from gathering berries in our field, we exclude them from gathering health and happiness and inspiration. . . . We thus strike only one more blow at a simple and wholesome relation to nature" (*WF* 58). In other words, the majority of people have been forcibly excluded not just from gathering up some supplementary nutrition, but from entering into rich moral relationships with the wild: "It is a grand fact that you cannot make the fairer fruits or parts of fruits matter of commerce; that is, you cannot buy the highest use and enjoyment of them" (*WF* 5). Human relations to nature under capitalism, for those now fenced off the land, have been stripped of their most fulfilling content. The growing numbers of landless workers and the poor in the cities have been, to be precise, alienated from nature. They confront nature only in the marketplace as an alien object: "You cannot buy that pleasure which [a huckleberry] yields to him who truly plucks it. You cannot buy a good appetite, even. In short, you may buy a servant or a slave, but you cannot buy a friend" (*WF* 5). The comparison to slavery here is not accidental. Thoreau turns to this metaphor repeatedly. Of farmers who fence off their berry fields, he writes: "They have no other interest in berries but a pecuniary one. Such is the constitution of our society that we make a compromise and permit the berries to be degraded—to be enslaved, as it were" (*WF* 58–59). In other words, what is true of social relationships is true of human relations with nature as well: The moral content of such relationships is rooted in, flowers from, the material structure of a whole ecosocial order.

Wild Fruits envisions a potential alternative to capitalist ecosocial relations. It recounts a body of natural knowledge and experience of which the implied subject is an organic community living "a simple and wholesome" life on the land, "gathering health and happiness and inspiration" in the woods of New England. And more than envisioning such a utopian community, the text attempts as well to convoke it, to call it into existence by inaugurating the ritual harvest and consumption of wild fruits. For Thoreau, gathering berries is an activity for a sacramental party, a collective aesthetic experience. In the entry for "Viburnum Nudum," he writes, "September 3. Now is the season for those comparatively rare but beautiful wild berries which are not food for man. . . . Now is the time for *Beautiful* Berrying, for which the children have no vacation. They should have a vacation for their imaginations as much as for their bodies" (*WF* 120–21). Like gathering beautiful berries, eating wild apples demands a communal subject: "You cannot read at the same time, as when you are eating an apple. It is a social employment" (*WF* 219). Moreover, Thoreau's community of fruit pickers and eaters takes its identity and character from its particular environment: "The tropical fruits are for those who dwell in the tropics. . . . It is not the orange of Cuba but rather the checkerberry of the neighboring pasture that most delights the eye and the palate of the New England child" (*WF* 3). Not only is this community rooted in a specific place, its annual experience is tuned to the cycle of the year: "Our diet, like that of the birds, must answer to the season" (WF 107).

As utopian and apparently whimsical as this vision is, Thoreau recognizes that wild fruits can take on the meaning he ascribes to them only within an entirely new kind of society. Investing wild fruits with such rich meanings is a matter of artifice, of deliberately envisioning an alternative to the course of historical development he has described. This way of thinking is implied, for instance, in his description of the wild apple as "wild only like myself, perchance, who belong not to the aboriginal race here, but have strayed into the woods from the cultivated stock" (WF 79). Convoking such a community is a matter, then, of deliberately straying into the woods, of rewilding society, of collectively reviving lapsed ways of living on the land that were characteristic of native and agrarian cultures:

> It would be well if we accepted these gifts [of wild apples] with more joy and gratitude, and did not think it enough simply to put a fresh load of compost about the tree. Some old English customs are suggestive at least. I find them described chiefly in Brand's *Popular Antiquities.* It appears that "on Christmas eve the farmers and their men in Devonshire take a large bowl of cider, with a toast in it, and carrying it in state to the orchard, they salute the apple trees with much ceremony, in order to make them bear well the next season." (WF 76)

Consciously reinhabiting such lost lifeways can, for Thoreau, transform human relations with the land. Thus, after describing the experience of preparing and eating acorns for the first time, Thoreau concludes, "now that I have discovered the palatableness of this neglected nut, life has acquired a new sweetness for me, and I am related to the first men. . . . Nature seems the more friendly to me" (WF 182). Likewise, he reports with obvious pleasure on the new urban ritual of eating roasted chestnuts: "I have seen more chestnuts on the streets of New York than anywhere else this year—large and plump ones roasting in the street, and popping on the steps of banks and exchanges. Was surprised to see that the citizens made as much of the nuts of the wild wood as the squirrels. Not only the country boys—all New York goes a-nutting" (WF 213). Throughout the text, the prefix "a-" designates the ritual activities that bind together Thoreau's imagined community: a-strawberrying, a-huckleberrying, a-nutting. Besides, Thoreau did more than write about berrying as a ritual of communion: his journal is filled with accounts of berrying and nutting excursions to the Concord and other local woods. These excursions organized in material reality what Thoreau envisions in *Wild Fruits*.[18]

Given the social forces that Thoreau saw as responsible for alienation from nature, it is not perhaps surprising that he saw eating wild fruits as a democratic activity. He not only celebrates the way that "all New York goes a-nutting" so that there are "chestnuts for cabmen and newsboys" (WF 213), but he also ridicules, in anti-elitist terms, what he represents as overly cultivated fruits. Pears, for instance, "are a more aristocratic fruit than apples." He describes the extraordinary care that is taken to bring them to market, wrapped in tissue for wealthy customers. "Yet they have neither the beauty nor the fragrance of apples. Their excellence is in their flavor, which speaks to a grosser sense. They are *glout-morceaux*. Hence, while children dream of apples, ex-judges realize pears." Hyper-cultivated fruits are for hyper-cultivated members of the ruling classes: "They are named after emperors, kings, queens, dukes, and duchesses. I fear I shall have to wait till we get to pears with American names, which a republican can swallow. The next French Revolution will correct all that" (WF 127). By contrast with the overrefined pear that vitiates tastes and appetites, wild fruits invigorate the democratic consumer: "It takes a savage or wild taste to appreciate a wild fruit. What a healthy out-of-door appetite it takes to relish the apple of life, the apple of the world, then!" (WF 87). Now, renewed vigor is not just a matter of individual well-being, though health was of course a matter of grave concern for Thoreau; renewal is also a communal, even a political concern. It is no rhetorical accident that he defiantly celebrates the eating of chestnuts "on the steps of banks and exchanges." These institutions operate as synecdoches for the profit-driven social order that produces the debilitating alienation from nature he hopes wild fruits will cure. More generally, the democratic community of wild fruit eaters will be fortified to bear the general malaise of modernity: "We require just so much acid as the cranberries afford in the spring. . . . They cut the winter's phlegm, and now you can swallow another year of this world without other sauce" (WF 106).[19]

In one entry, for the "European Cranberry," Thoreau does seem to suggest that going a-berrying is a form of political escapism, an "absorbing employment" that "drives Kansas out of your head, and actually and permanently occupies the only desirable and free Kansas against all border ruffians" (*WF* 165). This last sentence implies the possibility that Thoreau's community is a compensatory fantasy and introduces this remark: "The attitude of resistance is one of weakness, inasmuch as it only faces an enemy; it has its back to all that is truly attractive" (*WF* 165). Thoreau seems here to ventriloquize quite directly the idealist politics of nonresistant moral suasion that characterized *Walden* and the 1840s. He even goes so far in this entry as to satirize political reformers and utopian socialists, including himself: "Our employment generally is tinkering, mending the old worn-out teapot of society. Our stock in trade is solder. Better for me, says my genius, to go cranberrying this afternoon for the *Vaccinium oxycoccus* in Gowing's Swamp . . . than go consul to Liverpool" (*WF* 166). It is tempting to conclude on the basis of this passage that gathering wild fruits is no more than another form of comeouterism, the isolato's way of abandoning modernity in hopes that it will collapse. But this is precisely the position Thoreau explicitly rejects not only in the contemporaneous John Brown essays, but also in much of the rest of the *Wild Fruits* manuscript, especially in its final pages. In effect, this anachronistic voicing of Thoreau's former individualism and idealism, localized as it is within a fragmentary manuscript, serves only to reinforce the text's overall communalism and materialism.

For some readers, the sweetest discovery in *Wild Fruits* will come in an untitled section that makes up the last six pages of the book. Leo Stoller combined this passage with material from several entries into an essay which was published in 1970 as a small book entitled *Huckleberries.*[20] But it is in *Wild Fruits* that this material has been restored to its original textual environment, where its comes as a culminating peroration. The passage, which appears to be a draft of material for a lecture, is an explicit argument in support of collective action to preserve large tracts of land as wilderness. Its first paragraph contains a precise abstract of its overall argument. Thoreau begins with a lament: "How little we insist on truly grand and beautiful natural features. There may be the most beautiful landscapes in the world within a dozen miles of us, for aught we know—for their inhabitants do not value nor perceive them, and so have not made them known to others." The problem is identified as one of recognizing the importance of wilderness; but more than that, Thoreau implies that people have been blinded by something quite specific: "if a grain of gold were picked up there or a pearl found in a freshwater clam, the whole state would resound with the news." So far, this is a consolidating restatement of themes Thoreau has developed throughout *Wild Fruits*. Next, though, he introduces a new thought: "Thousands annually seek the White Mountains to be refreshed by their wild and primitive beauty, but when the country was discovered a similar kind of beauty prevailed all over it—and much of this might have been preserved for our present refreshment if a little foresight and taste had been used" (*WF* 233). Thoreau is proposing explicitly here what he has elsewhere in his work only hinted at: conscious decision-making by the community to preserve wild land.

Thoreau next describes a "noble oak wood" at the town of Boxboro: "Let it stand fifty years longer and men will make pilgrimages to it from all parts of the country" (*WF* 233). Nevertheless, "it is likely to be cut off within a few years for ship-timber" (*WF* 235). Arguing that the "rising generation" should have an opportunity to learn what an oak or a pine is by observing the "best specimens," Thoreau argues that "it would be wise for the state to purchase and preserve a few such forests. If the people of Massachusetts are ready to found a professorship of Natural History, do they not see the importance of preserving some portions of Nature herself unimpaired?" (*WF* 235). Thoreau immediately comes to the point that such a goal conflicts with the ongoing trend of privatization of wild lands and turns to Native American ecosocial relations for an alternative model of land ownership: "Among the Indians the earth and its productions generally were common and free to all the tribe, like the air and water, but among us who have supplanted the Indians, the public retain only a small yard or common in the middle of the village, with perhaps a graveyard beside it" (*WF* 235). He next turns to English common law for a second precedent: "In some countries precious metals belong to the crown; so here more precious objects of great natural beauty should belong to the public" (*WF* 236). On this basis, Thoreau argues that rivers, upon which "the town, as a corporation, has never turned any but the most purely utilitarian eyes" should be held too "as a common possession forever" (*WF* 236). Not just rivers, but "central and commanding hilltop[s]" should likewise be preserved, for each is a "sacred place," a "temple" that should not be "private property" (*WF* 237). Thoreau concludes that "each town should have a park, or rather a primitive forest, of five hundred or a thousand acres, either in one body or several, where a stick should never be cut for fuel, not for the navy, nor to make wagons, but stand and decay for higher uses" (*WF* 238). Repeating what is clearly a key phrase for him, he maintains that each such tract of land should be held as "a common possession forever" (*WF* 238). The navy and wagons here stand in for the modern state and the market it protects. And it is in opposition to these institutions that the land must be protected. Crucially, Thoreau recognizes that preservation will require concerted conscious action: "It is for the very reason that some do not care for these things that we need to combine to protect all from the vandalism of a few" (WF 237). By implication, the rituals Thoreau represents in *Wild Fruits* will produce devotional experience on the land, which will in turn motivate the community to combine and take action in defense of what they will now see as the basis of their collective identity.

Wild Fruits, then, offers a second answer to the question framed by the "Economy" chapter of *Walden*. Where *Walden* offers an idealist and individualist solution to that problem, *Wild Fruits* offers a process for transforming ideas into motivating collective experiences and therefore into material forces for change. In another of the moments in which *Walden* hints at his future, Thoreau describes a transformative epiphany in which he merges his "intelligence with the earth" (W 138). This is a significant departure from the disembodied consciousness, the "transparent eyeball" of Transcendentalist orthodoxy. More and more, Thoreau saw understanding as a moment of active integration with the world, rather than one of contemplative separation or abstraction. And more and more, Nature was the material world of Concord *and* the Walden woods, rather than an ideal category, the Emersonian "NOT ME." On January 24, 1856, Thoreau meditated in his Journal on elms, the species that is the subject of the first entry in *Wild Fruits*: "I find that into my idea of the village has entered more of the elm than of the human being" for most people do not have "a tithe of the dignity, the true nobleness and comprehensiveness of view" that they do. This pessimistic assessment may seem to cut against his hopes for collective transformation of ecosocial relations, but it soon becomes clear that he has only certain human beings in mind. Elms "are free-soilers," for they "send their roots . . . into many a conservative's Kansas and Carolina, who does not suspect such underground railroads." Not only are Thoreau's elms antislavery activists, but like the ecosocial historian of *Wild Fruits* and the community he hoped to call together, they take "a firmer hold on the earth that they may rise higher into the heavens."[21] Perhaps, Thoreau remembered this vision of the abolitionist elms of Concord on the day he drafted several pages of *Wild Fruits* on the reverse sides of broadsheets he had printed to announce a memorial service for John Brown. And perhaps it was with a sense of the social and political importance of serious play that Thoreau inhabited the office of "captain of a huckleberry party."[22]

Notes

1. Henry David Thoreau, *Essays,* ed. Lewis Hyde (New York: North Point Press, 2002), 113.
2. *The Correspondence of Henry David Thoreau,* ed. Walter Harding and Carl Bode (New York: New York University Press, 1958), Ralph Waldo Emerson to Henry David Thoreau, Sept. 18,1843, 137; James McIntosh, *Thoreau as Romantic Naturalist: His Shifting Stance toward Nature* (Ithaca, NY: Cornell University Press, 1974), 23, 17, 37.
3. Ralph Waldo Emerson, "Thoreau," *Atlantic Monthly* 10 (August 1862), 248; Henry David Thoreau, *Journal 3: 1848–1851,* ed. Robert Sattelmeyer et al. (Princeton: Princeton University Press, 1990), 380. In his "Introduction" to Henry David Thoreau, *The Natural History Essays* (Salt Lake City: Peregrine Smith, 1980), Robert Sattelmeyer identifies "the central debate over Thoreau's career—whether his late years form a record of declining power and a straying from the vision that led to *Walden,* or whether they furnish evidence of significant new directions and works which he did not live to complete" (xxvi).
4. Robert Sattelmeyer, *Thoreau's Reading: A Study in Intellectual History* (Princeton: Princeton University Press, 1988), 19, 22; Ralph Waldo Emerson, *Collected Works,* vol. 1, ed. Robert E. Spiller and Alfred R. Ferguson (Cambridge: Harvard University Press, 1971), 39. See Sherman Paul, *The Shores of America: Thoreau's Inward Exploration* (Champaign: University of Illinois Press, 1958), 3–16, for a brisk statement of this position. Paul, arguing in 1958 against what was already a truism, attempts to recuperate what he nevertheless concedes is the "barrenness" of the Journal by arguing that "instead of signifying failure, his reliance on science signified a greater maturity and success: to be scientific for Thoreau was not to abandon the ultimate poetic use of the fact but to be public and objective" (396). This was valiant, but Paul's logic, and his subtitle, *Thoreau's Inward Exploration,* imply that had Thoreau truly turned outward, his significant exploration would have ended. See Laura Dassow Walls, *Seeing New Worlds: Henry David Thoreau and Nineteenth-Century Natural Science* (Madison: University of Wisconsin Press, 1995), 15–52, for the best account of Thoreau's negotiation in the 1830s with the inheritance of European empiricist and idealist theories of knowledge.
5. William Howarth, *The Book of Concord* (New York: Viking, 1982), ix, 20, 10, 20, 64, 80, 118. See *Emerson and Thoreau: Transcendentalists in Conflict* (Middletown, CT: Wesleyan University Press, 1966), in which Joel Porte argues that Thoreau was in fact a Lockean empiricist. Victor Carl Friesen, *The Spirit of the Huckleberry: Sensuousness in Thoreau* (Edmonton: University of Alberta Press, 1984), maintains that the key to Thoreau's thought is his lifelong immersion in sensory experience. In *The Idea of Wilderness* (New Haven: Yale University Press, 1991), Max Oelschlaeger argues that

Thoreau learns an "Indian wisdom," a holistic knowledge of nature, by intuitively understanding the physical world through immersion in its particulars (133–71). In *Writing Nature: Henry Thoreau's Journal* (Oxford: Oxford University Press, 1985), Sharon Cameron argues that Thoreau came to see the Journal as his "central literary enterprise," and that in it "he is writing his life so that it actually comes to comprise alternate—natural—phenomena" (3–4). Cameron reads the Journal as an extended meditation on how the mind apprehends nature, on the process of generalizing from a bewildering chaos of fragmentary information. See Robert D. Richardson Jr., *Henry David Thoreau: A Life of the Mind* (Berkeley: University of California Press, 1986), 362–84, for an account of Thoreau's intense engagement in the late 1850s with the Agassiz-Darwin controversy and his abandonment of Platonic idealism for Aristotelian empiricism. Perhaps the most unequivocal statement of this position comes in Robert Kuhn McGregor, *A Wider View of the Universe: Henry Thoreau's Study of Nature* (Champaign: University of Illinois Press, 1997), a hagiographical reading that sees Thoreau changing from "a classically and staidly trained transcendentalist into a radical naturalist" and makes him the inventor of "the principle of biocentrism and the science of ecology" (5, 3).

6. Walls, *Seeing New Worlds*, 18, 147, 76–93, 4; Donald Worster, *Nature's Economy: The Roots of Ecology* (San Francisco: Sierra Club, 1977), 75, 78.

7. Henry David Thoreau, *Wild Apples and Other Natural History Essays*, ed. William Rossi (Athens: University of Georgia Press, 2002), 23–24. Sustained analysis of Thoreau's attitudes toward science begins with Nina Baym, "Thoreau's View of Science," *Journal of the History of Ideas* 26 (1965): 221–34.

8. Lance Newman, " 'Patrons of the World': Thoreau as Wordsworthian Poet," *The Concord Saunterer* n.s. 11 (Winter 2003): 155–72.

9. Sattelmeyer, *Thoreau's Reading*, 78–92. William Rossi, "Thoreau's Transcendental Ecocriticism," in *Thoreau's Sense of Place: Essays in American Environmental Writing*, ed. Richard Schneider (Iowa City: University of Iowa Press, 2000), 28–43, argues that Thoreau maintains "twin commitment to the metaphysics of correspondence and to a densely empirical knowledge of nature" (32). Ronald Wesley Hoag, "Thoreau's Later Natural History Writings," in *The Cambridge Companion to Henry David Thoreau*, ed. Joel Myerson (Cambridge: Cambridge University Press, 1995), 152–70, describes the kind of natural history that Thoreau practiced during this decade as a form of "humanistic science" that relied "on the personality and capacities of the observer" to illuminate "the human relationship to nature" (169). William Rossi, "Introduction" to Thoreau, *Wild Apples and Other Natural History Essays*, shows that in the late natural history essays, Thoreau "strikes at the root of an increasingly cultural as well as epistemological objectivism" (xix). Most recently, Alfred I. Tauber, in *Henry David Thoreau and the Moral Agency of Knowing* (Berkeley: University of California Press, 2001), argues that Thoreau was a " 'hinge' character residing between an ebbing Romanticism and a rising positivism" (ix), and that he "regarded epistemology as a fundamentally moral problem of situating objective knowledge within a humane context" (140). Laura Dassow Walls, "Believing in Nature: Wilderness and Wildness in Thoreauvian

Science," in *Thoreau's Sense of Place*, 15–27, argues that Thoreau developed "a radical view of nature as a self-generating, creative agent by incorporating Humboldtian proto-ecological science into traditional and romantic forms of natural theology" (17). Michael Benjamin Berger, in *Thoreau's Late Career and "The Dispersion of Seeds": The Saunterer's Synoptic Vision* (Rochester, NY: Camden House, 2000), 76–119, examines Thoreau's "epistemological mediations" in "The Dispersion of Seeds," concluding that he "critically examined, and to a significant degree productively reconciled, the claims of empiricism and idealism" (xii). H. Daniel Peck, in *Thoreau's Morning Work: Memory and Perception in "A Week on the Concord and Merrimack Rivers," the Journal, and "Walden"* (New Haven: Yale University Press, 1990), 39–114, argues that Thoreau thought of observation as "relational seeing" in which each interaction of observer and observed produced unique aesthetic phenomena that then required systematic categorization.

10. Sattelmeyer, *Thoreau's Reading*, 78, 50, 15; Walter Harding and Michael Meyer, *The New Thoreau Handbook* (New York: The Gotham Library of New York University Press, 1980), 135. Still the best account of Thoreau's radicalization in response to economic and political developments in New England is Leo Stoller, *After Walden: Thoreau's Changing Views on Economic Man* (Palo Alto: Stanford University Press, 1957). Stoller argues that, as with his ongoing negotiation between idealism and materialism, Thoreau made a long series of provisional compromises between perfectionism and direct action as theories of political action, "with the drift of the nation gradually modifying the proportions in favor of the direct assault" (36). Joan Burbick, in *Thoreau's Alternative History: Changing Perspectives on Nature, Culture, and Language* (Philadelphia: University of Pennsylvania Press, 1987), demonstrates that by combining his interests in Romantic history and historiography with the insights provided by the natural sciences, Thoreau "placed history within the natural world, where he found records of a story more capable of redemption than those of civilization" (3). John Hildebidle, in *Thoreau: A Naturalist's Liberty* (Cambridge: Harvard University Press, 1983), shows that Thoreau "applies the methods of natural history to the reading and writing of history generally" (25).

11. Howarth, *Book of Concord*, 134, 136, 139, 10; Walls, *Seeing New Worlds*, 4; Thoreau, *Essays*, 43–60. Susan M. Lucas, in "Counter Frictions: Writing and Activism in the Work of Abbey and Thoreau," *Thoreau's Sense of Place*, 266–79, argues from the evidence of the John Brown essays that Thoreau came to see writing as a way to inspire political action from principle.

12. Henry David Thoreau, *Walden*, ed. J. Lyndon Shanley (Princeton: Princeton University Press, 1971), 3. All further citations of this text will be parenthetical, using the abbreviation *"W."* For an important discussion of "representational accuracy," see Lawrence Buell, *The Environmental Imagination: Thoreau, Nature Writing, and the Formation of American Culture* (Cambridge: Harvard University Press, 1994), 81–114; and Lance Newman, "Thoreau's Natural Community and Utopian Socialism," *American Literature* 75.3 (September 2003): 515–44.

13. Michael T. Gilmore, *American Romanticism and the Marketplace* (Chicago: University of Chicago Press, 1985), 35–51.

14. See Joseph J. Moldenhauer, "The Extravagant Maneuver: Paradox in *Walden*," in *Critical Essays on Henry David Thoreau's "Walden*," ed. Joel Myerson (Boston: G. K. Hall, 1988), 96–106, for a concise reading of *Walden's* rhetorical strategies. Stanley Cavell, in *The Senses of Walden* (New York: Viking, 1972), 3–34, reads *Walden* as a "heroic book" that represents itself as a modern scripture and prophecy, a jeremiad directed at a fallen America.

15. Henry David Thoreau, *Wild Fruits*, ed. Bradley P. Dean (New York: Norton, 2000). All further citations of this text will be parenthetical, using the abbreviation *"WF."* For an account of the provenance of the manuscript, see 285–86, 287n. See Howarth, *The Literary Manuscripts of Henry David Thoreau* (Columbus: Ohio State University Press, 1974), 322–26, for a physical description of the manuscripts. Stephen Adams and Donald Ross Jr., *Revising Mythologies: The Composition of Thoreau's Major Works* (Charlottesville: University Press of Virginia, 1988), 240–52, give a brief account of Thoreau's work on the late natural history essays, but the authors "do not consider them major works," dismissing them as "pleasant" (241).

16. The late natural history essays "Autumnal Tints," "Wild Apples," and "Huckleberries," excerpted from the *Wild Fruits* manuscript, have only begun to receive serious critical attention in the past few decades, and even then only sporadically. John Hildebidle, in *Thoreau: A Naturalist's Liberty*, 69–96, provides a generic analysis of these as modified natural history essays in which Thoreau attempts "to bring to natural history a sense of form and myth" (90). In *Thoreau as Romantic Naturalist*, James McIntosh observes that "in the last essays, Thoreau consistently presents nature as a familiar ally, no longer as a problem" (280). He theorizes that, in the context of stable economic growth in the 1850s, Thoreau no longer appeals to nature as an alternative to socioeconomic crisis. Stephen Fink, on the other hand, in "The Language of Prophecy: Thoreau's 'Wild Apples,' " *NEQ* 59 (September 1986): 212–30, maintains that "the apparent modesty of 'Wild Apples' is a calculated and richly subversive rhetorical stance" designed to engage "the materialist and utilitarian interests of the public" in order to undermine those interests (214). Similarly, in "Thoreau's Extravagant Economy of Nature," *American Literary History* 5 (1993): 30–50, Richard Grusin argues that Thoreau borrows the language of market exchange in order to subvert it by showing that the "economy of nature" is one of extravagant interconnection. Robert Milder, in *Reimagining Thoreau* (Cambridge: Cambridge University Press, 1995), observes that in these essays there is "a synthesis of the poet and the naturalist in [the] activity of the moralist" (184), while in *Seeing New Worlds*, Laura Dassow Walls sees the essays as "a celebration of collective identity" in which "engagement with nature is a communal act" threatened by "the demands of the market" (215, 221, 222).

17. See Peter Blakemore, "Thoreau, Literature, and the Phenomenon of Inhabitation," in *Thoreau's Sense of Place*, 115–32, for a discussion of Thoreau's decision to ground his empirical observations of nature in a "reverence for home" (115).

18. Henry D. Thoreau, *Journal*, vol. 14, ed. Bradford Torrey and Francis H. Allen (New York: Dover, 1906), 12, 13, 56–57. See also *The Letters of Ellen Tucker Emerson*, vol. 1, ed. Edith E. W. Gregg (Kent, OH: Kent State University Press, 1982), 216. I am indebted to Sandra Petrulionis for pointing out the connection between Thoreau's imagined and actual berrying parties.

19. See Walls, *Seeing New Worlds*, 142–44, for a discussion of Thoreau's developing conception of knowledge production as a democratic and communal project.

20. Henry David Thoreau, *Huckleberries*, ed. Leo Stoller (Iowa City: Windhover Press of the University of Iowa, 1970), 166–202. Stoller's version of "Huckleberries" has been reprinted in three Thoreau collections: Thoreau, *The Natural History Essays*, ed. Sattelmeyer; Henry David Thoreau, *Collected Essays and Poems*, ed. Elizabeth Hall Witherell (New York: The Library of America, 2001); and Thoreau, *Wild Apples and Other Natural History Essays*, ed. Rossi. A small sample of the *Wild Fruits* manuscript is included in Henry David Thoreau, *Faith in a Seed: The Dispersion of Seeds and Other Late Natural History Writings*, ed. Bradley P. Dean (Washington, DC: Island Press, 1993). See McGregor, *A Wider View of the Universe*, 181–84, for a brief discussion of Thoreau's calls for forest preservation in "Huckleberries." Burbick, in *Thoreau's Alternative History*, 138–42, also discusses this essay, reading it as an articulation of "Thoreau's vision of the landscape as a new Eden, a utopian society that exists on the food nature provides" (139).

21. Emerson, *Collected Works*, 1:10, 8; Thoreau, *Journal*, vol. 14, 139–40.

22. Howarth, *Book of Concord*, 181; Emerson, "Thoreau," *Atlantic Monthly* 10 (August 1862): 248.

Thoreau, Homer, and Community

ROBERT OSCAR LÓPEZ

THIS ESSAY will seek to add to Thoreau studies by examining new connections between Thoreau's *Walden* and Homer's *Iliad*. In the process, it will also build on the work of other Thoreau scholars, to reflect on his conflicted thoughts about community and friendship in *Walden*. What Thoreau got out of reading Homer and how he felt about human relationships are more interconnected than one might guess. One can, for instance, come to notice Thoreau's conversation with the ghosts of ancient Greece in *Walden*, by beginning with a question that strikes at the notion of community: When Thoreau speaks, with whom is he speaking?

In *Walden,* Thoreau's ideal discourse community is hard to define. One important reason for this is that Thoreau usually does not seem sure about who is listening to him. He seems more certain about the wide range of social forces that he would prefer to escape. His position on social life appears unambiguous in *Walden* when he says, "wherever a man goes, men will pursue and paw him with their dirty institutions and if they can, constrain him to belong to their desperate odd-fellow society," adding that "I preferred that society should run 'amok' against me, it being the desperate party" (*W* 171).[1] It worries the author of *Walden* that men and women, if given the chance, institutionalize each other and halt their progress toward a truly free consciousness. As Lewis Leary puts it, Thoreau "advocated consciousness, yes; perception, certainly; but manipulation, no."[2] Of these three, manipulation is the only mechanism that involves live communication among people, rather than individuated and private thought. Community endangers both consciousness and perception insofar as all social intercourse is tainted by the prospects of manipulation and, therefore, corruption.

It would be rash to conclude that, because of his fear of human manipulation, Thoreau spits on all notions of human community. He is not a total misanthrope. He believes that noble virtues are available to anyone, in any locale or era where individuals find opportunities to cultivate their better instincts. As Bob Pepperman Taylor says of Thoreau, he "firmly believes that truth, heroism and virtue are universal attributes found in great individuals in all historical settings."[3] This idealism about human capability is closely linked to Thoreau's desire to be firmly rooted in the present rather than transfixed by the gleaming prestige of the past. Even though Thoreau is wary of his peers, he tries his best not to express his wariness as a smug preference for organic communities of an earlier golden age. He is hostile to historical nostalgia and refuses to grant to antiquity a higher place in the social order than his own time. The famous and enduring last words of *Walden* are "The sun is but a morning star" (W 333). The book's finale is a statement of proportionality. In thinking about the sun being as small as one dot of light, perhaps the reader can appreciate the enormous timeline that human potential inhabits.

Time is clearly on the author's mind in *Walden,* though his thoughts on human beings' relationship to history are complex and multilayered. Thoreau had a complex affection for dead geniuses like Homer, to be examined below, but this reverence for ancient ideas is still tempered by his desire to dismiss the grandiose claims of history's crumbling ruins and rotting tombs. Thoreau wants to stand outside of, and to condescend to, history itself: "Time is but the stream I go a-fishing in. I drink at it; but while I drink I see the sandy bottom and detect how shallow it is" (W 98). The past holds nothing necessarily magical. It is a natural reflection of everything he knows already. That is why Thoreau writes in *A Week on the Concord and Merrimack Rivers* that "the history we read is only a fainter memory of events which have happened in our own experience" (Wk 292).[4]

Eventually, though, his rejection of history fails, and he lapses into Homer worship, despite all attempts to see the claims of the past as shallow. These strides to treat history irreverently do not work, I will argue, due to his incurable bitter edge when Thoreau thinks about the human community accessible to him in the present tense. The ancients fill a gap left by the mediocrity of Thoreau's contemporaries. When he writes in *Walden* that "I never received more than one or two letters in my life . . . that were worth the postage," he is not only confessing but also causing his alienation from other people, in the very act of writing such an affront to anyone who took the time to try to contact him (*W* 94). As Stanley Cavell describes it, Thoreau "must undertake to write absolutely, to exercise his faith in the very act of marking the word,"[5] even where this exercise requires that he reject other human beings before they have been given the chance to reject him. All humanity must be dismissed, glibly if not cruelly, for the individual to find pure enlightenment. The ideal of meditation without compromising distractions becomes a desire for an absence of spoken language and a distrustful attitude toward conversation. Thoreau writes toward the end of his week in a riverboat with his soft-spoken brother: "the most excellent speech finally falls into Silence. . . . Silence is the universal refuge, the sequel to all dull discourses and all foolish acts, a balm to our every chagrin, as welcome after satiety as after disappointment" (*Wk* 292).

Thoreau is not necessarily looking for an escape from all conversation—only from the triviality of noise and chatter. The problem is that he never hears any discussion around him that can rise to his threshold of worthy dialogue. The imperfections of spoken exchanges ("dull discourses") drive him to silence. There is still a powerful appetite for better conversation, but it becomes internal and private. In the vast majority of circumstances, for Thoreau, the self is the most viable partner in discussion: "I should not talk so much about myself if there were any body else whom I knew as well" (*W* 3). The arguable word in the above sentence, though, is "about." Talking *about* one's self is not exactly controversial, but talking only *to* one's self is, because without an audience a book's authority dwindles down to the level of an easily forgotten journal.

Thoreau's ambivalent feelings about membership in a discourse community are evident in his mixed feelings about his target audience. The audience for a published book (with all its final polish and institutional authority) is different from the audience for a loosely organized journal. Since Thoreau produced both types of literary oeuvres, he could not have been unaware of the difference. Leonard Neufeldt has pointed out that Thoreau's "Journal turned out to be his largest work by far and, in his estimation, possibly his most important project as a writer."[6] Robert Sattelmeyer, agreeing that the Journal "became the major work of Thoreau's imaginative life," views the inception of Thoreau's personal writings as particularly important because of the fact that his friendship with Emerson both precipitated and was strengthened by his dedication to journal-keeping.[7] Yet despite the breadth of Thoreau's journals, Neufeldt points out that "Thoreau's 'failure' to be definitive on the purpose of his journalizing is part of a pattern noticeable throughout."[8] It was common for many different types of people in nineteenth-century Concord to keep journals—perhaps too common. If everyone who kept a journal fell into the sacred category of "author," then, as Neufeldt's research reveals, "authority" would be a badge conferred on Concord's "clergy, teachers, naturalists, businessmen, lawyers, housewives, unmarried women, students, and farmers [who] left journals behind ranging from a few page fragments to Bronson Alcott's fifty neatly bound volumes of approximately five million words."[9] The jump from the world of journals to the world of books involves an escape from the common din of the former into the respectable exclusivity of the latter. Perhaps with the respect of a published book comes an easier command of the audience's attention, readers' greater willingness to listen to the author and take him seriously, and ultimately a larger discourse community. The fact that Thoreau struggled to publish *A Week on the Concord and Merrimack Rivers* and *Walden* could reflect a hunger for that larger discourse community even as he sometimes hints, as noted above, that it is beneath him to jostle for society's approval.

The underlying crisis of *Walden* is perhaps not a search for a "redemption of language" as Stanley Cavell's work stresses,[10] but, I would propose, an unsatisfying search for an appropriate community to receive whatever meaning the writer's consciousness can generate. Cavell says that *"Walden* shows that we *are* there; every tongue has confessed what it can; we have heard everything there is to hear. . . . What is left to us is the accounting."[11] Cavell's argument would imply that Thoreau was certain that there was nothing left to confess and nothing left to hear; it assumes that he had truly given up entirely on talking and listening to people. But the reality of Thoreau's relation to other human beings is much more ambivalent. Thoreau wants to be heard and respected; he also wants companions but needs them to be free of hypocrisy and manipulation by having no conflict of interest. Such an argument oddly requires that they have no interest in him at all. He prizes neutrality as a condition for any acceptable social relationship (be it with friends or with a living audience), even though to most people the neutrality he prescribes could very well look like coldness, detachment, or indifference, none of which is conducive to friendship. "Individuals, like nations," Thoreau writes in *Walden,* "must have suitable broad and natural boundaries, even a considerable neutral ground between them" (*W* 141). The author wants to be social, but requires that any society with which he associates remain at a cold distance. He reveals his own uncertainty about how close an intimate friend should be suffered to approach when he adds that "If we would enjoy the most intimate society with that in each of us which is without, or above, being spoken to, we must not only be silent, but commonly so far apart bodily that we cannot possibly hear each other's voice in any case" (*W* 141).

His ambivalence about the value of a conversational community ultimately drives Thoreau to abandon his glib irreverence toward history, and to choose as his closest companions canonized ghosts like Homer. Live humans are too prone to speak, whereas the words of an ancient voice can still reach Thoreau in perfect silence. This is the difference, in his mind, between "garrulous and noisy eras, which no longer yield any sound" and the "Grecian or silent and melodious era" that is somewhere, but nowhere, and "ever sounding and resounding in the ears of men" (*Wk* 392).

It is no secret that Thoreau had persistent difficulty with notions of community and neither made nor kept friends easily. Harmon Smith notes in *My Friend, My Friend* that Emerson, one of his most important confidants, "found Thoreau's natural combativeness more and more difficult to deal with as the years passed."[12] Likewise, Sattelmeyer notes of the Thoreau-Emerson relationship that "by 1850, each was writing about the estrangement as accomplished, and looking at the other with a mixture of disappointment, anger, and resignation."[13] With living, breathing humans who come to him with their own compromises and political biases, Thoreau rarely finds any lasting satisfaction—not even in deciding he does not need them. "No word is oftener on the lips of men than Friendship," he ruminates in *A Week on the Concord and Merrimack Rivers* (264), even though his prognosis for the true value of human companionship remains bleak. "To say that a man is your Friend, means commonly no more than this, that he is not your enemy," he notes soon after, adding that "in our daily intercourse with men, our nobler faculties are dormant and suffered to rust" (*Wk* 266, 267). Yet the fact that he still desires a friend with whom he can chat is made clear, even if he makes long complaints about such a companion still being unfound among the living. "Think of the importance of Friendship in the education of men," he writes. "It will make a man honest; it will make him a hero; it will make him a saint" (*Wk* 267). In *Walden,* Thoreau ridicules townspeople for "the gossip which is incessantly going on there . . . as refreshing in its way as the rustle of leaves and the peeping of frogs" (*W* 167). At other times he admits that he is prone to the same rustle and peeping. In an earlier chapter he writes, "I love society as much as most . . . am naturally no hermit, but might possibly sit out the sturdiest frequenter of the bar-room, if my business called me hither" (*W* 140).

Solitude would be the prettier way to characterize Thoreau's situation; but since he never reconciles himself fully to a life without human company, the word "estrangement" is more apt. The ongoing estrangement from the social world around him, as well as from its languages, could very well be a key reason for his occasional turn to the Greeks. Robert D. Richardson Jr. points out that Thoreau's grounding in Latin and Greek was not necessarily outstanding, given the curriculum at Concord Academy and Harvard (where Thoreau attended) in the 1830s,[14] and that it is perhaps Thoreau's voracious absorption of modern languages that marks him as exceptional among his peers. In *Henry Thoreau: A Life of the Mind,* Richardson writes that "Thoreau is always thought of as well educated and well read in the classics—and no one has ever written a better defense of them—but it is not always recalled that he could read French, German, and Italian with ease, and, more important, that he was both inclined and prepared to think of literature in a broad, multicultural sense."[15] Notwithstanding Thoreau's aptitude for living languages, however, his intellectual trajectory from his youthful journals to the writing of *Walden* suggests that Greek and Latin often appeal to him precisely *because* they are not the languages in which other people speak anymore. Dead languages do not taint words with the alienation possible in social relationships with people who talk back to him. It is perhaps no coincidence, for instance, that in the fall of 1839, when Henry Thoreau and his brother John were both romantically interested in Ellen Sewall—and John seemed closer to winning the rivalry—Henry distracted himself from his hurt feelings by working on a translation of Aeschylus' *Prometheus Bound* and essays on the Roman satirist Persius.[16] Antiquity soothes Thoreau's injured pride, his resentments, and his annoyances with peers.

Even when Thoreau is not conversing with ancient writers, there are abundant traces in his writings of difficult emotions left over from unsatisfying interactions with other people. Human rejection, as a sign that the role of conversational companion has been inadequately filled, is an indispensable component in Thoreau's writing—and it is important to remember that the rejection is working in both directions. A perennial condition of his texts is that the reader can be driven to buck Thoreau's preaching and send him back to his ancient grotto with a dismissive flourish and a closing of his book. His posture is both defensive and offensive when he writes in the closing pages of *Walden*: "It is a ridiculous demand which England and America make, that you shall speak so that they can understand you. Neither men nor toad-stools grow so" (*W* 324). Who is spurning the other, and who—the reader or the author or both—is being disregarded? Rejection becomes simultaneous, a circle of chicken and egg with no traceable starting point. Indeed, despite the beauty of his prose, more than a few who read *Walden* find it difficult to like Thoreau's character enough to heed him. And this is a serious problem, given that, as Stanley Cavell says, "the hero of this book is its writer."[17] Bob Pepperman Taylor cites as Thoreau's social downfall his self-righteousness, something that sours many devotees who first embrace and then discard him after finding his moral self-referentiality untenable: "As I began to age, with family and job and all the other trappings and responsibilities of conventional American adulthood, I found (again like so many others) Thoreau beginning to get on my nerves. He seemed abrasive, self-righteous, arrogant."[18] Taylor's preface looks like the diary many people could have kept about their evolving relationships to this oeuvre. A tenth grader without much life experience can easily take Thoreau's words "There is not one of my readers who has yet lived a whole human life" (*W* 331) as an inspiration to see the future as boundless. To an adult the same words can feel like a blunt and uninvited criticism with little constructive value. Too much of a conventional adult life is already written, and fixed in a form that possibly merits Thoreau's contempt. Taylor is only one person with very specific circumstances, but who *doesn't* have some very specific circumstance that excludes the subject from Thoreau's ideal discourse? And more important, given the fact that Thoreau seems inclined to talk only to the worthies who could transform him into a saint or a hero, with whom exactly is Henry David Thoreau having his elaborate conversation?

Enter the Greeks

At times in *Walden,* Thoreau is having the conversation with the reader, as imperfect as the reader must necessarily be. As William Cain puts it, "*Walden*'s point of view and its social and economic criticism are strenuously individualized: this author is speaking to *you,* and it is your life that he tells you must be changed."[19] At other times, Thoreau is speaking to himself. But there is a special group of people whom Thoreau will find irresistible: those who have never tried to manipulate him, or estrange him, or suffer his estrangement. These latter companions have not only staved off compromises in the past but are guaranteed to make no ugly compromises in the future. These ideal interlocutors are already dead. They are the great geniuses from humanity's distant past. "The works of the great poets have never yet been read by mankind, for only great poets can read them," Thoreau writes in *Walden,* adding that on a pile of the greatest poets' works, "we may hope to scale heaven at last" (*W* 104). He pretends not to fetishize their antiquity for its own sake; rather, he claims that his pantheon is based merely on an objective measure of their talent. The authors of great books "are a natural and irresistible aristocracy in every society, and, more than kings or emperors, exert an influence on mankind," he adds (*W* 103).

In particular, the Greeks help Thoreau with some of his most troubling blind spots, such as his chronic naïveté about the cruelty of the animal world. At one point in *Walden,* Thoreau observes a war between black and red ants in the forest. He introduces it by saying, "I was witness to events of a less peaceful character," betraying a hint of a loss of innocence, at which point the allegory of the Trojan War calibrates his prose again, since he redeems the bellicose event by imagining that two of the red ants are Achilles and Patroclus (*W* 228). "I felt for the rest of that day as if I had had my feelings excited and harrowed by witnessing the struggle, the ferocity and carnage, of a human battle before my door," he concludes (*W* 231). The showdown between two races of insects was not a small incident in Thoreau's mind, but rather a haunting one, as evidenced by the fact that two of his books mention it. Years earlier, the war between the ants had worked its way into Thoreau's own poetry in *A Week on the Concord and Merrimack Rivers*:

> Here while I lie beneath this walnut bough,
> What care I for the Greeks or for Troy town,
> If juster battles are enacted now,
> Between the ants upon this hummock's crown?
>
> Bid Homer wait till I the issue learn,
> If red or black the gods will favor most,
> Or yonder Ajax will the phalanx turn,
> Struggling to heave some rock against the host. (*Wk* 301)

Even as he bids Homer to wait while he watches the war between black and red ants, Thoreau can articulate the war only by using Homer's tropes. Despite the attempts in both books to shrug off the authority of history and find personal validation in the language of the present tense, Homer's value still overshadows Thoreau, prefixing the terms, the meanings, and the lessons that the war between the ants can offer.

Throughout *Walden* Thoreau wants to claim a personal wholeness simply through his own ability to experience and to observe. Nonetheless, he must go outside of his views about the redemptive value of the natural world in order to assimilate the violence he witnesses. Homer's tropes of nature, with a piercing clarity that Thoreau finds beyond his grasp, point to an underlying predatory force, not only in animals and birds but in the forcefulness of water, wind, and fire. Thoreau's fascination with the *Iliad* may be a search for the missing component in his own representations of the cosmos. In Homeric time and space, gone is the relaxing and ennobling tranquility of man's experience in nature. Gone is the peace of mind in the setting of untamed rivers and wild forests that Thoreau tries to celebrate as golden silence. Thoreau is too complex to limit himself to the pastoral optimism of Virgil's *Eclogues* or the bucolic idylls of Theocritus—in turning to Homer, he chooses to face the tougher side of the natural world. When Homer likens human relationships to the interaction among animals in the wilderness, the comparison, if anything, adds a brutality and unfeeling aggressiveness to the human side of the equation. For instance, in Book XVII of the *Iliad*, as Menelaus battles Hector for the body of Patroclus, Athena wishes to embolden Menelaus. To keep him from relenting, she instills in him μυιης θαρσος, *muies tharsos*, or "the courage of a gadfly," eager to bite since it finds the blood of men λαρον, *laron*, or "sweet."[20] Homer's choice of attaching the genitive-possessive form of the word *muia* meaning "fly," to *tharsos* meaning "courage," precludes human beings from claiming romantic virtues like bravery as their unique entitlement. For Homer, the divinely inspired force that causes mosquitoes to suck the blood from someone's bare arm equals the masculine adrenaline that leads men to clash on the battlefield. Everything human is also animalistic; everything animal also has its traces of humanity. Homer's Greek threatens Thoreau's project of withdrawing from the corruptions of society and finding purer contemplation in nature. If the *Iliad* is any index, nature will only show him all the deleterious influences that drove him away from the manipulations of social life in the first place.

It is not only when Homer likens humans to animals that their blood-thirstiness and violence increase. When people behave like naturally occur-ring elements, their terror expands. In Book XX, as Achilles goes on his mad rampage to drive the Trojans from the beachhead, he is compared to θεσπιδαες πυρ, *thespidaes pur,* or "all-consuming forest fire," as well as a wind that scatters everything in confusion and goads the fire even further.[21] The natural world mirrors human aggression and cruelty so well precisely because in all forms of physical existence, whether living or inanimate, there is an innate order of strong and weak. Violence is ubiquitous. Many of Homer's most memorable similes, usually beginning with Greek lead-in words like ως, *hos,* or "just as," match relationships of vicious and tranquil beings to the mysteriously imbalanced social relationships among humans. In Book XXII, as Achilles chases down Hector at the walls of Troy, they are lik-ened to a κιρκος, *kirkos,* or hawk, and a τρηρωνα, *trerona,* or dove (the ac-cusative form). The strength of the simile lies in the fact that nature traps both the hunted and the hunter in a game of flight and pursuit that can only delay, but never abort, the inexorable murder of one by the other.[22] Homer reminds Thoreau that if he takes his fellowship with nature too seriously, it will not be a retreat at all. He will see in events like the war of the ants every-thing that disgusts him about the social conflicts of town life.

The Greeks, though dead and invisible, rupture Thoreau's isolation; they bring to him a humanity outside of himself that he must come to terms with. Thoreau almost never allows the value systems of others to impinge or make any demands on his own. "The only obligation which I have a right to assume, is to do at any time what I think right," he claims in "Civil Disobedience" (*RP* 65),[23] with a confidence that "what I think right" flows from a pure, pal-pable, coherent, and distinct self. But the Greeks, present cognitively while absent physically, repeatedly threaten the integrity of that self. In *Walden,* he admits that only one item, of all the possessions that he may have lost to visi-tors in his unlocked cabin, still felt lacking to him:

> Yet, though many people of every class came this way to the pond,
> I suffered no serious inconvenience from these sources, and I
> never missed any thing but one small book, a volume of Homer,
> which perhaps was improperly gilded. . . . I am convinced, that if
> all men were to live as simply as I then did, thieving and robbery
> would be unknown. These take place only in communities where

some have got more than sufficient while others have not enough. (*W* 172)[24]

Homer is the failure in Thoreau's wholeness. Homer's book is the only thing that he "missed." This statement could imply that it was either the only thing stolen or the only theft that caused him any grief. Either way, Homer ruptures the self-sufficiency and self-referentiality of Thoreau's world in *Walden*. Homer's epic, the site of Thoreau's excess, surpasses simplicity (being gilded) and throws the equilibrium between him and his neighbors out of balance. It is his, but it is also alien enough to him that it can be taken away.

Homer's disruption of Thoreau's independence appears in another section of *Walden*, when Thoreau is cataloging the "Visitors" whom he has entertained at Walden Pond. Not surprisingly, he has had few visitations that he considers noteworthy. At one point Thoreau reminisces that "Many a traveller came out of his way to see me and the inside of my house, and, as an excuse for calling, asked for a glass of water. I told them that I drank at the pond, and pointed thither, offering to lend them a dipper" (*W* 150). Walter Harding does not conclude from this statement that Thoreau experienced Walden in the total absence of human company. Diaries and letters belonging to members of the surrounding community point to a healthy stream of visitors (including notables like Emerson, Hawthorne, and the Alcotts). "The only guests that Thoreau did not welcome," Harding clarifies, "were the curious—and there were plenty of them."[25] The fact that so many people tried to pry into his solitary life at Walden reveals that Thoreau was interacting enough with the larger community to get something of a reputation. Life at Walden was not a total withdrawal from society. Nonetheless, the fact that Thoreau wanted to exclude the curious, as Harding claims, still reflects a powerful desire to withdraw from human relationships, even if he found it impossible to do so completely. In discouraging all but a small circle from seeking his friendship, he seals his world off from any intruder who might compromise his independence. At one point he says that in the winter months, "For human society I was obliged to conjure up the former occupants of these woods," a statement that reveals simultaneously his loneliness and his ostensible ability to cure his loneliness with his imagination (*W* 256).

At a rare and pivotal moment while at Walden, one person enters his life and excites Thoreau more than anything that he can conjure with sheer mental concentration. Almost half of "Visitors" is devoted to describing Alek Therien, a French-Canadian woodchopper, close to Thoreau in age, who truly attracted Thoreau's affection. It is this individual whom Harding says Thoreau "immortalized" in *Walden* by dwelling so long on their ambivalent friendship.[26] Thoreau writes: "He interested me because he was so quiet and solitary and so happy withal; a well of good humor and contentment which overflowed at his eyes" (*W* 146). Later he adds, "I occasionally observed that he was thinking for himself and expressing his own opinion, a phenomenon so rare that I would any day walk ten miles to observe it, and it amounted to the re-origination of many of the institutions of society" (*W* 150).

Therien's role in the unfolding of *Walden* is crucial for many reasons. He seems to be the only living person whose character is virtuous enough to hold the author's attention for several pages. Thoreau sincerely seems to like him; he notes that "he thoroughly believed in honesty and the like virtues" (*W* 150). Thoreau's confession is uncharacteristically emotional, revealing a loss of command over his own passions. He admits, after all, that he would walk ten miles to observe the man's honesty; and he also states with a small bit of concern that "it amounted to the re-origination of many of the institutions of society," as if hinting that Therien's charm threatens to compromise Thoreau's isolation. But the long reflections on this unique friend end with a cold disavowal, when Thoreau concludes disapprovingly, "If I suggested any improvement in his mode of life, he merely answered, without expressing any regret, that it was too late" (*W* 150). Ultimately, the man's failure to match Thoreau's intellect leads to an ungenerous assessment: "Yet his thinking was so primitive and immersed in his animal life, that . . . it rarely ripened to any thing which can be reported" (*W* 150).

It is informative to trace this ambivalent contact with the woodsman to the first point of interaction. The Canadian man is introduced into the narrative not by his own name, but by Homer's: "Who should come to my lodge this morning but a true Homeric or Paphlagonian man,—he had so suitable and poetic a name that I am sorry I cannot print it here,—a Canadian, a woodchopper and post-maker. . . . He, too, has heard of Homer" (*W* 144). "Alek" is certainly a name with "poetic" potential since "Alexander" is the name for Paris, the Trojan prince and abductor of Helen, in the *Iliad*. For important reasons to be examined below, however, Thoreau does not want to draw any parallels between Alek Therien and Paris. Instead he prefers to compare his friendship with Therien indirectly to the friendship between Achilles and

Patroclus. Although Thoreau alludes to there being some reason for leaving the man's identity anonymous, within the text of *Walden,* Homer's name replaces Alek Therien's name as the way to mark and to value this unexpected acquaintance: "To him Homer was a great writer, though what his writing was about he did not know. A more simple and natural man it would be hard to find" (*W* 145).

Homer authorizes Thoreau's love for the stranger. While Thoreau states that Therien knows enough English to converse with an American, it is the Greek language that at first unites them. He notes, "Some priest who could pronounce the Greek itself taught him to read his verse in the testament in his native parish far away; and now I must translate to him, while he holds the book, Achilles' reproof to Patroclus for his sad countenance" (*W* 144).

Thoreau's quoting of this passage bears directly on the meaning of the Canadian's arrival. "Achilles' reproof to Patroclus" comes from the opening of Book XVI of the *Iliad.* To analyze the significance of this section, I have block-quoted Thoreau's version of his translation and juxtaposed it against my translation of the original Greek from Homer's text. What is not included in the allusion is just as important as what appears in *Walden.* In my translation from the Greek, the words that Thoreau chooses to omit from his gloss are in bold.

Walden:

I must translate to him, while he holds the book, Achilles' reproof to Patroclus for his sad countenance.—"Why are you in tears, Patroclus, like a young girl?—"

> "Or have you alone heard some news from Phthia?
> They say Menœtius lives yet, son of Actor,
> And Peleus lives, son of Æacus, among the Myrmidons,
> Either of whom having died, we should greatly grieve." (*W* 144)

Iliad:

And so, they were waging wars around the ship with well-built benches, when Patroclus came before Achilles, the shepherd of those people, gushing warm tears just as a spring, bubbling up from black depths, pours dark water down a steep side of rock. Bright, swift-footed Achilles,

**seeing him, was wonder-struck, and calling to him directed
these winged words to him:**

"Why such crying from Patroclus, just like a tenderly young girl
**who, rushing beside her mother, begs to be embraced and
picked up, and clutching at her mother's skirt, rushing at
her, blocks her way? She keeps gazing at her with tearful
eyes until she is picked up. . . . Just like that girl, Patroclus, you pour heavy tears.** Is there perhaps some announcement for the Myrmidons, or for myself? Well, as such what news
do you release from Phthia? They say Menoitos, the son of Actor,
still lives, and Peleus son of Aeacus still lives among the Myrmidons. Greatly would we be grieving, you know, over either of those
having died. **Or is it you're lamenting the Achaeans, who are
getting destroyed on the hollow ships on account of their
own offenses—speak up! Hide not in your thoughts, so
that we both can know.**[27]

It is highly unlikely that this passage of *Walden* is strictly objective translation. The *mise en scène* for his reading of Achilles' reproof to Patroclus hints
that Thoreau's interaction with Therien is at once a parallel to, a translation
of, an interpretation of, and a revelation of, the meaning of Achilles' words to
Patroclus. First, one ought to consider the mysterious physicality of the moment. Thoreau translates while the woodsman holds the book—the book has
collapsed the "considerable neutral ground" that, only three pages earlier,
Thoreau has emphasized as a necessary buffer to keep human interaction
from collapsing into meaningless chatter. Is the woodsman sitting and
Thoreau standing? Are they both standing, and if so, does the author have to
hook his arm around Therien's shoulder to get a good look at the book? Or are
they sitting, side by side, so that one man's left arm brushes the other's right?
Whatever the configuration, Therien, regardless of his various faults that
Thoreau will catalog, has ripped a vulnerable hole in Thoreau's safe zone.
They are touching and—could it be?—*feeling* each other. Would this not
cheapen Thoreau's ideal of silent abstraction? Would it not cheapen the
"natural aristocracy" to which Homer belongs, by giving it into the crude
hands of a simple-minded man who does not understand him as well as
Thoreau does?

The reading of the book is already a dramatic moment in itself. Thoreau is making a friend and touching another human being, allowing himself to become entangled. It is no minor detail, then, that at this point of male bonding, bordering on outright homoeroticism, the passage of the *Iliad* that he is reading deals with Achilles and Patroclus, classic archetypes of friendship. Thoreau's sexual orientation is open to different interpretations, though one should proceed with caution in trying to apply labels of "straight" or "queer" to him, since one might run the risk of sexualizing relationships that could just as easily be viewed as intense social interest between companions. The value of pondering the extent of eroticism in Thoreau's interaction with Therien lies, perhaps, not in whether one can prove that he was really "gay" all along, but rather in what it tells us about Thoreau's view of bodily closeness and emotions such as longing, affection, and jealousy—sentiments that *Walden* as a whole prefers to skirt rather than to confront. Walter Harding, analyzing Thoreau's hostility toward marriage (and women in general) after being rejected by Ellen Sewall and Mary Russell, characterizes Thoreau's negotiation with his sexuality by proposing that "Thoreau was able to sublimate his love for the opposite sex in a worship of the world of nature and, as he once put it, falling in love with a shrub oak."[28] Thoreau found that his love for Ellen Sewall and Mary Russell ended, respectively, in rejection and frustration.

Harding's heteronormative spin on Thoreau's libido is not airtight, however. Robert D. Richardson Jr. points out that in 1839, Thoreau wrote a poem to Ellen Sewall's younger brother Edmund in the "conventions of Elizabethan love poetry" designed to "articulate rather than repress the strong surge of affection Thoreau felt for this 'gentle boy.' "[29] While the fact that Edmund was only eleven and Thoreau was twenty-two would cause the twenty-first-century reader some alarm, the age difference between the author of the love poem and its object may have actually made the entire exercise safer within the social norms of the 1830s. Richardson claims that since "it never crossed their minds that there might have been a physical attraction or longing behind all this, there was no reason for writer or reader to express or conceal the emotional attraction," adding that "as in the case of Whitman, a strongly affectionate nature was in some ways freer to express itself (when it chose) before Freud made us so complexly self-aware of all the possible implications of our feelings."[30]

Richardson is somewhat more comfortable than Harding with the possibility that Thoreau's erotic life included occasional attractions to the same sex. If homosocial or homosexual attraction was a dimension of Thoreau's interior life, then it developed somewhat early in his adulthood (at least by 1839) and possibly coexisted with his love for women like Ellen Sewall. Neither Richardson nor Harding, though, chooses to explore the full range of possibilities in Thoreau's admiration of Therien, who becomes a character in *Walden* in the mid-1840s, the point at which, as Walter Harding states, Thoreau "slipped into the pattern of the confirmed bachelor."[31] There is no dramatic age difference between the author of *Walden* and the Canadian wood-chopper to render the relationship sexually "safe" the way that the eleven years of difference between Thoreau and Edmund Sewall made the 1839 love poem safe. The heightened attention to Therien in the text of *Walden*, allusions to Achilles and Patroclus, and the details about the two men huddling together to read from the same book, leave this scene of the book open to speculations about homoeroticism. Whether Thoreau desired Therien as a friend or as something more, clearly Thoreau desired him, and his longing is significant regardless of the final verdict about the author's sexual orientation. The chapter "Visitors" in which this scene appears focuses on Thoreau's struggle to balance his ideals with his need for human company—and that is what Book XVI of the *Iliad* is about as well. The *Iliad's* basic plot lines depend upon Patroclus's death inspiring Achilles to kill Hector, so loyalty between male friends forms the crux of the entire epic.

The friendship between Achilles and Patroclus is something that Homer can depict, but that Thoreau cannot express in terms of his own experience in *Walden*. Thoreau has gone to great lengths to avoid allowing anyone to control his passions as much as Patroclus controlled those of Achilles. The story of their relationship, which Thoreau is obsessed with, weakens his position from within—first, intellectually, because he knows Homer's theme shatters his ideal of "considerable neutral ground"; and second, personally, because his fascination with the story has brought him into the arms of a charming woodsman whom Thoreau desires as a friend but cannot accept on qualitative grounds. This section of *Walden* is a vivid case of literature acting as a pander. Dante, one of the few post-antiquity authors whom Thoreau classes as a genius (W 104), includes in the *Divine Comedy* a warning about the compromising effects of literature. In Canto V of the *Inferno*, Paolo and Francesca are sentenced to be blown around by strong winds for having been lustful and adulterous. Francesca laments that it was the physical experience of reading about the affair of Lancelot that caused her and Paolo to approach each other too closely. She explains that "One day, to pass the time away, we read of Lancelot—how love had overcome him. We were alone, and we suspected nothing. And time and time again that reading led our eyes to meet, and made our faces pale, and yet one point alone, defeated us."[32] Reading a book together, according to Dante's schema, is doubly threatening to one's piety, because both the dreamy fancies of the story itself, and the physical proximity that results from sharing the same book, can assault even the strongest person's resistance to temptation. This, then, is perhaps the danger of the *Iliad* to Thoreau, as he reads to Therien. It is both sexuality and passionate devotion between friends (set in the troubling context of larger social institutions clashing with individual conscience) that the *Iliad* poses as its temptation.

Thoreau idealizes the *Iliad* based on its aesthetic grandeur and then finds himself unable to translate the central theme, close friendship, into real life. Even his translation from Greek into English, while linguistically impeccable, fails, because he says that Therien, after hearing it, remarks "That's good" and nothing more, going on his way to bring a bundle of oak bark to a sick man (W 144). The woodsman shows more interest in charity than Thoreau does, and seems more connected than Thoreau to other people in Massachusetts.

Also important are the nuances of the Greek in *Iliad* XVI. The first word of the book is ὡς, *hos*, a particle that usually introduces similes and stands in to say, "meanwhile." The word ὡς leads to a backdrop, either through a comparison or through narration of simultaneous events. It smacks of connectedness, relatedness, the inability of events or thoughts to be truly isolated. The first lines of Book XVI frame the moment by stating: "and so, as the men were making war around the ship with well-carved benches." At this point in Homer's epic, Achilles has tried to stay out of the war based on his individual perception of what is just. He burns with righteous anger over Agamemnon's ostensible misdeeds toward him. But the petty rivalry of other men continues even as Achilles sulks; the story, the cosmos, and the society of the *Iliad* all connect the sulking individual to the greater drama of social life with the simple word *hos*. And what is the moment that has required this framing? It is the arrival of the weeping Patroclus, who comes with the intent of forcing Achilles out of his isolation. Patroclus, using pathos and affect, means to drag Achilles back into the fray, despite Achilles' insistence that his independent conscience entitles him to stay out of the battle.

The passage in Book XVI is full of words that emphasize the raw physicality of passionate contact. Not only is Patroclus crying, but he is also touching

Achilles' body, so much that Achilles emphasizes repeatedly his similarity to a distraught daughter clinging to her mother's body. Achilles' comparative phrase ηυτε κουρη νηπιη, *eute koure nepie,* or "like a girl of tender age," should be enough to drive home the point. Yet he repeats it even more insistently by declaring, "τη ικελος Πατροκλε," *te ikelos, Patrokle,* or "Patroclus, that girl do you resemble." Achilles' redundant likening of Patroclus to a weeping girl (and his corollary comparison of himself to Patroclus's mother) is based on the physical experience of Patroclus's desire for contact. There is the reference to the girlish way of grabbing a mother's skirt, ειανου απτομενη, *heianou haptomene,* or "having taken hold of her mother's dress," and even more important, the word describing what Patroclus and little girls desire: ανελεσθαι, *anelesthai,* or "to be swept up and held." Strangely, Thoreau omits the fleshy references to bodily contact and the analogy of Achilles/ Patroclus to mother/daughter. He skips directly to the dry description of Myrmidons, the sons of Aeacus and Actor, and the grief one would show to fallen fighters. Though the lines about Patroclus touching Achilles probably speak more directly to what is on Thoreau's mind, he chooses to skip the most intimate exchange and includes, instead, arcane place names, clumsy genealogies, and frigid portrayals of grief. Grief is thematically less menacing than the delicate compromises that come with wanting to be held, coddled— loved—by someone who may not share the same vision of right and wrong.

The aporia in *Walden* cannot be interpreted, however, as Thoreau's decisive conclusion that human intimacy is irrelevant, because the text of *Walden* reveals (perhaps unwillingly) through its *mise en scène* that intimacy has prompted this passage as Thoreau's body is pressed close to the woodsman's while he reads the *Iliad.* Just as Patroclus's demand for Achilles' physical attention is jarring in the *Iliad,* so Thoreau is jarred by Therien's body, one might suggest, into telling only half the story and leaving it to the reader to excavate the real significance of the allusion. If this gloss on the *Iliad* is an unintentional disclosure of Thoreau's internal tension about human intimacy, so too is the strange fact that Thoreau summarizes the first twenty lines of Book XVI by calling it "Achilles' reproof to Patroclus." What in Achilles' words is truly a rebuke? Patroclus's tears are compared to the deep, warm water that comes from a spring. Achilles likens him to a delicate and tender little girl, a taunt based on behavioral norms, but he does not respond to Patroclus's eagerness by cursing him or pushing him away. Rather, he asks "what news do you bring?" And then, rather than spurning the intimacy, he demands even more connectedness by issuing the command, "speak, do not hide things in your mind; speak so that we both can know." Achilles' reproach is directed not at Patroclus but rather at Agamemnon, whom Achilles accuses of acting unjustly. Rather than scolding Patroclus, Achilles seems more interested in finding out what could cause such a lapse in his friend, whom he considers so close to himself that anything in the other's mind is an equal entitlement of his own.

This chapter of *Walden* may have been a subtle turning point for Thoreau; if so, it would be appropriate, since the passage he translates marks the crucial turning point in the *Iliad*. Up until Book XVI, Achilles has done, in effect, what Thoreau has done up to that point in *Walden*. In bitterness and disappointment over his unfair treatment by Agamemnon, Achilles has sworn off all intercourse with the larger society of the Greeks to protest the latter's injustice. The image of a man withdrawing from his people to protest the society's moral corruptions would have resonated powerfully for the self-described hermit of Walden Pond. Thoreau's withdrawal from society would not have involved such a hostility to bourgeois marriage were it not for the fact that he fell in love with and proposed to the same woman, Ellen Sewall, as his brother John. Emerson prodded Thoreau unsuccessfully to overcome his bitterness about Ellen Sewall. In their social circle, Thoreau's stubborn grudge against bourgeois marriage had achieved, as Harmon Smith describes it, "the status of myth," and "his celibacy was always referred to in terms of the crushing blow Ellen's rejection had dealt him."[33] Marrying, for Thoreau, would have meant entering all the trappings of society that *Walden* disdains. His refusal to marry, conversely, went hand in hand with his refusal to engage in many of the social events that occupied contemporaries like Emerson. It meant staying out of circulation—and that is (in quite a different context) what Achilles is doing in the first fifteen books of the *Iliad*.

Angry over his disagreements with Agamemnon about ownership of the captive woman Briseis, Achilles has withdrawn from the war and from almost all social activities. He has carved out a space of self-sufficiency where he entertains himself with Patroclus and detaches himself from the implications of the Trojan War. In Book IX, Odysseus visits Achilles and Patroclus in their reclusive tent and begs them to re-enter the war; but Achilles remains steadfast about abstaining, and he persuades Patroclus to follow suit. In Book XVI, Achilles and Patroclus develop a difference of opinion, and the plot line of the *Iliad* turns. Patroclus grieves for the Greeks who have died, while Achilles stays stubborn about his withdrawal and refuses to sympathize with them. In the line immediately after Thoreau stops his translation, the true reproof between Achilles and Patroclus occurs, but it is the reverse of what Thoreau represents: Patroclus harshly criticizes Achilles rather than vice versa, and the cause for Patroclus's harsh judgment of his friend is based on Achilles' refusal to abide by the dictates of community. Patroclus cannot insulate his emotions, as Achilles does, from the suffering of the Greeks whom they are refusing to help. Patroclus scolds his friend:

συ δ'αμηχανος επλευ, Αχιλλευ
μη εμε γ'ουν ουτος γε λαβοι χολος συ φυλασσεις,
αιναρετη. τι σευ,αλλος ονησεται οψιγονος περ,
αι κε μη Αργειοισν αεικεα λοιγον αμυνης;

You have become unworkable, Achilles!
May the anger that you guard over never seize me.
You—cursed in your virtue! I ask: how will another, one of your
   posterity, be profited, if, let's suppose, you fail to protect the
   Argives from a disgraceful death?[34]

   Patroclus's response to Achilles focuses most critically on the malfunctioning link between Achilles' private world and the public world that obligates both of them. The words in Greek all point to a distortion in Achilles' system of logic. It has become too individuated and lacks reasonable input from outside. According to Patroclus, Achilles has become αμηχανος, *amechanos,* or "dysfunctional," a negation of the verb that means to devise, construct, or put into use. The verb *phulassein,* usually meaning to guard or protect, is instead used by Patroclus to describe Achilles' actions toward his own χολος, *cholos,* or "anger" personified. Rather than worrying as he should about the fate of his friends and his own children, Achilles, driven by self-righteousness, bestows upon his own emotions (and the most destructive ones at that) the nurturing tendencies that he should instead be directing toward other men. Whereas Achilles wishes, in the earlier analogy, to liken himself to Patroclus's mother, Patroclus refuses the metaphor, coldly and brutally, instead placing Achilles in a linguistic no man's land, where no words that imply a harmony with the social world ought to be applied logically at all. The very notion of "virtue" or "honor" that Achilles believes entitles him to retire into a private world and disregard the problems plaguing the others, is tied by Patroclus's speech to a curse, at the moment that he brazenly addresses his friend through a vocative, crying "you—cursed in your honor!" Patroclus uses the strange word αιναρετη, *ainarete*, a brutal compound wedding the adjective αινος, *ainos*, or "grim," with αρετη, *arete*, the important Greek word for virtue or honor. The stubbornness of Achilles' attachment to his individual conception of honor has blinded him to the importance of community and, as Patroclus's words hint, made him a grim and undesirable human being.

Achilles must choose at this point. He may sacrifice his position and succumb to the exhortation of his closest friend, or else he may hold steady in his conscience and risk losing the other's company. Achilles' dilemma represents the danger of friendship and the conversation that friends bring. Friendship with heightened emotions produces anxiety in Thoreau and makes him flee from social settings in search of silence and secluded discussions with ancient ghosts. Friends make demands, argue, and pressure one to make ideological compromises. Friendship is always a possible window through which the hypocritical and corrupted ideas of larger society will infiltrate the sanctuary of individual conscience.

Thoreau probably would have understood Achilles' protest against the Greeks as a matter of conscience. Achilles, Homer makes clear, does not abstain from the war out of fear, but out of his own sense of moral rectitude. He responds to Odysseus's pleas to join the war, in Book IX, by making a rational argument incorporating philosophical observations about human nature:

> τι δε δει πολεμιζεμεναι Τρωεσσιν
> Αργειους, τι δε λαον ανηγαγεν ενθαδ'αγειρας
> Ατρειδης; η ουχ Ελενης ενεκ'ηυκομοιο;
> η μουνοι φιλεουσ' αλοχους μεροπων,ανθρωπων
> Ατρειδαι; επει ος τις ανηρ αγαθος και εχεφρων
> την αυτου φιλεει και κηδεται

> What obligates the Argives to make war with Trojans?
> What moreover brought the people of the Atreides to this place
>   and has them huddling and assembling?
> Or was it not on account of Helen with her beautiful hair?
> Or, of all the men who live, are the only ones who love their
>   wives

The sons of Atreus? After all, any good and sensible man
Loves and concerns himself with the woman who is his.[35]

Achilles consistently offers rational arguments for his decision. In Book
XVI, even his love for Patroclus is not enough to derail his principles. Despite
his best friend's personal attacks, he stands firm on his logic, drawing boundaries of relevance in his surroundings, and refusing to back down from them.

αλλα τοδ αινον αχος κραδιην και θυμον ικανει
οππστε δη του ομοιον ανηρ εθελησιν αμερσαι
και γερας αΨ αφελεσθαι, ο τε κρατει προβεβηκη

But this soreness enters my heart and soul
When a man, who exceeds in power, would desire to block a man
    similar to him
And snatch back his prize![36]

Citing his actions based on a rational analysis of Agamemnon's use of
authority, Achilles remains in his self-imposed isolation, bucking even his
best friend's most desperate pleas. He ends up losing Patroclus, avenging
Patroclus, bringing about Hector's death, and thereby making the central
story line of the *Iliad* possible. Immediately following his rhetoric of detachment, Achilles still refuses to go to battle but places his armor on Patroclus
and sends him to combat with specific instructions not to storm Troy. Hector
slays Patroclus in battle and steals Achilles' arms, thereby precipitating the
moment of grief that afflicts Achilles, jolts him out of his isolation, and
prompts him to rejoin the Greeks.

Thoreau says that he kept Homer's *Iliad* on his table at Walden, sustaining
himself through his heavy days of work with "the prospect of such reading in
the future" (*W* 99–100). The *Iliad* is something he seems to leave aside at
times, when there is work to be done, and then revisits later. There is a climax
to his study, though—a "prospect" for a future time when the epic's wisdom
will come to him in its purest and most enlightening form. But what exactly is
the wisdom that he hopes to glean from Homer? The *Iliad* is nothing without
the crucial break in Achilles' isolation and his final surrender of perfect independence, all because his love for Patroclus makes his self-referential ideology impossible to sustain. In the *Iliad* death is everywhere, and upon death,

the meaning of a human's life is permanently translated into the way he is remembered by his community. Patroclus's funeral games are necessary because Achilles can only memorialize his love publicly, in a social environment. Then the epic ends with the funeral of Hector, and the beautiful lamentations made by three women who recount their respective relationships to him: his mother Hecabe, his wife Andromache, and his friend Helen. Hector is defined purely according to his reputation as it endures in the memory of those socially related to him. He is respectively his mother's favorite son, the world's most faithful husband, and Helen's best friend. Thus Thoreau's fondness for the *Iliad* could be an obsession with social connectedness and may have reflected back, in one way or another, on the unresolved status of the self-reliant integrity he seeks in *Walden*. Without the collapse of Achilles' self-referential ethics and his subsequent submission to the standards of a larger community, there is no story; rather, there would be only endless war devoid of higher meaning.

If one removes the fantastic acts of gods, the *Iliad* portrays humanity in two molds, both senseless and irrational: either violence or affection. The social brings threats of extermination or kindness in excess of one's natural needs. In the *Iliad*, nature is a mirror, but it shows only what the battlefield shows: a grid of grudges and passions, culminating in violence, that tie together the animal world as they unify the human world. No reader can say with any certainty what lessons for his own life Thoreau gleans from the narrative, because Thoreau performs no exegesis in *Walden*. His analyses are internal and private. It is tempting to suppose that he saw in Achilles' change of heart the inevitable in himself: At some point, he would have to engage society at large, even with its imperfections.

Yet the *Iliad* is still a brutally physical book, and a book about war. It represents a set of challenges to Thoreau's integrity; but ultimately it does not win him over. Thoreau never lends the lumberjack his armor, nor lays down his life for Therien's sake. The encounter with his Homeric friend from Canada culminates with Thoreau's dismissing the man as too simple, too brutish, too mired in his animal nature. There is still a natural tendency in Thoreau that resists war. The man who wrote *Walden* and the avid reader of Homer's *Iliad* is still the same author who spent the night in jail because he opposed the war against Mexico. The lesson of Achilles and Patroclus must have had an impact on Thoreau, but he also must have wanted his version of their drama to be about sacrificing one's liberty for the sake of a universal humanity, and not about avenging a friend. The theme of friendship and interpersonal loyalty in the *Iliad* needed to morph, for Thoreau, into a more generalized concern for other people, for a community much larger than acquaintances and neighbors, for society and humanity itself—an entity that could obligate him based on principle and conscience rather than on personal affection. The *Iliad* teaches its readers a great deal about the twin themes of love and violence, but Thoreau was one reader determined to rewrite the epic with a nonviolent way of expressing love. Homer and Thoreau each came upon a turning point where their heroes—in Homer's case Achilles and in Thoreau's case himself—had to emerge from isolation and consummate their memberships in a larger discourse community. What came of the turning point, however, differed dramatically. Homer gave the world Book XVI and pushed gore and violence to new heights. Thoreau, determined to do better than his Greek forefather, gave the world "Civil Disobedience."

Notes

1. Henry David Thoreau, *Walden*, ed. J. Lyndon Shanley (Princeton: Princeton University Press, 1971).
2. Lewis Leary, "Your Mind Must Not Perspire: Thoreau on Observation, Perception, and the Role of Consciousness," in *Cast of Consciousness: Concepts of the Mind in British and American Romanticism*, ed. B. Taylor and R. Bain (New York: Greenwood Press, 1987), 151–59, 158.
3. Bob Pepperman Taylor, *America's Bachelor Uncle: Thoreau and the American Polity* (Lawrence: University of Kansas Press, 1996), 31.
4. Henry David Thoreau, *A Week on the Concord and Merrimack Rivers*, ed. Carl F. Hovde et al. (Princeton: Princeton University Press, 1980).
5. Stanley Cavell, *The Senses of Walden* (Chicago: University of Chicago Press, 1992), 29.
6. Leonard Neufeldt, "Thoreau in his Journal," in *Cambridge Companion to Thoreau*, ed. Joel Myerson (Cambridge: Cambridge University Press, 1995), 107.
7. Robert Sattelmeyer, "Thoreau and Emerson," in *Cambridge Companion to Thoreau*, 25.
8. Neufeldt, "Thoreau in his Journal," 108.
9. Ibid., 109.
10. Cavell, *Senses of Walden*, 92.
11. Ibid., 30.
12. Harmon Smith, *My Friend, My Friend: The Story of Thoreau's Relationship with Emerson* (Amherst: University of Massachusetts Press, 1999), 2.
13. Sattelmeyer, "Thoreau and Emerson," 28.
14. Robert D. Richardson Jr.'s study of Thoreau's reading habits, *Henry Thoreau: A Life of*

the Mind (Berkeley: University of California Press, 1986), points out that the curriculum at Concord and Harvard both emphasized the classics to such a degree that Thoreau's grasp of ancient languages "sounds impressive, but it was, of course, required of all students and was taught in a less than promising atmosphere." Because of the brutality of the classical teaching methods, Richardson muses that "Thoreau's interest in classics thus grew almost in defiance of his formal schooling. But grow it did" (24).

15. Ibid., 13–14.
16. Ibid., 5.
17. Cavell, *Senses of Walden,* 5.
18. Taylor, *My Friend, My Friend,* ix.
19. William Cain, "Henry David Thoreau, 1817–1862: A Brief Biography," in *A Historical Guide to Henry David Thoreau,* ed. Cain (Oxford: Oxford University Press, 2000), 31.
20. Homer, *Iliad,* ed. E. H. Warmington, M.A. (Cambridge: Harvard University Press, 1967), XVII.570–72. This is the standard version of the *Iliad* known to classicists as the "Loeb Classical Library." It includes a translation into English by Dr. A. T. Murray, but all translations from Greek to English used in this essay were made by the author.
21. Ibid., XX.490.
22. Ibid., XXII.139–40.
23. Henry David Thoreau, "Resistance to Civil Government," in *Reform Papers,* ed. Wendell Glick (Princeton: Princeton University Press, 1973), 63–90. The essay was retitled "Civil Disobedience" in its 1866 reprinting; debate continues whether that title is authorial.
24. An interesting irony is that Walter Harding argues that Alek Therien, who figures importantly in the second half of this essay, actually borrowed the volume and never returned it. See *The Days of Henry Thoreau* (New York: Dover, 1982), 191.
25. Ibid., 196.
26. Ibid., 190.
27. Homer, XVI.1–20.
28. Harding, *Days of Henry Thoreau,* 104.
29. Richardson, *Henry Thoreau: A Life of the Mind,* 58.
30. Ibid.
31. Harding, *Days of Henry Thoreau,* 110.
32. Dante Alighieri, *Inferno,* in *Divine Comedy,* tr. A. Mandelbaum (New York: Alfred A. Knopf, 1995), V.127–32.
33. Smith, *My Friend, My Friend,* 160.
34. Homer, XVI.29–32.
35. Ibid., IX. 337–42.
36. Ibid., XVI. 52–54.

"And What Became of Your Philosophy Then?"

Women Reading Walden

SARAH ANN WIDER

It grieves me to be obliged to interrupt him in the middle of some quaint sentence or beautiful thought just because the sun is touching a certain bush down by the water's edge, which is a sign that it is lunch-time and that I must be off. Back we go together through the rye, he carefully tucked under one arm, while with the other I brandish a bunch of grass to keep off the flies that appear directly we emerge into the sunshine. "Oh, my dear Thoreau," I murmur sometimes, overcome by the fierce heat of the little path at noonday and the persistence of the flies, "did you have flies at Walden to exasperate you? And what became of your philosophy then?"

ELIZABETH VON ARNIM, *The Solitary Summer*[1]

WE ARE NOT yet unpacked. There is a chaos of suitcases in the bedroom and a labyrinth of boxes in the hall. A semester with Colgate's New Mexico study group has ended, and we return to upstate New York with scant time before the semester begins. *That* is a textbook definition of disorientation. "What—how—when—where?" I wake on this winter morning as did Thoreau wondering over questions that I am not yet certain how to ask. The only thing I can say for sure is that the mice who moved in with my daughter's stuffed animals during our absence are no longer evident. The essay on *Walden* that I would like to be writing cannot for the moment compete with the stashes of seed in sweaters and the compact black reminders of digestion on shelves and in drawers. Those mice clearly enjoyed an extended stay in my daughter's room. I have cleaned that room in a mad housewife's frenzy. It is what some might now call clean, but I am as foul as they come. I have been laboring in quiet desperation. There is nothing akin to beautiful housekeeping in my thoughts. Thoreau's words sit on the shelf, undoubtedly accompanied by the ubiquitous mouse turds. I smile grimly at this house on the edge of the woods where I don't even have the common courtesy to welcome the mice in from the cold.

Two days later, I have not awakened to an answered question though I am certain of the woods and the gray daylight and the burning desire to unpack the thoughts in my mind rather than the boxes that still line the hall. Those boxes no longer communicate urgency. The study group report remains unwritten, and the small black calling cards left behind by the mice now draw only a slight flicker of attention. I settle at the counter that serves as my desk, books and papers companionably strewn from one end to the other. I stare out the window, not so much to steady the ideas careening wildly through my head but to place myself. Companionship with sheetmetal-gray skies, strangely green grass from unseasonably warm temperatures, and plentiful rain. I see what is there, but I am not there. I am still in New Mexico, desert dry, craving the colors of sunset written daily into sandstone.

At first I think the disorientation is pure homesickness. I grew up in New Mexico, lived into my third decade in desert clarity, and although calendar time now tells me I have spent half my life as a neighbor to maples and oak, tamarack and pine, and yes, the stone buildings of an eastern college, I am nonetheless never quite all here in this place known familiarly as "CNY"— central New York. I assume the disarray in my mind is simply the well-known gap between the place I love and the place I live. I stare back at my notes on *Walden's* readers; I look again at the snatches of things I have written over the years, words for a talk at this conference and that conference, essays I could never call finished. They are here on this desk, and I see their connections but cannot write them into a meaning I trust. The old methods of written discourse trouble me in ways they once did not, and now my thoughts refuse to rest in the well-worn forms of scholarly argument. I am no longer a thinker willing or even able to streamline thought, for every time I attempt it, I see falsification.

Elizabeth von Arnim's taunt to Henry David Thoreau returns. She challenged him, "And what became of your philosophy then?" What has become of my philosophy now? In my case, I am plagued not by flies and heat but by a critical methodology inadequate to my material. I pause. Philosophy has been superseded by story. For what I have to relate are stories about reading *Walden,* and not simply about a single reading but a palimpsest of readings. *Walden,* I have come to believe, is a book no one reads just once. In each of the stories I now think of, Thoreau's words speak directly, and their presence suggests prior readings. His lines function like a perfectly provocative synecdoche. They stand for the whole from which they were taken, and at the same time they become part of the whole in which they are placed. But identity is complicated by nature, and the quoted words, now on their own in another's text, remind the reader that their source is elsewhere. Like an erratic left behind by a glacier, they illustrate a separate set of forces. What remains unsettled is how those prior forces now come into play. They evoke a distance, a space the eye might not otherwise see.

We are, at times, resisting readers as Judith Fetterley so aptly described, now a quarter of a century ago. It is curious, and a good story, how we come to measure that resistance. I came of age as a reader before her book taught me to see the woman reader's hard row to hoe. Like Laura Dassow Walls, I was busy in my own bean field, impervious to criticism. Walls and I virtually grew up as readers in the same years, and like her, I never felt myself "radically excluded" by the gender-specific language of Emerson or Thoreau. In her discussion of women reading Thoreau, Walls points directly to the ways of reading I know by experience and see reflected in the comments of other women readers. As she notes in her 1993 essay, "*Walden* as Feminist Manifesto," Thoreau handily reduced "gender conventions" to "rubble."[2] For many women readers, he has long been a liberating force, giving rousing support to our difference. For those of us who found that gendered norms were the direct road to quiet (and sometimes not so quiet) desperation, Thoreau's words reinforced the alternatives we envisioned. Rereading Walls's essay, I see again why *Walden* has served as the "point d'appui" for so many women. Given the "gender fluidity" he creates in his writing, Thoreau opens possibilities. Rather than perpetuating a world of "binary [and mutually exclusive] oppositions," he envisions that "ideal house" where "housekeeping is no longer a woman's chore but a necessary and beautiful aspect of the economy of living."[3]

In my own years of reading, I have begun to accumulate stories about this ideal house. It began through conversations with Gail Baker, whose own work on the houses women represent in writing still speaks new thoughts to my understanding.[4] It continues in the slight glimpses of actual reading found in women's journals. And in the stories now pressing most in my thoughts, this startling transformation of setting into place speaks provokingly through the words and also through the houses themselves.

Imagine a cabin in the woods by a pond. Boat access only. You cannot reach this house by road. And once you canoe or row (or now motor) across the water, a 700-foot path greets you. Twitchell Lake is just inaccessible enough to keep out the curious city-bred tourist. There are other places in the Adirondacks for them. Life at Twitchell requires a commitment to the land. As the original owners of this house wrote, "We wanted our cabin to belong to the land. As far as was necessary we would make ourselves over to fit the forest rather than, in the midst of such wildwood build a dwelling that might stick out like a sore thumb on the hand of Pan."[5] Their guiding aesthetic was the desire to be unobtrusive. My colleague Ellen Kraly, who now calls this place her second and true home, recalls her initial response: "Here was this cabin that seemed to glow from the inside out. . . . It did seem to me then very much an imagined place."[6]

Ellen and I agree that this cabin, called "B Mark W" by the original owners, is hardly a cabin of Thoreauvian proportions. Its scale certainly exceeds the tidy 15 x 10 of Thoreau's cabin, and yet it apparently functioned (and continues to function) as that "more populous house" Thoreau ascribed to a golden age. As it did in the 1920s, so eighty years later it invites the visitor to "pay your respects to the fire." It is a house where you can see "so necessary a thing as a barrel or a ladder, so convenient a thing as a cupboard," and unquestionably it is a place "where to be a guest is to be presented with the freedom of the house, and not to be carefully excluded from seven eighths of it" (*W* 244).[7]

It is also a house where Thoreau's words held their place and where celebrations of *Walden* found a home. This was above all a reader's cabin. Even the original plans distinctly mark a home for books where to this day the five shelves begin at one window and turn the corner to the next. The presence of a place for books is no surprise. One of the original owners was a high school

English teacher and the other a librarian and writer. An Oberlin graduate, Adelaide Breckenridge taught at Peabody High School in Pittsburgh for forty years, from 1913 to 1952. Those first years at Peabody must have been heady ones. Peabody boasted students who would define the literary world. The poet and critic Malcolm Cowley was one of that crowd, as was the literary critic Kenneth Burke, James Light, theatrical director of the Provincetown Players, and Mary Blair, leading actress with the Players.

Adelaide's fellow house designer and companion and partner of many years, Katharine Whited, worked at the Carnegie Library in Pittsburgh and wrote, or at least was rumored to have written, numerous westerns. The pen name she guarded so closely in her life still remains an unsolved mystery, and the only evidence we have of her writing are two articles about life in the Adirondacks (one about the cabin published in *Country Life* in 1930) and three poems typed as if to be submitted for magazine publication but apparently never accepted.

It is no surprise that this "deliberate place" would hold so many books. The unexpected good fortune is the fact that many of Adelaide's and Katharine's books remained in the cabin despite two changes of ownership. The books on their shelves form a part of the house, and among them Ellen found a home-made quotation book that apparently was as much a part of the place as the two women themselves. A notebook reclaimed from other uses (pages are cut out and what was once a page of accounting is now pasted over with a newspaper clipping), it now holds others' words—passages hand-copied in, quotations cut from newspapers and magazines. There are a number of clippings stuffed into the book, a few with handwritten notations suggesting their inclusion. The handwriting on these selections is neither Katharine's nor Adelaide's. The quotation book was apparently common knowledge among the friends who came to the cabin, and submissions were welcome, if not always accepted.

The contents vary widely. It is a quirky book, one that celebrates the spirit of miscellany. A passage from "The Courtship of Miles Standish" is next to a page of one-sentence quotations on doing one's own work. Clipped quotations titled "The Librarian" and "The Pessimist's Year" stare at each other across facing pages and are partnered by a newspaper clipping on friendship and one titled "Fox Trot Fodder" about the trivial conversation overheard at a dance. Several pages contain a hand-copied record of bird migrations. And yet, this apparently random organization looks different upon closer examination. While no clearly labeled categories organize this collection of words, two major and intertwined strands emerge. These are words that speak about the power of friendship and the desirability of life in the woods.

Thoreau's words hold a notable place among these quotations. Several pages into the book is a page headed *"Thoreau,* Lines from *Walden."* Copied in by hand, four separate passages form a curious abstract of the book. The first quotation is one of the most famous, so often quoted that even in the 1930s it was stumbling into cliché. The different drummer begins the page, followed by Thoreau's witty overturning of time-saving proverbs. The well-known "stitch in time" turns into a relentless fretting that consumes the very time it purports to save. In contrast, the next quotation offers a truly time-honoring alternative: "This is a delicious evening, when the whole body is one sense, and imbibes delight through every pore." The final words on the page heighten such moments of union by way of sharp contrast: "What sort of space is that which separates a man from his fellows and makes him solitary? I have found that no exertion of the legs can bring two minds much nearer to one another." Whited's lines from *Walden* end by acknowledging distances that cannot be crossed.

I speculate on the readers of this page in the quotation book, thinking around and through the connections the four disparate passages bring about. Was it a shorthand for Katharine who copied these passages into the quotation book? Whose copy of *Walden* did she use, or did she carry these lines in memory? Were these passages that she and Adelaide talked over from Adelaide's teaching, or was *Walden* not a book for classroom fodder? No copy of *Walden* remained at B mark W when Ellen and her husband Scott bought the place, though there is a signed copy of *Walden Revisited,* George Whicher's 1945 centennial commemoration of the year Thoreau moved to the pond.

For those who leafed through the quotation book on a cabin-bound day, what did these lines evoke? Quotations do not speak in isolation. Taken from a context in which words flow before and after, this excerpting of fluid thought is designed to continue that forward-rushing movement. Whether the reader laughs to herself over her own remembered example of frenetically taken stitches, or recalls the companion passages in *Walden* that accompany the different drummer, she participates in and furthers the ongoing process of making meaning. Made to stand alone and apart, a quotation becomes the raw material from which the reader generates thought.

Were we to read this through the lens provided by Virginia Woolf in her centennial tribute to Thoreau, Thoreau's "alert and heroic" reader would return to model that "noble exercise." In her essay for the *Times Literary Supplement,* Woolf reminds her reader that there is no rest for the Thoreauvian reader. She comments, "We can never lull our attention asleep in reading Thoreau by the certainty that we have now grasped his theme and can trust our guide to be consistent. We must always be ready to try something fresh; we must always be prepared for the shock of facing one of those thoughts in the original which we have known all our lives in reproductions."[8] While Virginia Woolf might strike us as the unexpected reader of Thoreau, she clearly enjoyed returning to Thoreau's words as she worked on this essay. Although she relied heavily on H. S. Salt's biography, her prose sparkles most where the biography is not her primary source. In fact, her particular points of praise offer an admirable précis of the elements that would come to distinguish her own novels. Examining the "value of simplicity," she defines it as "intensification, a way of setting free the delicate and complicated machinery of the soul."[9] She describes the experience of reading *Walden* as one of "beholding life through a very powerful magnifying glass," and what else are her famous extensions of time than such magnification? And in the narrative technique Thoreau so aptly developed, she identifies a distance she would come to perfect in her own writing. "When we have read his strong and noble books, in which every word is sincere, every sentence wrought as well as the writer knows how, we are left with a strange feeling of distance; here is a man who is trying to communicate but who cannot do it. His eyes are on the ground or perhaps on the horizon. He is never speaking directly to us; he is speaking partly to himself and partly to something mystic beyond our sight."[10] Here is the reader's experience of reading *Mrs. Dalloway* or *The Waves* or *To the Lighthouse.* That strange feeling of distance, the writer's gaze focused beyond our line of vision, conveys the vast interiority of human life in which "no exertion of the legs can bring two minds much nearer to one another." The words Katharine Whited chose to conclude her "Lines from *Walden*" act as a necessary guarantor that the "way things are" are not the way they need to be.

This assertion and cultivation of distance is and remains one of Thoreau's most powerful appeals to the woman reader. Whether lines speaking from a quotation book or narrative strategy described and in turn developed, this assessment of distance measures much of the value women readers have found within Thoreau's writing. Such use of distance is, in Virginia Woolf's words, one of the most "fruitful discoveries" women have made from a text that does not always prove welcome or welcoming to its readers. When we find ourselves "radically excluded," there is always another possibility inviting our participation. We turn to explore the distancing space and see what makes us solitary and measure the power available in such distance.

Nowhere is this cultivation of distance more potently demonstrated than in Elizabeth von Arnim's *The Solitary Summer*. Published in 1899, it takes *Walden* as one of its founding texts, though in good Thoreauvian fashion, it tests this foundation for solidity. Sure enough, the mud and slush of opinion and prejudice make for slippery footing. Some places in *Walden* offer no hard bottom, and individual experience finds the weak spots out.

Von Arnim might well seem an unlikely person to create a Thoreauvian setting in her own backyard. Born to a society family, married into the German landed aristocracy, she would seem more at home in Edith Wharton's Newport than Henry Thoreau's Concord. She herself was well aware of the odd mix her experiment represented. And it is precisely here—in the implausible combination—that she found her closest affinity to Thoreau. Could she turn from the stifling social scene and set up her observer's point on the margin of her society? Could she, despite the expectations established for the Count von Arnim's wife and for the mother of his children (at the time, they numbered four: he kept trying for a son, much to his wife's dismay)— could she live without hurry and waste of life? Her answer was a sturdy, if somewhat ironic, "yes," written into her second book. *The Solitary Summer* takes *Walden* and pushes its boundaries to see exactly how far the Concord writer can speak to a circumstance that was similar only in the reader's imagination.

The differences are striking. Not only are the two writers separated by half a century, but they are divided by nationality, by gender, by class. What could the man who built his single-room house on borrowed land have to do with the well-to-do titled woman who decided to spend the summer at her husband's country estate? Much more, von Arnim claimed, than appearances would allow. Her decision *was* an act of defiance, a clear statement against her society and her husband, whom incidentally, she calls "The Man of Wrath." She chose to be alone for the summer, rejecting the notion of summer gatherings, of in-town visiting, of anything that would disturb her purpose. Her book opens with a declaration of intent:

> Last night after dinner, when we were in the garden, I said, "I want to be alone for a whole summer, and get to the very dregs of life. I want to be as idle as I can, so that my soul may have time to grow. Nobody shall be invited to stay with me, and if any one calls they will be told that I am out, or away, or sick. I shall spend the months in the garden, and on the plain, and in the forests. I shall watch the things that happen in my garden, and see where I have made mistakes.[11]

One might well hear an echo of "I went to the woods because I wished to live deliberately." And like Thoreau, von Arnim meets dimwitted resistance. The response to her plan mirrors the skepticism and the mental myopia he observed in many of his Concord neighbors. Where they bothered him with questions about what he did or thought or ate "out there," she encounters a comparable lack of imagination. Her husband's first response is, "Mind you do not get your feet damp."[12] He goes on to forecast complete failure in unequivocally demeaning terms. "You will find it a very long summer," he tells her. "People will think you are mad . . . you will catch cold, and your little nose will swell . . . you will be sunburnt and your skin spoilt." His final blow is dealt to her character. A summer alone, he says, will make her "dull." She turns aside all his charges and finally silences his words by reflecting on how limited they are. When he predicts that dullness will result from her experiment, she breaks off the conversation and remarks to herself and to her reader, "It often amuses me to reflect how very little the Man of Wrath really knows me."[13]

She holds to her plan, taking the summer as her own, and if that were all there were to it, an escape to the country with a Thoreauvian echo, the connection might seem more a function of my reader's imagination than of her intention. But Thoreau is not simply a whisper in this text; he is part and parcel of it. She spends every May morning reading Thoreau, at first in the garden, and then, at a farther distance from the house, all appropriately by the pond. This is her morning work, altered in June when the garden takes its own precedence. But in May, Thoreau is her "companion," her "morning friend" with whom she spends the hours from dawn until noon.[14]

She figures her reading as a conversation: his book is the author embodied. Describing her daily encounter with Thoreau, she reminds the reader how important place is. Books and their authors must be carefully situated.

Thoreau has been my companion for some days past, it having struck me as more appropriate to bring him out to a pond than to read him, as was hitherto my habit, on Sunday mornings in the garden. He is a person who loves the open air, and will refuse to give you much pleasure if you try to read him amid the pomp and circumstance of upholstery; but out in the sun, and especially by this pond, he is delightful, and we spend the happiest hours together, he making statements, and I either agreeing heartily, or just laughing and reserving my opinion till I shall have more ripely considered the thing.[15]

Her characterization is friendly, but humorous. Thoreau "speaks" without interruption; he speaks on and on and on. . . . Whether she "agrees heartily" or reserves judgment until her own thoughts have ripened, she remains the alert reader never lulled to sleep by his continuous prose. She keeps her statements to herself, but not for long. Morning comes to its literary end bringing a daily ripening with it. Her morning work cannot be continued in the way Thoreau advises. While she allows him to speak without interruption through these particular hours of the day, not all hours are equal. For individuals differently stationed, time rarely offers similar prospects.

He can afford to ignore the midday meal. She cannot. When she sees that the sun touches "a certain bush down by the water's edge," she knows, however inconvenient it may be, that she must "interrupt [Thoreau] in the middle of some quaint sentence or beautiful thought."[16] At noon, she closes the book even though, in her imagination, he continues to speak. "I know," she writes, "that inside his covers he is discoursing away like anything on the folly of allowing oneself to be overwhelmed in that terrible rapid and whirlpool called a dinner, and of the necessity, if one would keep happy, of sailing by it looking another way, tied to the mast like Ulysses. But he gets grimly carried back for all that, and is taken into the house and put on his shelf."[17]

Thoreau sounds his warning. She takes heed but cannot follow, for his words, though well intentioned, are impractical. In a moment where her reserved opinion ripens into its own witty commentary, she acknowledges that Thoreau is right in theory. "Luncheon," she agrees, "is a snare of the tempter." She would avoid it if she could, but two considerations stand in the way. The first is her own hunger. A growling stomach easily drowns out Thoreau. Taking him at his most literal, she contrasts his disembodied words with her corporeal presence. She comments, "I still happen to have a body attached to my spirit, which, if not fed at the ordinary time, becomes a nuisance."[18]

At the same time, she acknowledges his further point about the disruptive significance society attaches to a meal. Who needs a two-hour event when an apple in the pocket will do? Thoreau alive certainly kept body and spirit together; Thoreau dead can afford to speak primarily to spirit, but dead or alive, Thoreau never faced the same demands that she, as a woman, does. She comments, "I would perhaps try to sail by it [the meal] like Ulysses if I had a biscuit in my pocket to comfort me, but there are the babies to be fed, and the Man of Wrath, and how can a respectable wife and mother sail past any meridian shallows in which those dearest to her have stuck? So I stand by them."[19]

Such an effort is not without its cost. She is "punished"—her word—for her dutiful actions. In the morning, she sees herself as "almost a poet . . . very nearly a philosopher, and wholly a joyous animal"; at noon, she confronts the reality of her role as the dull wife and mother who can only show concern about "cutlets and asparagus and revengeful sweet things."[20] It is clear where she would rather be, and clear as well, that Thoreau's possibilities are not wholly hers.

Well aware how much separates her from the Thoreau she reads every morning, von Arnim uses these differences in good Thoreauvian fashion. They cut both ways, revealing limitations on each side of this conversation. She unabashedly states that her "philosophy" has not advanced far enough to let her household dispense with doormats and furniture. Her statement reminds us of what Thoreau chose not to say. Who can afford to dispense with certain household amenities?—not the wife, not the mother, but the man without children. Setting the question of spouse aside, for von Arnim's "Man of Wrath" is an entirely different topic, the babies must be fed. She cannot indulge in the Thoreauvian luxury of living from one biscuit to the next.

Nor does she imagine that Thoreau, the man or the persona, would in the least understand the actual constraints of her situation. Her "morning friend," fair weather of sorts, "turns his back on [her]" when she returns to the library in the afternoon. She will not take him off the shelf until early the next morning when once again they can resume their friendship. It is, in fact, a friendship entirely dependent upon *Walden*'s presence and Thoreau's absence. Were she to have met the Thoreau of Walden Pond, she readily acknowledges that he would have had little or nothing to do with her. "During his life," she writes, "I imagine he would have refused to notice anything so fatiguing as an ordinary German woman, and never would have deigned discourse to me on the themes he loved best."[21]

Death markedly improves the situation by lessening the authority of the person who authored the text, offering the reader a different place for response. There is an undeniable advantage for the reader of a later generation. Von Arnim comments, "but now his spirit belongs to me, and all he thought, and believed, and felt, and he talks as much and as intimately to me here in my solitude as ever he did to his dearest friends years ago in Concord."[22] She assumes Thoreau's spirit and participates in his thoughts precisely because the particular judgment of a single individual can more readily be suspended in the text, the verdict postponed through multiple rereadings.

Von Arnim's success stems from her invitation to and inclusion of multiple readings. Multiplicity, in this case, is a matter of necessity and bluntly foregrounds the limits she invariably faces. Even in her opening statement—her rousing declaration of intent for the summer—we see the problem within her own space. Von Arnim's image smacks of society and its seemingly inescapable malaise. She wants to "get to the very dregs of life," and the unsavory mud of bad wine leaves a bitter taste in the reader's mouth. It is a poor substitute for the life-giving marrow that Thoreau sought, and thus these opening lines immediately call into question what this first-person speaker will be able to accomplish.

That question remains thought-provokingly unanswered. While von Arnim succeeds in managing her solitary summer, the book concludes with an uneasy October conversation between husband and wife. Their words only confirm the absence of understanding between them. While she flaunts her success in front of him, he refuses to acknowledge it. She tells him "as a matter of fact . . . I never spent a happier summer." He says nothing but amply expresses his opinion with a look that requires no words to convey its skepticism. He then holds her to her initial vow. The summer was to be a time for soul growth. "If I remember rightly," he inquires, "your chief reason for wishing to be solitary was that your soul might have time to grow. May I ask it if did?" She replies, "Not a bit," and he is satisfied with his victory, but the reader knows how mistaken he is. Why should she admit success? If she does, she will be taunted; she may also forfeit the opportunity for another summer spent like the one she has just enjoyed. A second try, a second chance, another attempt, and her plea will placate his need for dominance.

Like Penelope she will keep unweaving the work whose completion seals her fate, so that she never need find herself silenced within someone else's narrative. She will keep the conversation open, and in so doing keep her mental distance from her husband.

Not knowing he has lost, he claims victory, rises from his chair and takes possession, "drawing [her] hand through his arm." The conversation degenerates into classic misogyny. The topic is "woman," and he claims authority: she is dishonest, incapable of judgment, and invariably the "natural enemy" of other women. Von Arnim laughingly dismisses the Man of Wrath's words. He takes laughter for agreement, and as their exchange continues to his apparent advantage, he grows increasingly affectionate. He little realizes how ineffectual either his words or his gestures are. In a comment made to the reader, presumably kept from the husband, von Arnim notes, "and when people begin to look affectionate I, for one, cease to take any further interest in them."[23]

The status quo remains—as far as the "Man of Wrath" can see . . . which is not very far. And in turn, the reader is offered a choice. Can von Arnim's crisply satiric voice maintain the necessary distance so that the reader's inside knowledge explodes the structures of privilege on which Elizabeth's German garden is based? The twenty-first-century reader might well ask the same question of *Walden.* One need not look far to see the extent of Thoreau's privilege, and as much as he sought to minimize its import or effect, there is the unalterable reality that Thoreau came to his experiment placed far differently from the Canadian woodchopper or the Irish immigrant. Can *Walden* speak its revolutionary message even in the midst of privilege, even against the privilege of its writer? What can the first person do?

The answer to that question briskly turns, as von Arnim well knew, on the reader. In her opening chapter of *The Solitary Summer,* a chapter akin to *Walden's* "Reading," she outlines her own practice. Unlike Thoreau, she minimizes the generalizations. She makes no large claims and uses only herself as example. At the same time, her tack is certainly consonant with the Thoreauvian heroic reader. She is not reading as a "paltry convenience," but for the absolute force that motivates good and rewarding work. She reads what she *loves,* in a world that cannily keeps the romance out of that word. Her husband loses credibility through affection. As he draws her arm through his, she steps aside and promises the reader a different story. Where affection operates within a system of subordination, all the while pretending it does not, love acknowledges the unyielding reality of reciprocity. "Everybody must love something," she comments, "and I know of no objects of love that give such substantial and unfailing returns as books and a garden."[24] Such returns are made possible precisely because there is no romance in this love. It is, plain and simple, the best of manures. In phrasing that might well be called Thoreauvian, she remarks, "love, after all, is the chief thing. I know of no compost so good."[25]

The witty observer creates precisely the space a reader needs to stay awake. The odor—or perhaps I should say "stink"—of this language is not likely to lull anyone into luxury. For example, when von Arnim reports her husband's words, they invariably sound rotten. His pronouncements occur with little commentary interwoven around them. They are bare, bald statements devoid of supporting structures, and they collapse under the weight of their own condescension. Von Arnim's speaker may well accentuate their fall by highlighting her own unspoken comments, but her remarks only point out the inherent weaknesses. As Thoreau so artfully shows in *Walden,* incrimination is a simple matter because it is always a reflexive function. All incrimination is self-incrimination. Every unsound idea will finally break apart due to its own discord. One need only keep a distance and subtly remark the flaws.

This advocacy of distance is perhaps the greatest gift Thoreau offers his marginalized readers, for within that space lies the large, revolutionary prospect that a markedly different perspective can successfully challenge the dominant one. It is little wonder that Thoreau called for a different way of reading when he wrote *Walden.* In themselves, rising rates of so-called literacy did not cheer him. It only meant piecing together the most threadbare of meanings. Surveying the readers of his day, he commented, "Most men have learned to read to serve a paltry convenience, as they have learned to cipher in order to keep accounts and not be cheated in trade." In contrast, he set forth a different kind of reading. No mere tool designed to get ahead in a system based on distrust, it might be classified as necessary work, the very way for living deliberately: "but of reading as a noble intellectual exercise they know little or nothing; yet this only is reading, in a high sense, not that which lulls us as a luxury and suffers the nobler faculties to sleep the while, but what we have to stand on tiptoe to read and devote our most alert and wakeful hours to" (*W* 104). Here is one's morning work, yet I cannot help but stumble in my reading. I have long ceased to believe in generic "men," and don't care to style myself one, especially in this account book of reading. For once I am glad to be excluded if it means I am more likely to know something of that "noble intellectual exercise." And yet, there is much more work to be done for that possibility to open into a space worth staying awake in. There are passages where you wonder if the reader is best advised to snooze through language that betrays its bias so bluntly.

For example, from just a few pages earlier in the "Reading" chapter of *Walden*, Thoreau seemingly closes down the possibility I have just opened. In his first description of right reading, I am drawn to the vigor and heroism of this noble exercise. *If only* we approached the written word with such urgency. Rather than emptied markers of meaning, words might then become vital, empowering agents of change. But I am stopped in this thought by the very nature of Thoreau's language. Structured into his call for the heroic reader is a cultural bias that if left unquestioned truncates the promise this passage holds. His words on the "mother tongue" make me realize how much distance I must build into the craft of meaning. If these words are to speak beyond their bias, they cannot speak alone. We need space, time, and plenty of other voices to untwine the prejudice written within this passage.

> To read well, that is, to read true books in a true spirit, is a noble exercise, and one that will task the reader more than any exercise which the customs of the day esteem. It requires a training such as the athletes underwent, the steady intention almost of the whole life to this object. Books must be read as deliberately and reservedly as they were written. It is not enough even to be able to speak the language of that nation by which they are written, for there is a memorable interval between the spoken and the written language, the language heard and the language read. The one is commonly transitory, a sound, a tongue, a dialect merely, almost brutish, and we learn it unconsciously, like the brutes, of our mothers. (*W* 100–101)

What prospect, then, for me or for any woman to become the esteemed "alert and heroic reader?" Certainly we continue to read—whether in the Adirondacks, in London, in Germany, in New Mexico or central New York. And we keep our necessary distance so that one thought does not crowd out another possibility. What if I don't want to escape the mother tongue but desire to relearn it and speak it fluently?

That question held, and still holds, and perhaps will always hold currency for any reader who does not match the identity Thoreau so readily assumed. My hackles rise when I read that passage on the spoken word, not solely for the way it diminishes women but for the ignorance it perpetuates about language. There is no inferiority in spoken language. Language does not "progress" from oral to written, and the written word carries so many liabilities that its association with maturity is overestimated, to say the least. I recall numerous conversations with Joseph Suina, one of my colleagues from New Mexico. As we talk about the ignorance—the racism—institutionalized within mainstream education, he describes the limitations created by written language. The written word isolates its readers. It devalues human presence and human interaction. Just take the book off the shelf and enter your self-enclosed world where the sound of real human voices is silenced into a pale imitation. Dependence upon a written language affects the very nature of human relationship. If one's source of knowledge lies within the covers of a book, then the individual reader is indeed that single, solitary self; community is subsidiary, an afterthought or luxury, constituted or dissolved by the limited understanding of limited individuals. This diminishment of relationship is why certain cultures choose not to force the mother tongue into the written word, why at Cochiti Pueblo, for example, Keres will not become a written language. Talk to anyone in any of the Pueblos and you will hear concerns about loss of the mother tongue, a loss due to the ubiquitous "father tongue" that *is* the written English language. But hear as well how far from transitory the mother tongue is. *Beowulf* looks pretty ephemeral in comparison to certain songs and certain stories whose currency today can be measured in thousands of years. The songs continue in this very moment, but who, outside a literature class, remembers *Beowulf* or any number of written pieces whose life has indeed become a shelf life, date expired, for whom there was no community to keep those words alive?

What keeps words vital? Not simply marks on a page. The written word labors within and against its own isolation. What chance for a reader who will speak life back into the silent words? When do readers undertake that noble exercise and question the very premises that bind a meaning in a text or attempt to bind readers to that meaning? The reader, we would like to think, opens and claims the necessary distance in which time can be taken and other voices can be heard. We would like to think that, whether in the imagined possibilities offered by Katharine Whited's quotations selected for her

Twitchell Lake readers or the conversational space von Arnim opens between herself and her reader, a space inviting the reader in and keeping out the dominant language that now sounds as tinny and hollow as it is.

In reading, we do as we always must and bring some semblance of the real human voice back into the written word. As Thoreau commented, it is, after all, always the first person who does the speaking in any piece of written discourse, and there is no better way to make that voice heard than by creating a conversation for others to enter. And sometimes conversation begins with disagreement, though we trust it will not end there. The best promise for opening such conversation appears within the quotation Katharine Whited placed as the last of the lines to represent *Walden* in her quotation book: "What sort of space is that which separates a man from his fellows and makes him solitary? I have found that no exertion of the legs can bring two minds much nearer to one another." That is very good news indeed. Where proximity essentially premises the continued dominance of one perspective over another, the real necessary of life is distance. No matter how dominant are particular views on written language, other voices continue to speak. No matter how close the Man of Wrath draws to his wife, he will not penetrate her thoughts. Those proceed directly to a place bound neither by conventional relations nor by the biases of a dominant culture. Within a society structured by corrosive conventions, a woman seeks as much space as possible between herself and her fellow man.

She too loves a broad margin to her life, especially since the open space of that margin is precisely where the reader touches the page. Literally the point of contact between writer and reader, it is also where voices can speak extravagantly. This is the space where reader turns writer, marking her own response in the margins. It is also the figurative space where silenced perspectives claim voice. Out of bounds, the words can be heard on their own terms. And when writers choose to build those margins into the body of their texts, then the revolutionary space opens within the words themselves, and not beside them, a necessary distance well worth cultivating.

Notes

To Ellen Kraly, my continued thanks and pleasure over the ongoing opportunity of working together on women's representation of the Adirondacks. And to Joseph Henry Suina, words that cannot be said, except in the certainty of ongoing, thought-provoking conversation.

1. Elizabeth Von Arnim, *The Solitary Summer* (London: Macmillan, 1899), 25.
2. Laura Dassow Walls, "Walden as Feminist Manifesto," *Interdisciplinary Studies in Literature and the Environment* 1:1 (Spring 1993): 139.
3. Ibid., 138.
4. Gail Baker, "Woman's Sense of Living Space," unpublished essay. I was fortunate to have been in the Emerson/Thoreau/Margaret Fuller and the Philosophy and Literature seminars that Gail team-taught with Paul Schmidt at the University of New Mexico.
5. Katharine Whited, "Our Wildwood Home: Two Women Solve the Country House Problem." *Country Life* 57 (January 1930): 47.
6. E-mail exchange, July 25–26, 2001.
7. Henry David Thoreau, *Walden,* ed. J. Lyndon Shanley (Princeton: Princeton University Press, 1971).
8. Virginia Woolf, "Thoreau," *The Essays of Virginia Woolf, 1912–1918,* vol. 2, ed. Andrew McNeillie (New York: Harcourt Brace Jovanovich, 1987), 136.
9. Ibid., 135.
10. Ibid., 137.
11. Von Arnim, *The Solitary Summer,* 3.
12. Ibid., 4.
13. Ibid., 6.
14. Ibid., 24, 26.
15. Ibid., 23.
16. Ibid., 24.
17. Ibid., 25.
18. Ibid., 25.
19. Ibid., 26.
20. Ibid.
21. Ibid., 26, 24.
22. Ibid., 24.
23. Ibid., 190.
24. Ibid., 30.
25. Ibid., 20.

Bibliography

Baker, Gail. "Woman's Sense of Living Space." Unpublished essay.

Fetterley, Judith. *The Resisting Reader: A Feminist Approach to American Fiction.* Bloomington: Indiana University Press, 1978.

Thoreau, Henry David. *Walden.* Ed. J. Lyndon Shanley. Princeton: Princeton University Press, 1971.

von Arnim, Elizabeth. *The Solitary Summer.* New York: Macmillan, 1899.

Walls, Laura Dassow. "*Walden* as Feminist Manifesto." *Interdisciplinary Studies in Literature and Environment* 1.1 (Spring 1993): 137–44.

Whited, Katharine. "Our Wildwood Home: Two Women Solve the Country House Problem." *Country Life* 57 (January 1930): 47–48.

_____. Quotation book. B Mark W on Twitchell Lake, undated.

Wider, Sarah Ann, and Ellen Percy Kraly. "The Contour of Unknown Lives: Mapping Women's Experience in the Adirondacks." *Biography* 25:1 (Winter 2002): 1–24.

Woolf, Virginia. "Thoreau." *The Essays of Virginia Woolf, 1912–1918,* vol. 2. Ed. Andrew McNeillie. New York: Harcourt Brace Jovanovich, 1987. 132–40.

Walden and the Georgic Mode

MICHAEL G. ZISER

LYRIC POEM, experimental novel, literary almanac, spiritual autobiography, travelogue, jeremiad, homily, and philosophical treatise—*Walden* has traditionally defeated every critical effort to stabilize its generic identity. Indeed, as many readers have noted, polygeneric restlessness is a rhetorical tactic well suited to a book written in defiance of the spirit of conventionality that is the essence of *genre,* "a literary form that has clear superficial features or marks of identification."[1] At the same time that critics have ruled any generic pigeonholing both impossible and undesirable, however, they have reached a tacit consensus on the question of *Walden's mode,* a broader compositional category that "derives its identity not from any formal convention but from a particular perspective on human experience."[2] In the case of *Walden,* the modal designation "pastoral" has established dominion over the outermost formal frame of Thoreau's pivotal book, with far-reaching consequences for subsequent formal, thematic, and historical scholarship. The present essay reopens the question of *Walden's* pastoralism, arguing that the book's assumptions about man's nature and situation place it as firmly in a different mode, the georgic, that Thoreau found in Roman, British, and American texts and reinvented for himself as he strove to resolve the inherent difficulties of his life as a laborer, philosopher, and artist. Elevating the georgic to a status equal to that enjoyed by the pastoral in studies of Thoreau and American literature more generally accomplishes at least four things: it allows pastoral, a vital framework for understanding *Walden,* to recuperate from its procrustean overextension; it rescues *Walden* from interpretive stalemates created by logic of the pastoral; it permits apparently contradictory existing scholarship on familiar Thoreauvian themes (language, nature, reform) to coexist peacefully under a new conceptual rubric; and it encourages the comparison of *Walden* (and texts influenced by it) with new kinds of literary and extraliterary objects.

The Pastoral Background

To understand the stakes involved in splitting the georgic away from the pastoral, one must return to Theocritus and the origins of identifiably pastoral treatment of the countryside and the nonhuman world. The *Idylls* established the pastoral model of a shepherd's colloquy and inaugurated most of the form's distinctive themes: the singing match, the coquettish milkmaid, the wholesome and leisurely rustic life, and the lost lover. Mixed in with these prototypical pastoral set pieces were forays into the unglamorous lives of slaves and housewives and other less exalted members of the rural community. Vergil's *Eclogues,* which established the conventions for all self-conscious later pastorals, followed the *Idylls* in most particulars except its panoramic rural gaze, opting instead to focus more cleanly on the interplay between shepherds alone, situated as they now were not in a quasi-realistic Sicily but in the imaginary realm of Arcadia. Four major consequences follow upon these Vergilian innovations. First, the pastoral scene was shorn of much of its broad agrarian context, effectively establishing the pastoral convention of isolation in the countryside in place of the manifestly interdependent village life of the *Idylls.* In its place, Vergil introduces an element of political allegory that would become a prominent part of Renaissance pastoral from Petrarch's sonnets to Sannazaro's *Arcadia* to *The Shepheardes Calender* to *As You Like It* to *Comus.*[3] This redefined social context of the *Eclogues* allowed Vergil and his followers to dispense with extraneous details about the broader environmental context of the representative pastoral anecdote. Fourth, in trying to recreate what was, to first century B.C.E. Roman readers, the exotic mystique of Theocritus's Greek Sicily of more than two hundred years before, Vergil exchanged his predecessor's naïve representations for a decidedly sentimentalized view of the Arcadian countryside. Bruno Snell, the most perceptive chronicler of this transition, notes the "air of unreality" that descends over Vergil's Arcadia and most subsequent pastoral works.[4]

These alterations both strengthened and weakened the association between the natural world and pastoral form as the tradition was translated from Greece and Rome (via Italy) to England. On the one hand, the *Eclogues* and its imitations made it clear that the pastoral's true home was the alternative to the city. (In fact, that was precisely what was interesting about it—it offered a counterpoint to the complexity of city life, and of the cares that beset its urbane readers.) But the countryside was now important mainly as a symbol of simplicity to contrast with urban sophistication, and it becomes the vehicle for what some influential critics call the defining strategy of the pastoral—"the putting of the complex into the simple."[5] As productive as this development may have been for literature, it nevertheless drew the pastoral's twin allegiances into conflict with one another: as repository of natural facts, it affords the nonhuman world a heightened significance; as fiction, it provides an alternative space in which fantasy or allegory can unfold without the constraints of physical laws or the resistance of natural objects. In fact, the simplification described by Empson when carried to an extreme could lead to a complete withdrawal from and extinguishing of the world in favor of the freer imaginative realm of the mind.[6] This trade-off of physical relationships with natural objects for a pastoral mood effectively precludes any sustained consideration of the natural world or the human place in it: in the contest between the pastoral's roots in environmental realities and its aspirations to pure fictivity, fictivity won. (That the best examples of the pastoral sustain an ironic and a critical attitude toward this conventional derealization does little to mitigate the underlying problem of environmental inattention.) The contradiction is perhaps best illustrated with a line from Andrew Marvell's "The Garden," a touchstone for students of the pastoral, which ends on the note of "annihilating all that's made / to a green thought in a green shade"; that is, by sublimating social cares and natural forms alike into reverie.

It was this classical and Renaissance version of the pastoral—radically redefined from a set of historically and formally circumscribed generic conventions involving the contrast between urban complexity and rural simplicity to a much broader, more flexible strategy of literary representation that works by "putting the complex into the simple"—to which Leo Marx appeals in his seminal translation of the pastoral vocabulary to American soil, *The Machine in the Garden*. In Marx's view, classic American writing forms a tradition of complex, self-aware pastoral simplification characterized by a deliberate withdrawal from the world of nature, history, economics, and technology into the simplified, protected, and elevated space of imaginative literature. Marx moves quickly from *The Tempest* to *The Great Gatsby* in his attempt to establish the preeminence of the pastoral in American letters, but his argument includes an influential and explicit analysis of *Walden*'s pastoral attributes, both generic and modal. Citing Thoreau's occasional allusions to Jacobean and English Romantic pastoral poetry, his self-stylization as a shepherd "tending the flocks of Admetus," and the symbolic quality of his Concord landscapes, Marx argues that Thoreau like other American authors relocates the pastoral hope of a harmonious integration of the self with the natural world out of history and into his own writerly imagination.[7]

Although Marx's explication of American pastoralism focuses on very large currents in American technological and intellectual history, his emphasis on questions of craft, an archetypal "pastoralism of mind," and political disengagement provide a compelling context for at least three other kinds of traditional pastoral scholarship on *Walden*. Charles Anderson's *The Magic Circle of Walden*, for example, follows through brilliantly on the formalist implications of Marx's pastoral thesis, remarking the poetic yield of Thoreau's apparent absorption in the artistic. The marvelous tradition of biographical and phenomenological readings of *Walden*, exemplified by the works of Sherman Paul and H. Daniel Peck, lays particular stress on the book's imaginative preservation of pastoral scenes and perceptual moments. In making the important assessment of Thoreau's evasion of or engagement with nineteenth-century economic and cultural structures, political criticism has likewise proceeded by interrogating the ideological meaning of pastoralism as a cultural and literary formation. Although many of the critics sampled above have had serious misgivings about Marx's particular findings and general conclusions, their diverse scholarship touching on the generic and modal attributes of *Walden* has nonetheless usually retained Marx's assumption that Thoreau's great work is an example—perhaps *the* primary example—of the complex American pastoral.[8]

The extremely high quality of the critical work that has emerged from such diversely pastoral approaches speaks for itself. At the same time, however, this very fertility may be seen as an indication rather of the inadequacy of the pastoral frame to *Walden* than of its suitability: a bad fit, after all, brings more work to the tailors. Indeed, *Walden*'s peculiarities have obliged the most perceptive scholarship—including Marx's—to embroider notions of the pastoral nearly beyond recognition, revealing in the process the ultimate limits of this capacious literary category and rendering it subject to concrete critique. The fragile pastoral consensus about the mode of *Walden* has been particularly threatened of late by ecocritical assessments of Thoreau's work, which have reexamined the naturalism Marx discounts as softheaded nature worship, to find in *Walden* and elsewhere (especially the late writings) a serious engagement with ecology and a flirtation with ecocentric ways of enacting the relationship between the aesthetic and the natural that seem to portend the pastoral-preservationist strain of twentieth-century American environmentalism.[9] Such criticism, while positioning itself against formalist and ideological pastoral scholarship, has frequently made its new claims in the name of the pastoral, recovering the mode's deep investment in the facts of the natural world after its suppression in urbane Vergilian and Renaissance eclogues. For ecocritics, the pastoral's most salient characteristic is not its formal conventions or attitudes but its subject matter: the pastoral is "all literature . . . that celebrates the ethos of nature/rurality over against the ethos of the town or city."[10] In redefining the mode from stylized retreat to willful engagement with the empirical details of nature, ecocriticism is exerting enormous pressure on internal contradictions of the mode buried since Theocritus, which threaten to destroy the pastoral's coherence as a teleologically definable conceptual framework. The reaction among some traditional pastoral scholars has only deepened the split, as demonstrated by Leo Marx's attempt to defuse the contradiction in a pair of dismissive reviews on ecocritical scholarship about *Walden* in the pages of the *New York Review of Books*.[11] If the pastoral is a mode in which the simple was being put into the complex, pastoral criticism has succeeded in bringing complexity out of what had once appeared simple. An alternative to this impasse is the georgic, a mode that does not depend on the assumption that creative assertion requires retirement from the material world and thus breaks the pastoral cycle between speculation and inattention.[12]

The Georgic

The georgic, or didactic writing about the natural world as apprehended through human labor practices, has a long history in Western literature. Thanks to Robert Sattelmeyer's painstaking scholarship, we know that Thoreau was well acquainted with the formal georgic, whose roots can be traced back as far as Hesiod's pessimistic agricultural calendar, *Works and Days*, though the mode derives its modern name from Vergil's much later four-part masterpiece on field agriculture, viticulture, animal husbandry, and bee-keeping.[13] Thoreau read these latter *Georgics* with great care, alluding to them as often as to the pastoral *Eclogues* and the epic *Aeneid*. More surprisingly, he also studied relatively obscure Roman agricultural works—georgic in content if not always in form—of Cato, Columella, Palladius, and Varro, citing them frequently in his published works as well as in the *Journal* (with particular frequency there around the 1854 publication of *Walden*).[14] The English inheritors of the georgic tradition in the three centuries leading up to his own were also favorites of Thoreau: for instance, Thomas Tusser's *Five Hundred Points of Good Husbandry* (1573), John Evelyn's *Sylva* (1679), and especially James Thomson's *The Seasons* (1730) and William Cowper's *The Task* (1785). Such works did not constitute extraordinary reading material for a man of Thoreau's era and education, but some of the less literary works about agricultural history (such as Henry Phillips's *History of Cultivated Vegetables* [1822], to take a late example) and agricultural science (such as the annual report of the U.S. Department of Patents, for which he developed a strong taste) certainly did. Much of the early New England literature from which Thoreau drew his prodigious knowledge of regional history—William Wood, Edward Johnson, John Josselyn—contains a significant amount of agricultural content or is written from the perspective of writers who have pragmatic rather than meditative designs upon the land. Indeed, he often referred to these early American georgic writers alongside Roman ones. His continual engagement with such works in *Walden* and elsewhere puts Thoreau in line with this New England agricultural tradition.[15] Furthermore, as Robert Gross has shown, "The Bean-Field" chapter of *Walden* responds quite directly to the agricultural reform literature—both technical and hortatory—of antebellum Massachusetts.[16] Such reading material shares few external, generic formal markers—only a common concern with man's active, pragmatic, and specific relationship to the natural world around him. This makes it less a generic subcategory of the pastoral mode than a mode in its own right. Further, its capaciousness means that Thoreau's immersion in the formal and informal georgic does not signal a wholesale endorsement of any particular generic or modal assumptions so much as a critical reinterpretation that adds depth to the classical, British, American, and New England georgic traditions.[17] *Walden*, to remake a phrase from Leo Marx, is best understood in literary historical terms as a complex georgic.

If *Walden*'s prehistory was in part georgic, so in part is its legacy. The bibliographer Loren Owings has exhaustively demonstrated that the book served as a major influence on the enormous body of georgic "country-house" literature that came into print after the Civil War.[18] Apart from this chain of literary inheritance, the notion that Thoreau was a hands-on agrarian writer makes a kind of intuitive sense, as *Walden* not only inspired but even served as a guide for countless back-to-the-landers whose experience has been, and was in conception, as much georgic as pastoral.[19] As many readers have noted, *Walden*'s didacticism often carries over from its agricultural contexts into metaphorical practices of self-cultivation, becoming in places a personal conduct manual aimed at those who "find it labor enough to subdue and cultivate a few cubic feet of flesh" (*W* 5).[20] Indeed many critics, Stanley Cavell most persuasively, have understood *Walden* as at base a deeply didactic how-to manual for leading the philosophical life, a georgic of self-inquiry.[21] The historical argument for *Walden* as emerging from and feeding into a georgic tradition is thus as strong as or stronger than the pastoral lineage fancifully sketched by Leo Marx and left unquestioned by most subsequent scholarship.[22]

But historical argument can only go so far in explaining the claims a particular work makes upon the imagination, and the continued success of Marx's pastoral proposition likely has less to do with his idiosyncratic literary historiography than with the power of the pastoral as an explanatory model independent of any historical tradition. Its tenacity may in part be due to a notable congruence between the conditions of reading generally and the pastoral drama of withdrawal, nostalgic reduction, preservation, and elevation: we often read literature in leisured seclusion, our belated interpretations necessarily involve a restriction of our circle of attention, and the valued text survives in our imaginations not as full presence but as exalted memory to be recharged by subsequent rereadings.[23] Given the operation of so powerful a pastoral analogy at work within our reading practices, perhaps it is no surprise that the pastoral should remain a particularly hard critical legacy to overcome. For the purposes of the present essay, what this means is that in describing the difference it makes to read *Walden* as a complex georgic rather than as a complex pastoral, we will also be obliged to examine deeper questions about how texts are to be read and used. If we want—without concluding our mortal careers —to front the Thoreauvian task of casting light on both of *Walden*'s surfaces, the one written and the one read, we must turn the passive act of reading modeled on the pastoral into a cooperative creative act between text and the world.

In order to realize this larger georgic promise of *Walden,* we need to work our way through some of the specific generic and modal differences between the georgic and the pastoral. Although critics since Joseph Addison have tended to view the pastoral and the georgic as opposed if overlapping modes of representing the country life, rarely have the distinctions been spelled out with precision. In what follows I want to sketch the differences in the two modes' attitudes toward a defined set of subjects—time, audience, register, the body, labor, and reference—in the particular context of *Walden* and make a brief case for *Walden*'s adherence to the georgic alternative. My intention is not to provide an exhaustive comparison of the two modes but simply to concentrate on the differences most relevant to Thoreau.

A major part of Marx's definition of the pastoral hinges on its deliberate detachment from the flow of history into a clearly bounded realm, logically and often grammatically in the past tense (though occasionally, as in the prophetic or utopian pastoral, in the distant future). In contrast, the georgic points to the present, alternating between a tenseless imperative mood and a mythological mode in which pastness is rendered inoperable as a concept. (Mythological inset is in fact more characteristic of the classical georgic than of the pastoral, and therefore Thoreau's myth-making and myth-bending place *Walden* even more firmly within the former genre.) The book pays its closest attention to the possibilities of the present rather than the losses of the past: it positions itself in the moving dawn, the georgic "nick"—not the pastoral niche—"of time."

> Men esteem truth remote, in the outskirts of the system, behind the farthest star, before Adam and after the last man. In eternity there is indeed something true and sublime. But all these times and places and occasions are now and here. God himself culminates in the present moment, and will never be more divine in the lapse of all the ages. And we are enabled to apprehend at all what is sublime and noble only by the perpetual instilling and drenching of the reality which surrounds us. (*W* 96–97)

Where the pastoral is marked by a nostalgic orientation to a lost moment in the past, the georgic is primarily concerned with the projection of continuous tradition from the present into the future, a goal that implies a sense of time as duration. In a journal passage that well illustrates the temporally splayed vision of his georgic, Thoreau turns from present despair to eternal confidence to alight at last on a distended present moment of resolution, transcribing the immanent theology of the above passage into agronomical terms:

> Hosmer is overhauling a vast heap of manure in the rear of his barn, turning the ice within it up to the light; yet he asks despairingly what life is for, and says he does not expect to stay here long. But I have just come from reading Columella, who describes the same kind of spring work, in that to him new spring of the world, with hope, and I suggest to be brave and hopeful with nature. Human life may be transitory and full of trouble, but the perennial mind, whose survey extends from that spring to this, from Columella to Hosmer, is superior to change. I will identify myself with that which did not die with Columella and will not die with Hosmer.[24]

Thoreau remarked this peculiar persistence of concrete agricultural experience through the millennia at several points in his journal, and the Roman agriculturalists appear pivotal in directing his thoughts away from the phenomenon of loss and toward the notion of the earth as a compendium of human and natural history that can never fully disappear. Though *Walden* has its nostalgic moments—childhood memories of the pond, the undertone of mourning for John—these are balanced by its pragmatic immersion in the lingering traces of local history found both in books and on the landscape, a recognition of history not as fossil but as the loam in which the present flowers. This tendency to view the natural world as built up out of, but not completely determined by, successive human histories posits human labor inside the referential transaction between nature and language in a way that makes estrangement an impossibility—a state of affairs not predicted by Emerson's breezier pronouncements in *Nature* and only incompletely articulated in his later examinations of the subject.[25]

The emphasis on the perpetual need for principled exposure to the environing and historical world points up another difference. While the pastoral as part of its nostalgic strategy stresses completion by modeling closure in its songs and arguments, the georgic often comes in the form of an open-ended almanac or manual whose instructions are meant to be followed year in and year out without the appearance of any final product. The georgic provides half of a meaning: acknowledging that its end lies somewhere outside of itself, it relies on its readers or community of users to complete it. *Walden* repeatedly registers just this anxiety in wondering whether its readers will have ears to hear and eyes to see the wisdom it offers. On a formal level, it does all it can to resist closure, and bears marks of Thoreau's later experiment, in the Journal, with a permanently open-ended form that follows, meditates on, and attempts to anticipate the seasons in a way that recalls English agricultural "kalendars."[26]

By enveloping itself in an impermeable boundary, turning its attention away from lateral concerns and toward the correspondence of its world with a higher one, the pastoral establishes itself in an anagogic register, encouraging allegorical uses and making it the natural mode of Platonic philosophy and Christian allegory. The pagan georgic, on the other hand, is always resolutely in a metonymic—one might even say an ecological—mode where the lateral relationship between things, people, and activities is more important in structuring the composition than the higher significance of any one thing. As a result, the georgic is always in the midst of a process of negotiating its own rules and borders. That is, it focuses not on the state of being sanctified or profaned but on the texture of security and vulnerability, registering the contact of world and integument—thus Thoreau's minute attentiveness to his skin and clothes. The crucial Thoreauvian state of "extravagance," described in terms not of pure ecstasy but of "being yarded" or extended bodily across a disciplinary boundary, is a georgic trait exemplified by a milk cow jumping a fence rather than by a bison pasturing on the open prairie.[27]

As we have already begun to see, the most immediate and important distinction between the two modes has to do with their attitudes toward labor. The pastoral is primarily the mode of *otium,* or the leisure both of the shepherds represented in their withdrawal from the world and of the poet who composes his verses about them in retirement. On the contrary, the georgic, which derives from "earth-work," is devoted to *negotium,* or the engagement and toil involved in running a farm. By analogy to the pastoral extension of poetically represented to poetically enacted leisure, the georgic's internal theme is the labor involved in writing a literary work. Despite the flirtations with idleness that might lead us, following some Concord townspeople, to class him among the pastoralist malingerers, Thoreau was profoundly interested in the technical aspects of work, as the physical competence eulogized by Emerson reveals. More important to him still were the spiritual fruits that might be had from physical discipline: "But labor of the hands, even when pursued to the verge of drudgery, is perhaps never the worst form of idleness. It has a constant and imperishable moral, and to the scholar it yields a classic result" (W 157). The counterintuitive rhetoric of idleness in such statements is designed not to supplant labor as a value but to jolt the neighbors out of the mistaken notion of work under which they were laboring. Thoreau's own major artistic task, as Nicholas Bromell has shown, was the reconciliation of manual and intellectual labor announced in *Walden*'s first play on words—"[I] earned my living by the labor of my hands only" (W 3).[28] Thoreau's most searching inquiry into these subjects coalesces around the "The Bean-Field," whose limited agricultural subject matter therefore serves as a portal into its more broadly georgic thematization of labor in the world.

"The Bean-Field" is also the place of Thoreau's most sustained meditation about the relationship of labor—both manual and intellectual—to the natural world on and within which it works, and thus has a special relevance for Thoreau's ecocritical readers. As David M. Robinson writes, it is where his vision of an agrarian alternative to the spiritually bankrupt social structures of the nineteenth century comes up against an incipient ecological interest in nature for its own sake.[29] The chapter as a whole is an elaborate attempt to reconcile the first vision, which entails a vigorous assertion of human labor and will over nature, with the second, which requires a submission to non-anthropocentric whims of the natural world. By one reading, the chapter enacts a movement from the first value to the second: the account of labor and anxiety giving way to a "relinquish[ment] [of] all claim to the produce of his fields" (W 166). More characteristic than this turn away from solicitude, however, is a realignment of ideal human labor with the labor of natural creatures (birds with their seeds, squirrels with their chestnuts). (Hence the dabbling in gathering modes of subsistence—the huckleberry, the groundnut, the wild apple.) In some cases this means a de-emphasis on traditional forms of human toil, as Thoreau justified his days spent observing phenomena: "sheer idleness to my fellow-townsmen, no doubt; but if the birds and flowers had tried me by their standard, I should not have been found wanting" (W 112). At other times it meant stressing the laborious coming-to-being of natural phenomena, as in the famous sand-bank passage in "Spring," where natural phenomena are viewed as the fruit of experimental aesthetic labors: "When I see on the one side the inert bank,—for the sun acts on one side first,—and on the other this luxuriant foliage, the creation of an hour, I am affected as if in a peculiar sense I stood in the laboratory of the Artist . . ." (*W* 306). This nonpastoral vision of becoming not the leisured enjoyer of a bounteous earth but, in George Perkins Marsh's term, "a co-worker with nature," lies at the heart of *Walden*'s georgic turn.[30]

We can put these two major themes—intellectual labor and field labor— together to get some better sense of Thoreau's understanding of the way the tools of his intellect, his words, refer to the object of his attention, the earth. The pastoral mode leaves us little choice but to understand reference as either a matter of direct and natural continuity with an object or of complete disengagement from it: that is the only way that an otiose relation between the word and the thing can be maintained. As we have witnessed, pastoral criticism seems to oscillate between notions of the abstracting movement of the imagination away from the factical on the one hand and, on the other, a wishful continuity with the natural world conceived of as origin. The pastoral oscillation between these two positions—Marx, reading it into *Walden*, called it the book's "contrapuntal theme" between empiricism and mysticism—has the effect of creating a permanent stalemate within students of nature writing between the tough—and the tender-minded, a stalemate that bears family likeness to other now-traditional divisions within the humanities (idealism and materialism, for example; or social constructionism and sociobiology).

Perhaps the most important thing about the georgic, then, is that it has a different implicit theory of reference, one that baffles the antinomies produced by the pastoral. Clearly, the georgic does not conceive of itself as a place for the unregulated play of the imagination: it is always ruled after the fact of its utterance by the intransigent physical world upon which it has designs. In fact, it was judged historically by its performance in the real world: Vergil's *Georgics* were used as an instruction manual into the eighteenth century. At the same time, the georgic does not pretend simply to imitate the world as it is, to deliver up through mimetic organic language discrete stable real a priori objects, to treat man's thoughts and words, in Wallace Stevens's rejected phrase, as "the intelligence of his soil." This kind of linguistic determinism, besides being suspect on theoretical grounds, is likely to be as unhelpful to the creative writer as it is to the creative agricultural producer, both of whom must, through labor, make the earth say "beans"—that is, something other than what it would say in their absence. As Thoreau wrote, "we would not deal with a man . . . as a mushroom" (*W* 165).

Against both of these pastoral possibilities, the georgic asks not *whether* language can successfully jump up from a real original to an imitation, but *how* it can jump down from abstraction and land with a degree of efficacy upon some object in the world, becoming not just a mirror of nature or a lamp, but something more akin to a hoe or a shovel or a seed drill "of nature." This is the relevance for the georgic of the fable of Antaeus that plays a significant role in "The Bean-Field." Antaeus is described in myth not simply as losing strength when separated from the earth—that would be the mushroom version—but as gaining strength when he is allowed to touch down again upon it. The "strength like Antaeus" of which Thoreau brags is thus not the strength of from-earth or on-earth so much as the strength of toward-earth. It is, finally, a question of direction: the georgic reverses the course of thought, viewing the real as a destination of meaning rather than as meaning's origin, understanding language fundamentally as experimental. Thoreau's puns, which tend to run backward from metaphorical to literal meanings, do so not in search of origins (as perhaps Heidegger's do) but in order to condense speculative verbal energies into a material form that can be set back beside the world. Indeed, Thoreau describes his alternative to both high-flying abstraction and mycological mysticism through an image of something coming down from above onto the earth. "We would . . . deal with a man . . . [as] something more than erect, like swallows alighted and walking on the ground" (*W* 165). This image not only captures the downward directionality of georgic reference, but also shifts the axis of attention from the vertical (metaphoric) register to the horizontal (metonymic) one—a rhetorical transformation characteristic of the georgic and of considerable interest to readers of Thoreau who wish to evaluate the degree of his apostasy from orthodox Transcendentalism.

There is still something unsatisfactory about this Antaeus image, which might be understood as an argument for our spiritual connection to the earth as a natural fact, like gravity, rather than as an accomplishment that requires our continual labor. This is why Thoreau does not identify simply with Antaeus but instead casts his crucial time in the bean-field by comparing it to the wrestling match *between* Antaeus and Hercules, with each of whom Thoreau identifies over the course of a well-known paragraph:

> What was the meaning of this so steady and self-respecting, this small Herculean labor, I knew not. I came to love my rows, my

beans, though so many more than I wanted. They attached me to the earth, and so I got strength like Antaeus. But why should I raise them? Only Heaven knows. This was my curious labor all summer,—to make this portion of the earth's surface, which had yielded only . . . wild fruits and pleasant flowers, produce instead this pulse. What shall I learn of beans or beans of me? I cherish them, I hoe them, early and late I have an eye to them; and this is my day's work. It is a fine broad leaf to look on. (*W* 155)

Note how Thoreau occupies all the positions: he is Hercules the laborer, he is Antaeus the principle of earthly resistance. His beans both call forth labor and subsidize it; in the double pun he introduces at the heart of the passage, the leguminous produce is said to "produce" his "pulse." Indeed the passage has a kind of systole and diastole, both in the alternated images of rising and falling in the sentences and in the rhythms of the sentences themselves. Thoreau's compression here of the two kinds of force represented by Antaeus and Hercules into one life-giving rhythm—a heartbeat—is a solution of the pastoral antinomy, a reconceptualization of the split opened by his earlier, fatal regard of the natural world as composed of "facts" that one might "face"—in which the self and the world are already in the process of being mutually, and productively, furrowed.

The Herculean labor of lifting Antaeus (raising crops, creating meaning) does not rupture a bond between earth and humans—it is, on the contrary, the way in which man and his language become more deeply embedded in the earth. That troubling statement, "Nature is hard to be overcome, but she must be overcome" (*W* 221), thus has both an ethical and a philosophical significance: this is how relinquishment happens, not through retirement but through exertion. Thoreau's ego disappears, let us remember, as he works: "It was no longer beans that I hoed, nor I that hoed beans" (*W* 159). It is by sinking labor—and that is *Walden's* master pun—into the earth that Thoreau is rewarded with insight into and intimacy with the more-than-human world. It is also how the words that make up his interior world of spiritual possibility get attached to the earth. By the end of the passage cited above, Thoreau's agricultural labor has become identical to Thoreau's work as a writer, which arranges things in rows and results in a "fine broad leaf to look on." In this way Thoreau vanquishes the pastoral assumption that a need to expend manual and intellectual labor in support of a particular relation to the environment is a sign of the inauthenticity of that relation—and thus opens up the field to authentically labored georgic nature writing.

As Thoreau said, much depends on how one is yarded. This essay has argued that the georgic—the mode of the yard as well as the field, the orchard, and the garden—is a better yardstick than the pastoral to take the measure of *Walden*'s extravagant meditations on the nature of time, history, the body, labor, and language. The *Walden* perceived through georgic eyes proves to be less an object of study than a tool for nourishment; our reading of it less an act of reception than of creation; its purpose, in the here and now, to show the way to a life of creative verbal and physical engagement with the world around us.

Notes

1. My definition of genre is that of Paul Alpers in *What Is Pastoral?* (Chicago: University of Chicago Press, 1996), 45. For a map to *Walden*'s specific generic chaos, see Linck Johnson, "Revolution and Renewal: The Genres of *Walden*," in *Critical Essays on Henry David Thoreau's "Walden,"* ed. Joel Myerson (Boston: G. K. Hall, 1988), 215–35; and Lawrence Buell, *The Environmental Imagination* (Cambridge: Harvard University Press, 1995), 397–423. The latter argues that Thoreau's genre jumping constitutes an extreme version of the polyglossic strategies of the novel as elaborated by Mikhail Bakhtin in "Discourse in the Novel," *The Dialogic Imagination*, ed. Michael Holquist, tr. Caryl Emerson and Michael Holquist (Austin: University of Texas Press, 1981), 259–422.

2. Leo Marx, "Pastoralism in America," in *Ideology and Classic American Literature,* ed. Sacvan Bercovitch and Myra Jehlen (Cambridge: Harvard University Press, 1986), 46. For a more explicit treatment of mode, see Alpers, *What Is Pastoral?,* 50.

3. Annabel Patterson's *Pastoral and Ideology: Virgil to Valéry* (Berkeley: University of California Press, 1987) is a marvelous comparative study of the political uses of the pastoral. She reminds us of the historical context of the *Eclogues* (the drawn-out reconsolidation of Rome after the civil wars) and points out the structural political content of the poem itself: the oft-quoted opening lines of the first *Eclogue* establish in their rhythmic alternation of *tu* (you) and *nos* (we) a political scenario boiled down to its bare bones.

4. Bruno Snell, *The Discovery of the Mind: The Greek Origins of European Thought,* tr. T. G. Rosenmeyer (1946; Cambridge: Harvard University Press, 1953), 281–90.

5. The formulation is William Empson's in *Some Versions of Pastoral* (Norfolk, CT: New Directions, 1960), 23. Alpers, a much more fastidious scholar than Empson, adopts the latter's essential definition in the wide-ranging and persuasive *What Is Pastoral?*

6. For the notion that the pastoral represents a flight from the material world, see especially the work of Richard Cody, *The Landscape of the Mind: Pastoralism and Platonic*

Theory in Tasso's "Aminta" and Shakespeare's Early Comedies (Oxford: Clarendon Press, 1969); and Renato Poggioli, *The Oaten Flute: Essays on Pastoral Poetry and the Pastoral Ideal* (Cambridge: Harvard University Press, 1975).

7. Leo Marx, *The Machine in the Garden: Technology and the Pastoral Ideal in America* (Oxford: Oxford University Press, 1962), 242–65.

8. Charles Anderson, *The Magic Circle of Walden* (New York: Holt, Rinehart, and Winston, 1968); Sherman Paul, *The Shores of America* (Champaign: University of Illinois Press, 1958); H. Daniel Peck, *Thoreau's Morning Work* (New Haven: Yale University Press, 1991). For the two kinds of political readings, see Rob Wilson's *The American Sublime* (Madison: University of Wisconsin Press, 1991), and especially Lawrence Buell's "American Literary Pastoral Reappraised," *American Literary History* 1.1 (Spring 1989): 6–29, as well as a subsequent qualification in *Environmental Imagination*, 31–52.

9. See Donald Worster, *Nature's Economy* (1977; Garden City, NY: Doubleday, 1979), 57–111; Max Oelschlaeger, *The Idea of Wilderness* (New Haven: Yale University Press, 1991), 133–71; and especially Buell, *Environmental Imagination*, 115–39.

10. Buell, *Environmental Imagination*, 23.

11. Leo Marx, "The Struggle over Thoreau," *New York Review of Books* 46.11 (24 June 1999): 60–64, and "The Full Thoreau," *New York Review of Books* 46.12 (15 July 1999): 44–48.

12. This may be the place to clarify a matter of terminology that stems from a bifurcated use of the term "pastoral." If we mean by pastoral, as Lawrence Buell suggests, any writing "preoccupied with nature and rurality as setting, theme, and value in contradistinction from society and the urban," then it is natural to see the georgic as a subset of the pastoral. Indeed, farming literature often is shelved among the nature writers in bookstores, and Thomas Lyons's well-informed taxonomy of nature writing includes farming books along a continuum with other more identifiably pastoral subjects. But, as Buell is acutely aware, the term "pastoral" refers not just to a field of inquiry—"nature writing"—but also to one of several particular orientations toward that field, and I think we use the term to denote both kinds of things at the risk of mistaking all literature about the environment as pastoral in the second, theoretically narrower sense, and therefore of ruling out from the beginning alternative approaches to environmental writing. Indeed, this double use has already sown confusion and rancor between those whose field is the pastoral in the first sense and those who approach the pastoral in the second sense as a theoretical and political problem.

13. Robert Sattelmeyer, *Thoreau's Reading* (Princeton: Princeton University Press, 1991). A discussion of the classical georgic tradition can be found in Thomas Rosenmeyer's *The Green Cabinet* (Berkeley: University of California Press, 1969). On the sixteenth- and seventeenth-century georgic, see Anthony Low's *The Georgic Revolution* (Princeton: Princeton University Press, 1981). The eighteenth-century English flowering of the mode is treated in Dwight L. Durling's *Georgic Tradition in English Poetry* (New York: Columbia University Press, 1935), and John Chalker's *The English Georgic* (Baltimore: Johns Hopkins University Press, 1969).

14. Thoreau read all the Roman agriculturalists, as he sometimes referred to them in the

aggregate, in a collected edition, *Scriptores Rei Rusticae* (Heidelberg: Commelini, 1595). His Journal reveals considerable engagement with these writers before, during, and after the revision of *Walden:* with Cato in the fall and winter of 1851; with Varro in January and February of 1854; and with Columella and Palladius in the spring of 1856.

15. Timothy Sweet's *American Georgics* (Philadelphia: University of Pennsylvania Press, 2002), an indispensable guide to the ecologic, economic, and philosophic significance of American agricultural writing from Stephen Parmenius in 1583 through George Perkins Marsh just before the Civil War, discusses the georgic dimensions of these writers. See also Christopher Grasso's *A Speaking Aristocracy* (Chapel Hill: University of North Carolina Press, 1999).

16. Robert Gross, "Culture and Civilization: Agriculture and Society in Thoreau's Concord," *Journal of American History* 69.1 (1982): 42–61. See also Gross's "The Great Bean Field Hoax: Thoreau and the Agricultural Reformers," *Virginia Quarterly Review* 61.3 (1985): 483–97, which views the chapter less as a satirical critique than as a "spoof" of Henry Colman's agricultural reform projects.

17. Notably absent from this genealogy, for understandable reasons of geography and circulation, are the British-American staple colony georgics discussed in David Shields's *Oracles of Empire* (Chicago: University of Chicago Press, 1991) and Joyce Chaplin's *An Anxious Pursuit* (Chapel Hill: University of North Carolina Press, 1993).

18. Loren Owings, *Quest for Walden: A Study of the "Country Book" in American Popular Literature with an Annotated Bibliography, 1863 through 1995* (Jefferson, NC: McFarland, 1997). On the course of the American georgic during this same time period, see Stephanie Sarver's *Uneven Land* (Lincoln: University of Nebraska Press, 1999).

19. See David Shi's history of the "voluntary simplicity" movement, *The Simple Life* (Oxford: Oxford University Press, 1985), 139–49.

20. *Walden,* ed. J. Lyndon Shanley (Princeton: Princeton University Press). The contribution of *Walden* to the didactic conduct-book genre is detailed in Leonard Neufeldt's *The Economist* (Oxford: Oxford University Press, 1989), 101–10.

21. Stanley Cavell, *The Senses of Walden* (New York: Viking, 1972), 25–26, 85–86, 111.

22. In a short but trenchant early response to Marx, James S. Tillman laid out a general case for *Walden's* georgic nature: see "The Transcendental Georgic in *Walden,*" *ESQ* 21 (1975): 137–41.

23. Thoreau himself was a perceptive reader of the pastoral, and appears to have recognized the internal constraints of the mode in both its naïve and complex forms. The chanticleer epigraph to *Walden* rallies a dream team of complex pastoral or near-pastoral intertexts—Chaucer's "The Nun's Priest's Tale," Spenser's *Faerie Queene,* Shakespeare's *As You Like It,* Quarles's poetry, Coleridge's "Dejection: An Ode"—only to signal its own post-pastoral intentions: "I do not propose to write an ode to dejection. . . ." If Thoreau's aim, as Marx would have it, is simply to critique the naïve pastoral in favor of the complex version, he would have put these complex precursors at the *end* of the book as a triumphant ratification of his argument. By placing them at the very beginning, he suggests that they represent a position he intends to move beyond.

24. *The Journal of Henry David Thoreau,* ed. Bradford Torrey and Francis H. Allen, vol. 8 (Boston: Houghton Mifflin, 1906), 245.

25. Post-*Nature,* Emerson's position becomes murkier and more difficult to detect. See Laura Dassow Walls, *Emerson's Life in Science: The Culture of Truth* (Ithaca, NY: Cornell University Press, 2003).

26. On the inconclusive quality of Thoreau's Journal, see Sharon Cameron, *Writing Nature* (Oxford: Oxford University Press, 1985). On Thoreau's phenological Kalendar and its antecedents, see Paul, *Shores of America,* and Peck, *Thoreau's Morning Work.* For a theoretical consideration of the agricultural calendar as mediator of experience and solvent of impersonal structure, see Pierre Bourdieu's earliest and best work on the sociology of cultural capital, *Outline of a Theory of Practice,* tr. Richard Nice (Cambridge: Cambridge University Press, 1977), 72–158.

27. There are other significant differences between georgic and pastoral that could be mapped in *Walden*—the pastoral situates itself within a community of texts (cf. "Lycidas"), the georgic within a human and natural community (cf. Wendell Berry's Port William Membership); the pastoral imagines a world sharply bifurcated into the city and the country, the georgic subsists in the borderlands between these two extremes— but to some extent these are implied in the other distinctions discussed here.

28. Nicholas Bromell, *By the Sweat of the Brow* (Chicago: University of Chicago Press, 1993), 80–98, 213–40.

29. David M. Robinson, " 'Unchronicled Nations': Agrarian Purpose and Thoreau's Ecological Knowing," *Nineteenth Century Literature* 48.3 (1993): 326–40. In our own day, the notion of stewardship as a privileged means of access to ecological understanding is best represented by Aldo Leopold's *Sand County Almanac,* and the many works of Wendell Berry. Michael Pollan makes the case for applied environmentalism in his essays on gardening: see *Second Nature* (New York: Dell, 1991). In *The Sunflower Forest: Ecological Restoration and the New Communion with Nature* (Berkeley: University of California Press, 2003), the pioneer restorationist William R. Jordan III spells out the implications of a physically engaged environmental ethic.

30. George Perkins Marsh, *Man and Nature: or, Physical Geography as Modified by Human Action* (1864), ed. David Lowenthal (Cambridge: Harvard University Press, 1965), 35. As Laura Dassow Walls demonstrates, Thoreau's growing interest in scientific observation (one major basis for his canonization as environmental saint) was likewise motivated by a desire for relational, engaged, and evolving knowledge. Thoreau's late writing revolves around experimental, embodied, and social practices rather than around isolated and disembodied facts, and thus can be seen as involving georgic inquiry into problems of active perception rather than of ontology. See *Seeing New Worlds* (Madison: University of Wisconsin Press, 1995), 147–57.

Thoreau's Divide

Rediscovering the Environmentalist/Agriculturalist Debate in Walden's *"Baker Farm"*

ROBERT E. CUMMINGS

AT A RECENT SYMPOSIUM sponsored by the Association for the Study of Literature and the Environment (ASLE), one particular question continually resurfaced in disparate discussions: How are environmental scholars and activists perceived by those who work or live on the land of environmental conflict? Throughout the conference, a generalized and growing concern for the relationship between environmentalists and people who work the land for a living was never far from formal and casual conversation. It seems that many environmental speakers and scholars are worried about a growing rift between themselves and agricultural workers, including both owners and laborers. But it might have surprised conference-goers to learn that while this conflict is troubling, it is by no means new. Because contemporary environmental issues may appear novel, we sometimes overlook sources of literary inspiration for treatment of these issues. The tension between environmental activists and agriculturalists is old enough not only to be foreseen by a nineteenth-century author such as Henry David Thoreau, but, as this essay will show, also important enough to warrant the focus of a *Walden* chapter.[1]

These contemporary conference-goers are worried that to the many people who work the land, professional environmentalists often seem at best out of touch, and at worst a threat to their livelihood. Environmentalists will arrive suddenly and unannounced at the scene of a land-use controversy with seemingly prepackaged judgments on complex issues that a farmer may have been engaged with for the better part of a career. In any given situation, the environmentalists tend to see a land-use issue, whereas the farmer sees a home and a job. Environmentalists—at least the professionals—are more likely to live away from the land that is central to a dispute, perhaps even in an urban area, while those who work the land often live on it (with the important exception of corporate agribusiness ventures). In the May/June 2002 issue of *Sierra*, Gerald Haslan reports on how difficult it was for Brian Blane, the head of California's largest pecan growing and processing organization, to join with environmentalists to defeat a common foe. Blane said, "A lot of farmers genuinely believe that environmentalists are out to destroy agriculture. Many things can be done that would be good for farmers and the environment, but suspicion keeps people from working together."[2] On the other side, Scott Dye, a Sierra Club organizer, reported, "Some farmers think a Sierra Club organizer will show up looking like their image of an environmentalist, with a long ponytail and sandals. . . . When I show up looking like an average farm kid, well, they're more likely to listen."[3] This conflict takes on many forms: it could include the flooding of arable fields by state agencies to create additional wetlands in Hennepin, Illinois.[4] It could be the debate over whether ranchers throughout the western United States should sell cattle-grazing rights in national parks back to the federal government.[5] And it is a truly international conflict as well, which could manifest itself in the Pumé of Venezuela, who seek to preserve an indigenous culture of hunting and gathering through the formal declaration of land-tenure rights in spite of the call of ecotourism developers and low-wage jobs that remove them from the land.[6] In all of these cases, those who garner practical knowledge from living on and working the land find themselves at odds with those who have cultivated a theoretical understanding of land use.

People who work the land are often tied to it for economic reasons that aren't always addressed in the environmentalists' pleas for sustainable land management. Individual, private farms in the United States are often held by several generations of the same family. The assets of a typical family farm frequently range into the millions of dollars, and the legal and tax codes that surround the operation of that family business are staggeringly complex. More often than not, people who work the land feel trapped by it. It's no secret that America loses a substantial number of family farms each year: from 1986 to

1999, an average of 1,517 U.S. family farmers each year sought the protection of chapter twelve of the bankruptcy code, a temporary chapter of the code written specifically to address this epidemic.[7]

Many people who work the land they have inherited yearn, like all of us, for the simple financial power to control their own fate. The losing business they have inherited often sprouts from depressed real estate values in the underlying property. They can look longingly at their neighbors who are "lucky" enough to sell out to real estate developers who convert pastures to sprawling residential subdivisions. These land owners observe the relative freedom of environmentalists and think, "How in the world can you make a living by trotting over the earth spewing unwanted advice? I'd give anything to leave this albatross." While these views summarize several anecdotes, they capture a prevailing sentiment of the tensions between those who work the land within our capitalist system and those who seek, either through political activism or scholarship, to preserve the wilderness experience for all who would share it. But "the news" of this split between contemporary environmental activist and contemporary land worker is, of course, not news at all. The split between a distanced, circumspect, informed, and privileged land-use perspective and a philosophy born of an everyday, necessary, hands-on practice is certainly as old as our touchstone of the American literary experience with environmentalism, Henry David Thoreau's *Walden*.

The production of an author with his own economic anxieties, his own diurnal gardening habits, and his own circumspect, writerly connection with the land, *Walden* is a text simply fascinated with the divide of consciousness fostered through the human connection with land. *Walden's* intense narrator casts the reader as witness to a self-conscious and activist land-use relationship, as opposed to the underrepresented thoughts of characters who work the land, such as the Fields. In this essay I propose that the tension between the two land-use perspectives, activist and agricultural, occurs in *Walden* in a previously overlooked nexus—the "Baker Farm" chapter. Thoreau's purpose in "Baker Farm" is not to take a stand in this divide, but rather to host an exploration of the two perspectives. Further, not only does Thoreau anticipate our contemporary divide on activist versus agriculturalist land use, but he also clearly indicates the depth and permanence of the division through the split between Thoreau the narrator and Thoreau the writer. The delicacy of the relationship between these two knowledge systems is handled most aptly through Thoreau's use of humor, a strategy of self-parody that allows the author freedom to speculate on the complex reception of his ideas by agriculturalist thinkers through the foibles of his activist narrator.

"Baker Farm" is a chapter often overlooked or, perhaps more often still, misread, as a misanthropic diatribe against the poor, ignorant, working-class bogger. In Thoreau's sketch of John Field's house, it is appropriate to conceive of the narrator as the nineteenth-century equivalent of the professional environmentalist of contemporary land-use conflicts. Like our professional environmentalist, Thoreau's narrator arrives at the farm suddenly, unannounced, quickly surveys the family's surroundings, and begins prescribing remedies for problems that he alone diagnoses. And just like those of our imagined contemporary family farmers, the Fields' reactions range from Mr. Field's bewilderment to Mrs. Field's anger. Additionally, the rupture between Thoreau and the Fields corresponds rather neatly to the contemporary tension between environmental scholars and agricultural owners. Thoreau's narrator is a character born out of an environmentalist's anxieties, a spontaneous growth of the writer's fears.

The presence of this anxiety suggests that this tension is not only an old one, but also perhaps evidence of an ideological divide between two types of knowledge: theory and practice. On one hand are Thoreau the narrator and our anecdotal environmentalists, interpreting observations of overall human interaction with wilderness, and attempting to formulate an exportable message based on their personal nature experience as well as a theoretically derived understanding. And on the other hand are the farmers and agricultural land workers, past and future, who employ a very different—and equally valid—knowledge based on the actual day-to-day living with the land. Thoreau's interaction with the Fields suggests that this divide was just as substantial for him as it is for us.

One Curious Narrator

As the creator of his own story, Thoreau plays the dual roles of author and narrator when he casts himself into the work. In the "Baker Farm" chapter, Thoreau the narrator is caught by a sudden downpour while on the way to a fishing pond on a neighbor's farm. He seeks shelter in "the nearest hut," which he believes to be uninhabited, but which proves to be the dwelling place of an

Irish-American laborer and his family. There, not unlike the prototypical environmental activist imagined in the preceding sketch, Thoreau freely and presumptuously offers his philosophy and advice to the family.

Thoreau the narrator first views the infant of the family, coldly describing her as "the wrinkled, sybil-like, cone-headed infant that sat upon its father's knee as in the palace of nobles, and looked out from its home in the midst of wet and hunger inquisitively upon the stranger, with the privilege of infancy, not knowing but it was the last of a noble line, and the hope and cynosure of the world, instead of John Field's poor starveling brat" (*W* 204). The narrator then transfers his paternalistic attitude to his address of the family generally. He presumes to know their qualities, merits, and inner thoughts—in short, the content of their character—all, apparently from glancing around this hut. He continues: "An honest, hard-working, but shiftless man plainly was John Field; and his wife, she too was brave to cook so many successive dinners in the recesses of that lofty stove; with round greasy face and bare breast, still thinking to improve her condition one day; with the never absent mop in one hand, and yet no effects of it visible anywhere" (*W* 204).

Thoreau's narrator assumes from the poverty prevalent in the Field house that the family is in need of his help, that their simple lifestyle devoid of possessions is something to be corrected, regardless of the fact that Thoreau the author has spent prior chapters of *Walden* extolling the virtues of materialist minimalism. There may be no evidence that their poverty is calculated, as is the author's, but the narrator never seems even to entertain that possibility. Here the narrator exhibits what one reader—Richard Bridgman—has called his "bigotry."[8] The narrator assumes that the Fields possess an ignorance that is responsible for their poverty, while his equally simple lifestyle is a product of his considered thinking. Such an assumption merely adds to the reader's perception of the narrator as arrogant. But the fact remains that witnessing the Fields' poverty is a challenge to Thoreau's own condition. Thoreau's narrator must then seize on the difference in causes for the same effect: the Fields are unintentionally poor and therefore unhappy, but Thoreau is intentionally poor and liberated. Conceptually it is this calculation, or deliberate determination to live lightly, that the narrator relies upon to separate his brand of poverty from the Fields'. Seeing the Fields living in a presumably miserable condition suggests the ultimate power of material realities (i.e., that being poor and doing without is an undesirable approach to living regardless of the ideology one attaches to it) and perhaps necessitates the elaborate narrative pontification of "Baker Farm" to gird up Thoreau's conception of his lifestyle's potential to yield desirable results for all who would partake in it.

Thus the poverty of the Fields is taken by the narrator as a direct challenge to the power of the worldview that drives his own style of living. The fact that Thoreau's narrator assumes that the Fields live in a poverty of ignorance, without exploring the opportunity that their poverty is a manifestation of conscious choices, reveals mostly anxiety about his own choices. His poverty is intentional, theirs is not; but does poverty in and of itself have the power to determine the narrator's fate? Over time will the material condition triumph over the spiritual will? In some manner then Field presents the narrator with a test case—if the narrator can export his perspective successfully to the Fields, then he will know that one's deliberate intention to live in poverty is more powerful than material consequences of living in that same poverty. Though John Field will, at least in the narrator's eyes, prove himself inept later in this chapter by failing to catch any fish, and thereby lead the narrator to conclude that John Field is beyond help, the narrator's approach to his visit in the Field house compels him to distinguish his own poverty from the Fields' on the grounds of intentionality.

This scenario's explicit discussion should remind us again of the contemporary split between environmental activists and agriculturalists. The heart of the debate between the activist and agriculturalist is appropriate land use and a general approach to living. Like our Sierra Club activists, Thoreau's narrator advocates a theory for sustainable living to those faced with the realities of warding off poverty. And like our contemporary California nut growers, the Fields listen warily as an uninvited guest professes his theories to them. But "Baker Farm" does more than provide us with an easy parallel for the casting of the actors in these contemporary debates—"Baker Farm" also captures the underlying fears that charge this debate with emotion. For the activist, the theory is just that: partially tested knowledge that the proponent truly hopes will be successful for the farmer if he or she will only adopt it. And Thoreau's lifestyle is still in the theoretical stages—it works for him, but he cannot honestly say that it will be successful for all who apply it. These fears can cause the activist to claim the truth of the theory with even greater certainty. Similarly, the agriculturalist fears the uncertainty of the advice as well. As the California nut grower states, he or she knows that there is validity in the activist's message, and is willing to grant that there is a problem dire enough to require new approaches. But the agriculturalist necessarily remains fearful of any proposition that asks him or her to gamble family assets on another's advice.

Yet in a nuance not mirrored in the contemporary split, the narrator's stance introduces the issue of ethnic bias. Thoreau's "Baker Farm" narrator betrays a sense of superiority in his relationship with this Irish-American immigrant family, based on his status of having arrived first in America. After looking around the cabin and noting its deficiencies, the narrator remarks, "There we sat together under that part of the roof which leaked the least, while it showered and thundered without. I had sat there many times of old before the ship was built that floated this family to America" (*W* 204). By claiming a prior relationship with their residence, the narrator implies a superior relationship with the space these immigrants inhabit due simply to his having lived longer in America. In this reflection it is easy to detect a callous attitude on the part of landed and established Americans toward recent arrivals. The narrator notes that the Fields' current home was not deemed worthy of inhabitation prior to their arrival: "I made haste for shelter to the nearest hut, which . . . had long been uninhabited" (*W* 203). The fact that the property had been, prior to the Fields' arrival, a sort of public shelter, additionally indicates a loss on behalf of the narrator and others who might have shared in its use; the Fields' possession of it as their residence now precludes its employment as a gentleman's fishing camp. Then the narrator reminds us that through the immigrants' very presence, the landed Americans are made materially worse: they have lost not only the use of the shelter for leisurely fishing trips, but they have also lost the ability to envision the leaky shelter as insufficient to pass as a person's primary residence. Thus the landed Americans are comparatively worsened through the presence of the impoverished immigrants. Rather than feeling wealthier through the immigrants' presence, the established Americans are disturbed by the presence of those who are desperate enough to occupy their cast-off housing. This perspective creates in the narrator an underlying tone of strained benevolence, which is revealed when he remarks that he hopes John Field does not read his commentary unless—reminiscent here of the "white man's burden" ideology—Field might improve himself by it: "Poor John Field!—I trust he does not read this, unless he will improve by it,—thinking to live by some derivative old country mode in this primitive new country" (*W* 208).

In this interaction with the Fields, the narrator seems to embody and give voice to the very sense of authority against which the majority of *Walden* rebels. This presentation of the narrator as condescending "bigot" cannot help but be a bewildering experience for the reader who has listened to the author insist on living by experiment and charting one's own course. Worse still, readers will note that this narrator's own "tight, light, and clean house" was originally the property of another Irish-American immigrant family; given the ramshackle condition of the Field house in comparison to his own, and given that the narrator has done (in his own view, at least) quite well with essentially the same materials, the narrator's experience with the same raw materials seems to further his conclusion that these immigrants simply lack the ability to live well in the land of plenty. As the narrator presents it, the poverty problem lies with the inhabitants—not with the raw materials, not with their new culture.

Though this discussion has only begun to look at "Baker Farm," we must stop at this point and acknowledge that the text has offered the reader a lot to absorb. Thoreau has presented himself as the "bigot" Bridgman describes—a character far removed from the thoughtful author who has inspired the reader in chapter upon chapter of witty observation and philosophical contemplation, ranging with ease from mundane daily chores to man's teleological fate, and the interconnections between. How is the reader to reconcile the extreme differences between the tone of the narrator in "Baker Farm" and the remainder of *Walden*? Most critics who have wrestled with this strange interlude in *Walden* have not framed "Baker Farm" as a focal point of the book, but rather as a transition between more substantial sections. Lawrence Scanlon's reaction is an accurate assessment of most critical attention when he states, "The tendency has been to ignore it entirely, or to treat it . . . as merely 'transitional' between 'The Ponds' and 'Higher Laws.' "[9] But for reasons introduced herein, I would like to argue that it is time to begin framing "Baker Farm" in terms of the activist/agriculturalist divide. In "Baker Farm" Thoreau casts himself as a rube. This fool-for-a-narrator plays an important role, however: by intersecting the heretofore theoretical and introspective *Walden* narrative with the daily life of the Fields' house, Thoreau is able to humorously project how his inspired advice for daily living might be received in a real household.

Like any theorist, Thoreau is looking for a pause to reflect on the practice of his ideas. "Baker Farm" provides that respite, and more, since we also need to account for the self-absorbed manner in which the narrator presents his material: one can envision many fictional ways to entertain the reception of Thoreau's inspired living without the ill-considered perspective of the "Baker Farm" narrator. The narrator's lack of tact is in fact proof of the endurance of the activist/agriculturalist divide. The author necessarily worries over the audience's reception of his or her ideas, and in "Baker Farm" Thoreau creates this brazen narrator out of an authorial anxiety over the potential reception of his message in order to fictionalize the worst possible presentation of his advice on living. In order to cope with the worst-case scenario of how his activist thoughts on informed living could be received, he steals the thunder of his harshest potential agriculturalist critics by fictionalizing the worst possible presentation of his ideas to the least prepared audience. Exorcising the authorial anxiety over the agriculturalist reception to the activist message is one of the purposes of "Baker Farm," and is the source of the tension that drives its humor. This approach can provide a compelling explanation for the unsolicited advice to which Thoreau's narrator subjects the Fields.

After hearing of a poor bargain Field has made for his bogging services, the narrator presumes to offer the following advice about how to overcome poverty: "I tried to help him with my experience, telling him that he was one of my nearest neighbors, and that I too, who . . . looked like a loafer, was getting my living like himself; that I lived in a tight light and clean house, which hardly cost more than the annual rent of such a ruin as his commonly amounts to; and how, if he chose, he might in a month or two build himself a palace of his own" (*W* 205). The narrator then continues to relate his philosophy of materialist minimalism: if you work hard, you must eat great quantities, but if you don't work as hard, and do without meat, butter, eggs, etc., then your demands will be proportionately less.

The narrator remarks, "I purposely talked to him as if he were a philosopher, or desired to be one" (*W* 205). This is certainly true: he is focused here on his abstract principles of simple living, and ignores some of the obvious problems of applying his philosophy to his neighbors' lives. First, and most important, Thoreau commits to material sacrifices for himself alone. His neighbors, however, must think about providing for offspring. Even if John Field were to agree with Thoreau's philosophy, his sacrifices would also be borne by his wife and children. Additionally, Thoreau the narrator doesn't seem to address his remarks to Mrs. Field. Whether or not it was customary to assume that the husband should make the decision for this family, Thoreau's address to the husband reinforces patriarchal authority, a traditional social dynamic that Thoreau's radicalism would certainly wish to resist obliquely if not directly. Last, and perhaps most problematic, the most glaring omission on Thoreau's part is that his own hut rests on Ralph Waldo Emerson's land: he lives, in a sense, on Emerson's good graces, a unique situation that few can choose to participate in. Never mind that in spite of his philosophy, Thoreau could traverse a two-mile walk home to his mother's house for a hearty meal at any time, a privilege that he availed himself of frequently. In light of these considerations, Thoreau can seem, at times, something like a boy who has pitched a tent in his mother's back yard. For him, the safety of home is never far.

Readers should not ignore that most of Thoreau's conversation occurs in front of Mrs. Field. And readers can certainly anticipate her reaction. Arriving on her doorstep, the town crank and self-described "loafer" attempts to extol the virtues of "doing without" to her husband in the midst of their grinding poverty. The critic Leonard Neufeldt characterizes the narrator's reputation this way: "Many Concordians viewed Thoreau pretty much as the narrator views Field: a ne'er-do-well who isn't eager to take good advice, wastes too much of his time in shiftless pursuits like fishing, and cannot figure out how to make a good living in an America of opportunity." [10] Mrs. Field, however, enjoys none of this comfort as she struggles to cope with hunger. She and her children depend completely upon her husband's labor for their current meager income and food. Surely only good manners prevent her from sending Thoreau's narrator out the door and on his rear when she hears him propose living on *less* food. And yet to the narrator's eyes, he's made a persuasive case for helping his neighbors. Through Mrs. Field's reaction to this argument, the reader, however, can clearly sense how Thoreau's remarks are received. Thoreau ends his discourse by pointing out that if this family were to follow his approach to farming, "they might all go a-huckleberrying in the summer for their amusement. John heaved a sigh at this, and his wife stared with arms akimbo. . . . 'You'd better go now, John,'" she adds, nudging him back to work "with glistening and hopeful face" (W 206).

Mrs. Field provides the comic foil for Thoreau's narrative bachelor. By gendering this conflict, and placing John Field in the middle of an argument between Thoreau's narrator and his wife, Thoreau changes a competition of lifestyles into a battle between a carefree bachelor and a mother busy with the serious business of raising a family. This gendered reception presents the impractical theoretical thinking as "bachelorized"—immature and selfishly conceived, not yet ready for a world of family responsibilities. Thoreau satirizes his theories on simple living by placing the narrator's advice to "go a-huckleberrying" against the stark relief of family responsibilities. Does this mean that Thoreau is abandoning these ideas? Of course not. Again, the role of "Baker Farm" within the larger context of *Walden* is to provide a safe place to relieve authorial anxieties over the agriculturalist reception of his advice on "light living." By placing this advice up against the hard demands of family living, represented here by the clash of a bachelor resting in the household of an exhausted wife, Thoreau maximizes the satire by sharpening the contrast between activist and agriculturalist into bachelor versus wife. Thoreau may not be the ponytailed Sierra Club environmentalist arriving at the family farm, but the underlying authorial anxiety over the impracticality of his message is more easily parodied in front of a stern Mrs. Field. For the comedy to work, there needs to be tension, and her "arms a-kimbo" stance provides this. Readers of "Baker Farm" have to ask themselves how it is that the thoughtful, philosophical, and contemplative character of the first part of *Walden* has transformed himself into this myopically self-centered giver of unwanted advice? If we see Thoreau's presentation through the light of the activist/ agriculturalist conflict, then "Baker Farm" fits back into the theme of *Walden*. Unfortunately, most critics—even those who have actively looked for humor—have not interpreted the chapter by this light.

The Critical Bog

A survey of recent critical readings provides a fairly accurate idea of the dour tenor of reader responses to Thoreau the narrator in "Baker Farm." The first readerly impulse is to simply digest these descriptions of the narrator's thoughts and actions as the author feeds them to us, open-throated like a baby bird in the nest. In *Dark Thoreau*, Richard Bridgman finds that "Baker Farm" evidences Thoreau's inhuman impulses, as he collapses the distinction between Thoreau the narrator and Thoreau the author. Bridgman argues that "In general, 'Baker Farm' is a disturbing chapter, for it seems to reveal a bigotry and megalomania in Thoreau that are difficult to credit."[11] Bridgman looks to Thoreau's other writings to find more incidents of anti-Irish sentiments, and finds that "Thoreau's pronouncements on the Irish were in general negative."[12] Bridgman also sees no palatable answers for the narrator's behavior in other readings of "Baker Farm" when he states, "At best, defendants of Thoreau on this matter have pointed out that, in time, Thoreau's attitude toward the Irish changed," referring to the work of three additional Thoreau scholars.[13]

Indeed, Bridgman's reading seems to be typical of most scholarship on "Baker Farm." Bridgman finds additional support for this reading of a "bigoted" Thoreau in the Field house in Leon Edel, whom Bridgman cites as characterizing the segment "as cruel as it is sanctimonious."[14] Bridgman also cites Frank Buckley who, in his article "Thoreau and the Irish," concludes in a dour tone that Thoreau's evaluation of the Irish is condemning: "The occasional praise of individual Irishmen do[es] not justify the conclusion that Thoreau after 1850 became a consistent friend and defender of the Irish. As his praise increased so did his condemnation, and when he found fault he was likely to include the whole race."[15] Thus, like many readers, Buckley too envisions Thoreau as pronouncing sonorous judgment upon Irish-Americans. Bridgman also cites George Ryan, who notes more broadly still that Thoreau was not alone in condemning the Irish immigrant. Ryan writes that both Emerson and Hawthorne tossed equally crude labels onto the Irish immigrants in efforts to decry their selfishness, drunkenness, and inability to contribute to and share in a prosperous America.[16] Although Thoreau offers at least one poem, "Johnny Riordan," as an entire work dedicated to admiring the Irish, the prevailing critical opinion considers Thoreau as sitting in judgment on Irish-Americans. For those readers, "Baker Farm" presents no exception to Thoreau's overall attitude toward the poor.

Yet these readings should leave us wholly unsatisfied, for they offer no way to make sense of "Baker Farm" in terms of *Walden* as an overall work. To view "Baker Farm" in this anti-immigrant light leaves the reader of *Walden* with an inspiring, meditative reflection on nature and individual experience, wrapped around an interlude of shortsighted arrogance and ignorance. The critic Charles Anderson attempts to address this gap in his book *The Magic Circle of Walden*.[17] Anderson's remarks seek to preserve the unity of the "Baker Farm" narrator's remarks and the author's remarks elsewhere in the book. It's an impossible task. Anderson takes his cue from the opening and closing of the chapter, those first and last paragraphs that provide a curious frame to a dialogue otherwise rooted in the narrator's visit to the Fields. Anderson concludes:

The economic lesson of Field's involuntary poverty set over and against Thoreau's voluntary poverty is only an illustrative episode. The real theme is a contrast between the elevated and the degraded life, between freedom through imagination and serfdom through stupidity, between a poet's desire to soar into the life of the spirit and a clod's resignation to being bogged down in squalid materialism. The pun was intended, for Field . . . is portrayed as a bogger . . . at heart as well as by trade, stuck in the mire of his miserable life. On the contrary, Thoreau is always presented as a vigorous and radiant youth . . . leaping the brook en route to Baker Farm, running down the hill to Fair Haven when he leaves it, and in the last sentence taking off on winged heels into the aspiring "Higher Laws" that follow in Chapter 11.[18]

Anderson does the reader a service by attempting to digest the entirety of "Baker Farm," including the imagery of its beginning and ending paragraphs. Yet this reading is as unsatisfying as others that ignore the visitation with the Fields: the rainbow and "talaria" imagery of the opening and closing paragraphs do indeed deserve attention, but they do not negate the problematic nature of the "bigoted" behavior of the narrator, especially when that behavior stands in such contrast to the overall tone of the book.

Perhaps the most conclusive look at humor in *Walden* is Michael West's *Transcendental Wordplay*.[19] This book-length study of punning in the American Renaissance is remarkable for its understanding of the nuances of nineteenth-century language as well as its dedication in mapping out underlying meaning based on the ear of that era's readers—meaning otherwise lost to most contemporary readers. Perhaps because of his penetrating critical stare, when West broaches "Baker Farm," his vision remains narrowly focused on the mechanics of puns, rather than on the overall context of "Baker Farm" within *Walden,* a context necessary for viewing the chapter's narrator with irony. West's reading of "Baker Farm" is consistent with that of most critics who label this chapter a "nadir." He further resists an ironic reading when he writes, "The Yankee animus against philanthropy that sparked some of his most brilliant and truthful pages in 'Economy' functions well in the abstract, but this theme resists dramatic treatment. . . . The sight of the celibate Thoreau airily patronizing Field and his family in the name of philosophy, urging him to drop his job, change their diet, and go a-huckleberrying, is as unsettling and vaguely repellant as it would be to see Socrates persuading Phaedo and company to commit suicide."[20] Could it not be, however, that this chapter, and this speaker, are to be laughed at rather than cried over? West seems to miss this possibility as he labors to define the chapter to fit his overall reading of "Scatology and Eschatology." West celebrates and investigates the humor of Thoreau's writing, but mainly at the sentence level, as he transforms John Field to a "merely symbolic entity" to escape the issue of the narrator's comparatively inhuman characterization of Field.[21] But wouldn't he and other analysts of Thoreau's humor better serve us if they instead placed the advice to go a-huckleberrying in context with the overall work? Instead, the image of Mrs. Field and the domestic necessities of the Field household command such sympathy from *Walden's* humorist critics that they abandon their ability to laugh at the narrator's foolish behavior.

What would cause such a serious reaction? Why would Thoreau include a chapter so far out of context with the overall tone of the work? The driving forces would be fairly powerful, indeed. Again, the most logical explanation for humor that the critics have missed is the ironic airing out of authorial angst. For chapter upon chapter Thoreau has journaled in relative isolation, and "Baker Farm" has become the place for the theorist to check back in with his audience. In other words, at some point the environmental theorist is driven to meet the agricultural practitioner, and the anxiety of this long-delayed meeting has run high. Reading the humor of "Baker Farm" on a fragmented, sentence-level perspective, rather than working the humor back into a larger reading of *Walden,* does not help.

Laughing All the Way to the Pond

Instead, a reader might look again at the opening paragraphs of "Baker Farm" with an awareness of the activist/agriculturalist debate and find that the sentence-level analysis of humor supports this reading. The first sentence is indeed quite poetic, focusing as it does on the natural imagery surrounding the narrator on his way to the pond. The trees are clearly incorporated with a spirituality: "These were the shrines I visited both summer and winter" (*W* 202). And yet there is an important clue in the second sentence that offsets the spiritual/tree imagery: "Instead of calling on some scholar, I paid many a visit to particular trees" (*W* 201). As he hints here, Thoreau is carefully constructing a split between a scholarly knowledge based on abstractions and a more meaningful knowledge based on first-hand experience. The difference between these two types of experience is quickly established. Given that most of *Walden* is Thoreau's effort to capture through writing his own participatory experiences with nature, here again we see that much of "Baker Farm" comes to focus on the anxieties born of trying to communicate that experience to others.

As stated above, it is humor's insistence on duality in meaning that makes it uniquely suited to capturing the dual existence of narrator and author. The critic Edward L. Galligan is already on this path when he writes: "Is there evidence in *Walden* itself that we are to take the book as comedy? Indeed there is. To perceive the evidence all one needs to do is adopt the simple, fundamental strategy of making a distinction between the writer and the narrator."[22] The reader's first clue to Thoreau's satire lies in the family names. "John" is used by Thoreau as a ubiquitous moniker for any American man, as opposed to "Jonathan" for any British man. The name "John" is Thoreau's equivalent of John Doe. Recall that *Walden*'s final paragraph begins with the sentence "I do not say that John or Jonathan will realize all this" (*W* 333). This statement indicates not only Thoreau's belief that "average" readers may not be able to grasp his more difficult conclusions, but also his tendency to use the name John as an anonymous pedestrian stand-in. Also, when we consider John's last name—Field—the reference to land and land-use questions becomes almost irresistible. When joined together, "John Field," can be read as "the everyman of the land."

Word play and trickery exist throughout *Walden*, alerting the reader to the author's playful sense of style. One of the more famous examples of punning occurs in "The Ponds," where Thoreau refers to the unsuccessful fishermen he encounters as members of the religious group the "Coenobites," or, translated for effect, the "see no bites." Humor also lies in the heart of the instructional story of the traveler who asks the boy if the swamp has a hard bottom before entering with his horse; when the horse sinks to its girth, the traveler asks the boy if he didn't just tell him that the swamp had a hard bottom, and the boy replies that it does, but the traveler hasn't gotten halfway to it yet. Readers should note that this story is central enough to the message of *Walden* to be repeated: it appears first in the "Economy" section and then reappears in the "Conclusion." In its own way, it prepares us nicely for the longer exposition of "Baker Farm" by prefiguring the role of the traveling outsider who is at the mercy of the humble local for practical knowledge of his environment.

Thoreau's narrator in "Baker Farm" has more local knowledge about their surroundings than the Fields do, but in most cases the displaced activist is at the mercy of the locals to gain his or her bearings. The anecdote also hints at the difficulty of those two groups—visiting activists and local agricultural-ists—attempting to transcend their communication gap.

In "Conclusion," Thoreau states, "It is life near the bone where it is sweet-est" (W 329). But the "Baker Farm" chapter offers a necessary and pragmatic counterpoint to his personal philosophy: it is only for those who elect it. How can it be otherwise? At the end of "Baker Farm," Thoreau's narrator requests a drink from his humble hosts before leaving. Here, Thoreau the author can-not resist elevating the pompous attitude of Thoreau the narrator yet another notch; the character states that when he asks for the water, he asks not be-cause he is thirsty, but because he was "hoping to get a sight of the well bot-tom, to complete my survey of the premises" (W 206–7). Once supplied with the requested water, Thoreau the character notes that the water contains impurities that have not yet settled. But the language that he uses to relate this conclusion is particularly revealing of self-deprecating intent; he states that "such gruel sustains life here, I thought; so, shutting my *eyes,* and exclud-ing the *motes* by a skillfully directed under-current, I drank to genuine hospi-tality the heartiest draught I could" (W 207; emphasis added). Interestingly, Merriam-Webster's etymology and definition of "mote" provide a key for read-ing this sequence. As one might suspect, the definition is "a bit of foreign matter in food or drink."[23] But more compelling still is the biblically inspired phrase that the dictionary's editors found to be integral enough to the overall usage of the word so as to include it with the definition. The editors tell us that "a mote in the eye" (recall again that Thoreau's exact phrasing places the word "eyes" near the word "motes") means: "a comparatively slight fault noted in another person by one who fails to see a greater fault in himself." Webster's also glosses the following quote from the gospel of Matthew as the source of the expression: "Why do you see the speck in your neighbor's eye, but do not notice the log in your own eye? . . . You hypocrite, first take the log out of your own eye, and then you will see clearly to take the speck out of your neighbor's eye" (Matt. 7:3–5). Considering Thoreau's consistent references to a wide range of spiritual texts and his explicit penchant for reworking common bibli-cally inspired sayings, it is more than likely that the placement of these phrases is intentional. Our narrator Thoreau is laughable in the Field house, with a log in his eye. And perhaps most important, our author is quite aware of this, as he reports on the narrator's ability to shut his eye: "Such gruel sustains life here, I thought; so, *shutting my eyes* . . . I drank the heartiest draught I could." Clearly ironic, Thoreau the author can't resist one last laugh at Thoreau the narrator when he reflects that "I am not squeamish in such cases when manners are concerned" (*W* 207).

We must think again that the tension of "Baker Farm," and therefore the power of its comedy, lie in the attempt to export Thoreau's philosophy to an unwilling audience. As Stanley Cavell notes, *Walden* is a project that situates itself in the gap between two communities. Cavell writes that Thoreau's problem concerning his readers "is not to learn what to say to them; that could not be clearer. The problem is to establish his right to declare it."[24] The best approach to establishing that right to declare a message to both sides of the gap, it would seem, is not only to present both sides of the issue in conflict, as is done in "Baker Farm," but also to present both sides of that issue throughout *Walden*. If "Baker Farm" works as comedic airing of tensions between the differing perspectives of agriculturalists and activists, it is only because the author has previously portrayed both of these groups with a convincing familiarity.

Surely no reader could come away from *Walden* without a profound respect for an author who can so movingly lament the loss of natural wilderness and still hold a deep and abiding respect for the individuals who make their living from the commodification of nature. In "Higher Laws," Thoreau writes: "Fishermen, hunters, woodchoppers, and others, spending their lives in the fields and woods, in a peculiar sense a part of Nature themselves, are often in a more favorable mood for observing her, in the intervals of their pursuits, than philosophers or poets even, who approach her with expectation" (*W* 210). We see this familiarity at numerous other points within *Walden*.

Though Thoreau does portray himself as the activist in "Baker Farm" through his narrator, he comes to his understanding of the differences between the two perspectives with honesty, as his chapters "The Bean-Field" and "Where I Lived, and What I Lived For" demonstrate. Thoreau may be ruminating on Eastern and Western philosophy, but he is honestly applying it to the business of day-to-day agriculture. His hands are as dirty as any of his farming neighbors. And though authorial angst over the reception of his philosophical ideas by those with practical minds drives "Baker Farm," this should not cause us to see Thoreau as out of touch with his practitioner neighbors. We cannot forget that in "Visitors" Thoreau spends a good deal of time observing and generally praising the working style of a Canadian logging acquaintance, Alek Therien.

Therien is portrayed by Thoreau as a character study into the consciousness of a simple working man. Thoreau writes: "In him the animal man was chiefly developed. In physical endurance and contentment he was cousin to the pine and the rock." He presents a man perhaps capable of a greater intellectual life but hampered by an education that has driven out his will to question and has left him subsumed by the desires of others: "He had been instructed only in that innocent and ineffectual way in which the Catholic priests teach the aborigines, by which the pupil is never educated to the degree of consciousness, but only to the degree of trust and reverence, and a child is not made a man, but kept a child" (W 147). It is interesting, then, to think of how characters such as Therien can inform our reading of John Field. Statements about the simplicity of working men cannot be taken alone—in the case of Alek Therien or elsewhere in the case of the farmer Hosmer, as simplicity is always offset by complexity. Writing of the complexity hidden within Therien's simplicity, Thoreau notes, "To a stranger he appeared to know nothing of things in general; yet I sometimes saw in him a man whom I had not seen before, and I did not know whether he was as wise as Shakespeare or as simply ignorant as a child, whether to suspect him of a fine poetic consciousness or of stupidity" (W 148). In fact, Thoreau specifically introduces our conflict between theorist and pragmatist in his descriptions of Therein when he states, "It would have suggested many things to a philosopher to have dealings with him" (W 148).

Similarly, in "Winter Visitors," Thoreau remarks that his farming neighbor, Edmund Hosmer, is also unlikely to meet the stereotypical land owner, who either fails to extract practical knowledge from working the land or fails to have enough "book learning" to philosophize. In introducing Hosmer to the reader, Thoreau even links him to Emerson's ideal individual as expressed in "American Scholar": "[Hosmer is] one of the few of his vocation who are 'men on their farms'; who donned a frock instead of a professor's gown, and is as ready to extract the moral out of church or state as to haul a load of manure from his barn-yard" (W 267).

But we should not look to "Baker Farm" for any such portrayal of complexity under the simple exterior of the working man. As the portraits of Therien and Hosmer indicate, these working men are complete individuals, with complexities to complement their simple exteriors—for those capable of looking. John Field is no different from Therien or Hosmer, but his narrator is different from Therien's and Hosmer's. "Baker Farm" asks the reader to choose between a world of complex characters, as developed in *Walden* outside of "Baker Farm," or a world where the "Baker Farm" narrator sums up the entirety of the souls of folks like John Field with a few anecdotes. In the last part of "Baker Farm," we see John Field fail to catch any fish, regardless of how the narrator attempts to accommodate him: "he, poor man, disturbed only a couple of fins while I was catching a fair string, and he said it was his luck; but when we changed seats in the boat luck changed seats too" (*W* 208). This portrait of John Field is consistent with the overall ironic narrative of "Baker Farm." There might be as much complexity to John Field as we see in Therien or Hosmer, but we won't get it from this narrator. It is doubtful that Thoreau the author would approach the Field household with the pat answers for their family's affairs that we hear from Thoreau the narrator. It is much more likely, given the sensitivity shown elsewhere for those who live close to the land, that the author would view the actions of his narrative persona as just as laughable as those of the confident traveler who charges into the swamp on horseback.

The comedy of "Baker Farm" is inspired by the genuine difficulty of addressing the conflict between theoretical speakers and wise practitioners. Thoreau's comedy is a way of highlighting the difference between the two camps and simultaneously paying tribute to both systems of knowledge. As we have seen, this is an active and ongoing conflict. Placing "Baker Farm" in the light of this current conflict both contextualizes those concerned with today's activist/agriculturalist divide and further informs *Walden*'s readers of the book's permanency and contemporary relevance. The tension between activists and agriculturalists, which leads to Thoreau's comedic exorcism in "Baker Farm," is therefore both contemporary and historical. Though comedy suggests a static divide between these two camps, perhaps even a sense of futility born of an immutable conflict, the following passage suggests that Thoreau places each camp's claims to truth within a sense of ultimate truth:

> No face which we can give to a matter will stead us so well at
> last as the truth. This alone wears well. For the most part, we are
> not where we are, but in a false position. Through an infirmity of

> our natures, we suppose a case, and put ourselves into it, and
> hence are in two cases at the same time, and it is doubly difficult
> to get out. In sane moments we regard only the facts, the case that
> is. Say what you have to say, not what you ought. Any truth is bet-
> ter than make-believe. (*W* 327)

Walden's conclusion underscores a connection between all human communities, as well as the necessity and urgency of effective communication between
individual approaches to truth. The link between audience and message is an
enduring problem for those in the environmental community and those who
work the land. Thoreau's comedy can be an effective tool to do more than
merely disarm the tensions between today's communities of workers and
scholars, as well as the gap between practical and theoretical knowledge—it
can raise a contextual awareness that each speaker offers a credible stance
rather than an exclusive hold on truth.

By casting "Baker Farm" as the relieving of authorial anxiety over the differences between activists and agriculturalists, this inquiry sees in *Walden*
the roots of an enduring land-use conflict. Though the immediacy of this
problem is easy to witness in contemporary land-use discussions such as
those at the ASLE conference mentioned at the outset, few articulate it as
well as Wendell Berry. It is fitting then that we, having traced its roots to
Thoreau, hand this conflict over to Berry. Fortunately, Berry also gives us a
glimpse of a way out, a strategy in which the environmental activist and the
agriculturalist can coexist. In his 2002 article for *Sierra,* Berry too sees the
necessity of closing the gap between two "sides" by actively conceiving of
their interconnectedness:

> I am a conservationist and a farmer, a wilderness advocate and an
> agrarian. I am in favor of the world's wildness, not only because I
> like it, but because I think it is necessary to the world's life and to
> our own. . . . As a part of my own effort to think better, I decided
> not long ago that I would not endorse any more wilderness preser-
> vation projects that do not seek also to improve the health of the
> surrounding economic landscapes and human communities.
> Whatever its difficulties, my decision to cooperate no longer in
> the separation of the wild and the domestic has helped me see
> more clearly the compatibility and even the coherence of my two

allegiances. The dualism of the domestic and the wild is, after all, misleading.[25]

Notes

1. Henry David Thoreau, *Walden,* ed. J. Lyndon Shanley (Princeton: Princeton University Press, 1971). Hereafter cited parenthetically in the text as *W.*
2. Gerald Haslan, "Growers and Greens Unite," *Sierra* (May/June 2002): 56.
3. Ibid., 58.
4. Associated Press, "Conservation Project Funded through Legal but Controversial Loophole," September 29, 2003.
5. Holly Fretwell, "Cash Crop: Proposal to Pay Ranchers for Grazing Permits Fraught with Problems," *Rocky Mountain News,* November 29, 2003, Saturday final ed., 12C.
6. Cultural Survival, Inc. "Into the Life of the Nation: Use and Self-Determination among Traditional Pumé Hunter-Gatherers in Venezuela," <http://www.culturalsurvival.org/special_projects/americas/pume.cfm>. 3 Feb 2004.
7. United States Department of Agriculture, Economic Research Service Briefing Room, "Bankruptcies: An Historical Perspective of Farmer Bankruptcy," <http://www.ers.usda.gov/briefing/bankruptcies/Data/Bankruptcies Table1.htm>. 10 Dec 2001.
8. Richard Bridgman, *Dark Thoreau* (Lincoln: University of Nebraska Press, 1982), 108.
9. Lawrence E. Scanlon, "Thoreau's Parable of Baker Farm," *ESQ* 47 (1967): 19–21.
10. Leonard J. Neufeldt, "'Baker Farm' and Historicism: The Rainbow's Arch," in *Approaches to Teaching Thoreau's "Walden" and Other Works,* ed. Richard J. Schneider (New York: The Modern Language Association, 1996), 129–37.
11. Bridgman, *Dark Thoreau,* 104.
12. Ibid., 108.
13. Ibid., 106. Bridgman offers the following authors for support: Walter Harding, *The Days of Henry Thoreau* (Princeton: Princeton University Press, 1982); George E. Ryan, "Shanties and Shiftlessness: The Immigrant Irish of Henry Thoreau," *Eire-Ireland* 13, no. 3 (Fall 1978): 54–78; and Frank Buckley, "Thoreau and the Irish," *NEQ* 13 (September 1940): 389–400.
14. Leon Edel, *Henry D. Thoreau,* University of Minnesota Pamphlets on American Writers, no. 90 (Minneapolis, 1970), 27.
15. Buckley, "Thoreau and the Irish," 397.
16. Ryan, "Shanties and Shiftlessness," 58–59.
17. Charles R. Anderson, *The Magic Circle of Walden* (New York: Holt, Rinehart, and Winston, 1968).
18. Ibid., 143.
19. Michael West, *Transcendental Wordplay: America's Punsters and the Search for the Language of Nature* (Athens: Ohio University Press, 2000).
20. Ibid., 452–53.
21. Ibid., 453.

22. Edward L. Galligan, "The Comedian at Walden Pond," *South Atlantic Quarterly* 69 (1970): 24.

23. *Webster's Third New International Dictionary of the English Language Unabridged* (Springfield, MA: Merriam-Webster, 1993), *s.v.* mote.

24. Stanley Cavell, *The Senses of Walden* (New York: Viking, 1972), 11.

25. Wendell Berry, "For Love of the Land," *Sierra* (May/June 2002): 50.

Leaving Walden

DANA PHILLIPS

IN THIS ESSAY, I am going to explore a couple of different but closely related matters. First I will reconsider Thoreau's reasons for moving out of
his family's home in Concord and to a cabin he had built beside Walden
Pond, in light of the difficulty he seems to have had in staying put at that
pond once he had made the seemingly momentous decision to try and live
there all by himself. Rather than taking him to task for this apparent inconsistency, as others have done, I am going to argue that his almost daily departures
from Walden and his frequent visits to the village where he had been born
were part of a deliberate strategy of estrangement. This strategy enabled him
to achieve some critical distance from his community despite living just a
short way down the road from its vital center, and allowed him to subject
Concord—and by extension, all of America—to a form of scrutiny in *Walden*
that strikes me as essentially comic. It strikes me this way because by focusing on the absurdities of human behavior both individual and collective, but
especially the latter, it calls into question the distinction between nature and
culture, as comedy so often does, and highlights the arbitrariness of our decisions about the things we count as facts.

The second matter that I will be exploring in this essay involves yet another
departure, both on my own part and on Thoreau's. After spending some time
perusing them, I am going to take a short hop from the pages of *Walden* to
The Maine Woods, where I will touch down in "Ktaadn." If in the first of these
texts Thoreau seeks to penetrate to the heart of his culture by conducting
a series of expeditions launched from a base camp located well within its
borders (truth be told), in the second he attempts a retreat to its utmost

periphery. From that outlandish and rather tenuous position, he is able to review his culture's assumptions about both itself and the nature with which it is surrounded in a manner that seems to me to have certain features in common with deconstruction. In "Ktaadn," Thoreau's presence in the Maine woods and his absence from both Concord and Walden are joined in a complex interplay with the presence in those same woods of moose and Indians, both of which manage to remain absent from Thoreau's sight while he travels through the backcountry. But what he does get to see includes a number of peculiar items left behind by loggers and other woodsmen, the most peculiar of which is a copy of an important text by his friend and mentor Emerson. Thoreau's sardonic remarks about this text and a few others that he comes across during his first journey to Maine have convinced me that "Ktaadn" is more adventurous and insightful, and less escapist, than most of its readers have realized. After spelling out some of the particulars of this conviction, I will return to *Walden* for one last look at its pages before I take leave of them for good, pausing just long enough on the threshold to make a few closing remarks about Thoreau's distaste for and fascination with factitiousness.

Concord

I suppose we all imagine that we know why Thoreau went to Walden Pond, just because we have his word for it. In a much-celebrated passage of "Where I Lived, and What I Lived For," he tells us that he "went to the woods" in order "to live deliberately, to front only the essential facts of life" (*W* 90).[1] But life being what it is (fleeting and uncertain), and *Walden*'s author being the kind of writer that he was (ever paradoxical and eminently self-aware), this statement of intention is actually less definitive than it sounds. For Thoreau, going "to the woods" meant moving his minimal worldly goods only a very short distance—less than two miles—to a tiny cabin situated in a patch of second-growth pines just outside Concord, his home town and a community with which he was intimately familiar. Arguably, if this was "going to the woods" in order "to live deliberately," it was so only by way of contrast with never venturing out of sight of the town commons, for fear that one might lose track of the latest fads and fashions.

Despite his insistence on the fronting of facts and on veracity, Thoreau is willing to overstate the circumstances of his withdrawal from village life, since doing so allows him to portray himself as someone who, because he is a stranger, finds that faddish and fashionable life essentially alien and alienating. When he writes about Concord, he displays little, if any, of the native son's affection for his birthplace, however fond he seems to be of the fields and remnant forests that surround it. He treats Concord as a wellspring of factitiousness and hereditary prejudice, and as a microcosm in which all the world's foolishness and pettiness are on display. His depiction of the village is so very distanced and unsentimental that he sometimes has been taken to task for being insufficiently aware of the value of community, hypocritical about the benefits it confers, and both ahistorical and apolitical in his treatment of it.

For instance, in 1865 James Russell Lowell recorded one of the first and most damaging dismissals of the author of *Walden,* describing him as an antisocial misfit and a hypocrite who sponged on his neighbors. "He borrows an axe," Russell wrote, and "his boards, his nails, his bricks, his books, his lamp, his fish-hooks, his plough, his hoe, all turn state's evidence against him as an accomplice in the sin of that artificial civilization which rendered it possible that such a person as Henry D. Thoreau should exist at all."[2] The harshest and most conservative critics of Thoreau's work have continued to take an *ad hominem* and rather narrow approach to it similar to Lowell's. Much more interesting, because more broad-minded and better informed and therefore more respectable intellectually, are the objections to his work raised in recent decades by some historicist critics. For example, in a discussion of Thoreau's failure to engage history and politics in his treatment of community, Sacvan Bercovitch argues that *"Walden* embodies the myth of American laissez-faire individualism" and is therefore a less original, less revolutionary work than it at first seems to be.[3] Michael Gilmore makes a case similar to Bercovitch's, but he makes it more negatively. Of *Walden,* he writes: "It is inspired by the agrarian ideals of the past, yet in making a metaphor of those ideals it fails as a rejoinder to the nineteenth century and creates as many problems as it lays to rest." According to Gilmore, because Thoreau is invested in certain ideals, he has to engage "in a series of withdrawals from history," which "disables the political" and marks his "forsaking of civic aspirations." The result is that "he mystifies the temporality of his own experience, presenting it as natural or removed from social time" and privileging the "symbolic value" of myth over "actual circumstances."[4] Gilmore has specifically in mind the (mis)-representation of two years' experience as one in *Walden* and the ordering of the book's chapters according to the cycle of the seasons, features of the text that have been praised by critics anxious to demonstrate its formal cohesion and signifying power, but unaware of or indifferent to the text's political meaning—or rather, as Gilmore would have it, its lack thereof.

Even the latter two of these criticisms of Thoreau, innovative and original though they may have been when they first appeared in print, strike me as obtuse.[5] In them I think we may glimpse something instructive about the stalemate that always seems just about to occur in *Walden* scholarship. What strikes one set of the book's readers as an excellence—for instance, the fact that such cohesion as it possesses has been achieved by means of an intense rewriting of its author's experience, both private and public, with the celebration, defense, and reinforcement of certain ideals in view—is likely to strike other readers as a deficiency, if not as a piece of overt dishonesty. Conservative readers of the book like Lowell were the first to raise the objection of dishonesty. In recent years, revisionist readers like Bercovitch and Gilmore, who are of a more radical bent, have been likely to find the book less than fully satisfactory not because it seems to them a dishonest or a slipshod performance, but because it succeeds only too well in a context in which success must be regarded as evidence of ideological complicity with a status quo that the book's author ought to have scorned more consistently and more systematically than he did. Since the difference between dishonesty and complicity strikes me as whisker-thin, I want to ask Thoreau's detractors, both conservative and radical/revisionist, the following questions: is *Walden* not intended, in large part, as a reassessment of the very ideas of community, history, and politics? If that's so, then why take its author to task for not valuing politics, history, and community more highly than he did? Who's to say that life in mid-nineteenth century Concord wasn't every bit as stultifying and just as unthinkingly conventional as he found it to be? And isn't it obvious, in any case, that he found it productive to pose as a lone wolf—and a skeptic?[6]

So that we might begin to answer these questions for ourselves, and in fresh terms, I'd like you to consider the following passage from "The Village," in which Thoreau describes how he often left Walden for an afternoon so that he could walk into town and view his fellow citizens from the detached perspective of natural history:

> Every day or two I strolled to the village to hear some of the gossip
> which is incessantly going on there, circulating either from mouth
> to mouth, or from newspaper to newspaper, and which, taken in

homœopathic doses, was really as refreshing in its way as the rustle of leaves and the peeping of frogs. As I walked in the woods to see the birds and squirrels, so I walked in the village to see the men and boys; instead of the wind among the pines I heard the carts rattle. In one direction from my house there was a colony of muskrats in the river meadows; under the grove of elms and buttonwoods in the other horizon was a village of busy men, as curious to me as if they had been prairie dogs, each sitting at the mouth of its burrow, or running over to a neighbor's to gossip. I went there frequently to observe their habits. (*W* 167)

This passage might be read as an illustration of its author's callous attitude toward his friends and neighbors, an attitude no good liberal ought to leave unchallenged. But viewing culture as if it were nature, gossip as if it were leaves rustling and frogs peeping, men and boys as if they were birds or squirrels or muskrats, and customs as if they were habits, while it may have been illiberal, did enable Thoreau to conduct some interesting social experiments. The result of the particular experiment described in "The Village" is something like a parallax view of the village's residents, in which we see them both as they appear in immediate context or *in situ* and in another frame of reference and another place altogether, one which is very strange and yet entirely familiar, or at least as familiar as leaves, frogs, birds, squirrels, and muskrats. If there is irony, or maybe just whimsy, in Thoreau's choosing to view the inhabitants of Concord from the perspective of natural history, there is also method, and I would argue that the method isn't purely or solely rhetorical. It's also anthropological, philosophical, and political.

The remove to Walden Pond places Thoreau at a spatial and a theoretical midpoint between two horizons, one representative of wild nature, which is embodied in a colony of muskrats, and the other representative of what I would like to call *wild culture,* which is embodied in the spectacle of muskrat-like townsmen darting from burrow to burrow and sharing tidbits of gossip as if they were tender shoots of forbs and grasses. And as Thoreau indicates, on any given day he is just as likely to strike out for one of the two horizons he enjoys from his vantage point at pondside as he is to strike out for the other. Such departures from Walden's shores are necessary, if the perspective he has gained there is to have any argumentative validity and rhetorical vitality. He needs to do more than just enjoy the fine vistas afforded

him by culture and nature: he must beat the boundaries of his domain in
order to gather some data and acquaint himself with the facts, such as they
are, if he is going to face them, which as he says in "Where I Lived, and What
I Lived For" is just what he had hoped he might be able to do. He must, in
short, leave Walden.

The passage I have quoted from "The Village" is in accord with what we
know about Thoreau's daily activities while he was resident at Walden, and
should have silenced those who disparage him for not having been more of a
hermit than he was and thereby violating his own principles. You know the
old argument: "Solitude, my foot! Thoreau's mother brought him covered
dishes, and Alcott all but tucked him into bed at night." If there is a contradiction implicit in his almost daily bending of his principles, it's one that the
author of *Walden* cheerfully admits. And besides, with him contradiction isn't
a potential flaw in his self-presentation, but is essential to the intellectual and
rhetorical registers in which he works. That is, he writes in order to contradict
himself, and others—especially others.[7] Those who find this objectionable
might as well object to the unpredictability of the weather, or to the reverse
flow of topwater currents in tidal rips.

With Thoreau's penchant for contradiction and his contrariness in mind, it
might be said that when it came to nature and culture, he was of one mind, in
that he was undecided about both. Whether he was at Walden or in Concord,
he found it hard to settle down, because he was always aware of another
horizon of possibility. Yet it would be foolish to deny that on his visits to Concord, more often than not he found the habits of its citizens distinctly
unnatural, even downright counterfactual, and much too tame. After all, as
wild animals go, muskrats aren't notable for the dangers they pose to larger
mammals. Muskrats are likely to bite you, if you provoke them, just as squirrels will—birds, too, for that matter. The willingness to defend itself of even
the smallest wild animal may be why Thoreau says in "Economy" that when
life in civil society becomes too enervating and depressing, you need to leave
town and city for the countryside, there to "console yourself with the bravery
of minks and muskrats" (*W* 8). But minks, muskrats, squirrels, and birds are
for the most part amicable creatures who pose no threat to humans either
individually or collectively, and who, with the possible exception of minks,
adapt to town and even city life with relative ease. And Thoreau knows this.
Hence his comparison of human beings to these animals, and his suggestion
that human speech is like the rustling of leaves and the peeping of frogs, puts

humans in a very different place in the scale of being from the exalted one they have long believed themselves to occupy. It seems that taking the human character into account must be a deflationary, reductive enterprise, like book-keeping or sociobiology (and let's not forget Puritan theology), if it is to offset their grandiose vision of themselves, which Thoreau suggests is just at much at odds with the cultural as it is with the natural reality of their lives.

With this thought in mind, we might consider going so far as to say that in his own way Thoreau was observant of a notion we now identify with the doctrine of social construction. This is the notion that something's status as a fact—the innate superiority of humans, for instance—is never value-neutral, but is always reflective of society's needs, wants, desires, and beliefs. "A fact," as Steve Shapin and Simon Schaffer put it (somewhat opaquely) in their book *Leviathan and the Air-Pump*, "is a constitutively social category."[8] And what they seem to mean by this statement is that facts are "social" all the way down. Facts never come to rest on the bedrock of the natural but float on a magma roiled by conflicting cultural, institutional, and political forces. Gradually, with the passage of time, almost any fact you care to name will get subsumed by these forces and will begin to melt away, to survive only as a half-forgotten historical curiosity—like the flat earth, the four humours, the ether, or the inheritance of acquired physical characteristics—if it survives at all.

Many so-called facts are actually an alloy of sheer factitiousness and of something else that may or may not be something truly substantive, according to some social constructionists. And at least one advocate of their point of view, especially when it comes to the study of science, speaks quite soberly of a "general metaphysical commitment to 'sociologism,'" though it's hard to imagine how the loopy universe that this gentleman posits, one which seems to be defined by a category mistake, could be the least bit functional.[9] But let us put this worry aside and not be too niggling, since metaphysics can, and will, take care of itself. The upshot of social constructionist thinking, and the matter of most immediate concern to us here, seems to be that since we are all sociable by nature (so to speak), none of us will get to handle the sterling article—to face any facts that aren't just ephemeral constructs, or the products of wishful thinking—so long as we can do nothing to overcome the circumstances of our birth, which require us to be nurtured by others of our kind. For those who see the world in this light, the only real alternative to sheer conformity is to engage in a certain kind of ideological critique, yet another deflationary enterprise—and one that tends to issue in little more than an increased awareness of the constraints that bind us all, as if we were inept spiders trapped in webs of our own weaving.

As I've suggested, Thoreau's understanding of the facts was similar, but it was also a lot more hopeful and much less passive. Like today's social constructionists, he was aware that much of what passes for fact is actually factitious or "soft," as Bruno Latour puts it. All too often, according to Latour, so-called facts are the products not of careful and disinterested investigation but of "idle speech, twaddle, prattle, and chatter in bars, at parties, at home or at work." But Thoreau was uncomfortable, famously so, with what Latour calls the "regime of circulation" by means of which "soft" facts get passed from person to person and begin to harden into prejudice along the way.[10] And that's why Thoreau would have regarded resting in the conviction that all facts are socially constructed as an outright begging of one of the most important questions we can ask ourselves about our lives. From his point of view, social constructionist thinking pays too much heed and yields too much ground to the factitious and the "soft," which a good Thoreauvian insists on putting to the test as if it were factual and hard, even in those cases when it seems palpably otherwise.

So while Thoreau's efforts to analyze the relationship of facts to society may run parallel to present-day constructionist attempts to do the same thing, his efforts run in the opposite direction much of the time, since he is unwilling to cede the epistemological (or, if you prefer, the cognitive) high ground to society, as constructionists are. For them, facts always take a back seat to values, which, while they may not go all the way down to bedrock either, nonetheless provide whatever metaphysical baseline and foundation a given society happens to have, even if its values are known to have been invented by corrupt demagogues and false prophets, and therefore seem bizarre, counter-productive, and delusional to outsiders. What counts, socially and metaphysically (hollow though this second adverb may be), is membership in the culture. Thoreau, in contrast, is more concerned about the relationship of his society to facts than he is about the relationship of facts to his society. For him membership in the culture is always inessential, provisional, and voluntary. So far as he is concerned, you can withdraw from the culture, if you like, and go live by the side of a pond in a shack literally of your own construction. If that's not enough for you, and if your now-distant neighbors continue to importune you for no good reason, you might choose to venture even further afield and affiliate yourself with a new culture—or, better yet, a new nature—entirely. Yet Thoreau is too honest intellectually to come down simply and squarely on the side of brute facts and immutable natural laws, and to oppose such facts and laws to values, as one kind of realist would do. Unlike the realist and the social constructionist, he recognizes that the issue of what counts as a fact, and the closely related (indeed, inseparable) issue of what worth said fact might have once it has been recognized as such, are still going to be live issues, regardless of whether we have persuaded ourselves that all facts have been constituted by nature or by men and women acting in social concert, or—the third, and the most plausible alternative—by large measures of both.

For the good Thoreauvian, cultural relativism isn't a recipe for complacency so much as it is a motivation for the intensified scrutiny of *all* cultures, east and west, north and south. So whatever new affiliations you might contrive for yourself, once you have said goodbye to the culture in which you were born, you will be under no obligation to regard them as binding. Your horizons will have shifted, of necessity, but there will continue to be at least two of them, with limit conditions established on the one hand by (what still seems to be) culture and on the other by (what still seems to be) nature. That is precisely why a good Thoreauvian must be less of a realist or a social constructionist, and more of a satirist. And when a satirical impulse is superadded, as it were, to a realist or social constructionist perspective and subverts it, the result is either a comical sort of surrealism or something that we might call *natural deconstruction*. I'll explain what I mean by the latter term in the next section of this essay; first I want to spend some time discussing a few examples of Thoreau's comical sort of surrealism.

One instance of what I mean by a comical sort of surrealism is provided by the memorable picture Thoreau paints in "Economy" of "the broad, flapping American ear" eagerly waiting to hear the latest trivial news from Europe—"that the Princess Adelaide has the whooping cough" (*W* 52). Because Thoreau was dissatisfied with the political and social scene of the 1840s and 1850s, and because he was dismayed by the shape that the new popular culture already was beginning to take, he does his best in *Walden* to make it appear strange and even nonsensical, but in an amusing way. Hence one of the most basic patterns of his prose, and the singular trend of his thought: the self-declared extravagance of *Walden* often takes an abrupt and comic turn, and issues in a striking form of grotesquerie that might seem at odds with the

Transcendentalist impulses of the book's author. But that Transcendentalism was in part a polemical expression of disgruntlement with the American scene ought perhaps to be emphasized more than it is. And that this disgruntlement could issue in potent forms of grotesquerie, which cannot be dismissed as Transcendentalist moonshine, is evident not only in the passages of social satire with which "Economy" and other chapters of *Walden* are punctuated, but in the depiction, early on in Emerson's "American Scholar," of the country's hard-pressed laborers as "so many walking monsters,—a good finger, a neck, a stomach, an elbow, but never a man" (*CW* 1:53). How this depiction squares with Emerson's description of himself in *Nature* as an equally monstrous "transparent eye-ball," which does seem to be an example of Transcendentalist moonshine, and whether the one moment in his writing really needs to be squared with the other at all, are of course good questions (*CW* 1:10).

Instead of pursuing those questions, I'd like to continue with my little survey of *Walden*'s comic-surrealist moments. In the third paragraph of "Economy," Thoreau begins by disavowing the urge to leave both Concord and Walden behind so that he might give his readers a report on the Chinese and the Sandwich Islanders (whose horizons, presumably, are as different from a typical New Englander's as can be). He instead turns to a consideration of a purely local matter, the various means of subsistence relied upon by his neighbors, farming in particular. And even though he, too, is Concord-born and bred, he approaches the lives of his neighbors as if he were a visiting ethnographer posted to Massachusetts from some place very far away and from another historical epoch entirely. He soon makes New England life seem anything but familiar and commonsensical.

"I have travelled a good deal in Concord," Thoreau writes, "and every where, in shops, and offices, and fields, the inhabitants have appeared to me to be doing penance in a thousand remarkable ways." He then offers what amounts to an exercise in comparative mythology, pitting Hindu and Greek feats of endurance and strength against the fortitude it takes to make it through the daily grind prescribed by the Protestant work ethic.

> What I have heard of Brahmins sitting exposed to four fires and looking in the face of the sun; or hanging suspended, with their heads downward, over flames; or looking at the heavens over their shoulders "until it becomes impossible for them to resume

their natural position, while from the twist of the neck nothing but liquids can pass into the stomach;" or dwelling, chained for life, at the foot of a tree; or measuring with their bodies, like caterpillars, the breadth of vast empires; or standing on one leg on the tops of pillars,—even these forms of conscious penance are hardly more incredible and astonishing than the scenes which I daily witness. The twelve labors of Hercules were trifling in comparison with those which my neighbors have undertaken; for they were only twelve, and had an end; but I could never see that these men slew or captured any monster or finished any labor.

And so on, and so on, for the better part of another page, until Thoreau has worked in references—and unfavorable comparisons—not only to the Brahmins and Hercules, but also to Iolas and the hydra's head, to Romulus and Remus, to the Augean stables, to the New Testament, and to Deucalion and Pyrrha (the last complete with a two-line quotation from Ovid's *Metamorphoses*, both in the original Latin and in Raleigh's English translation) (W 4–5). It is, to say the least, quite a performance. Thoreau drives home his point ("men labor under a mistake") again and again, and he drives it home so aggressively and mercilessly, and with such small sympathy for the American way of doing things, which he regards as bizarre, that some readers have found the ideas expressed in "Economy" either half-baked and naïve or offensive, or all three at once.[11]

I don't apply the word "performance" to this passage lightly. In fact, I think its performative aspect is worth dwelling on for just a moment. Obviously the passage is very much a display of knowledge—and not only a display of local but of esoteric knowledge as well. It is crammed with cultural references of the sort that Thoreau had gleaned from his reading while studying at Harvard and during his long hours of leisure at Walden Pond. In other words, the passage is a display of book learning. And yet it's more than just a sort of recitation. For all its erudition and despite its patina of worldliness, it has a genuinely American flavor, even a folk flavor. It smacks of that democratic variant of myth, the tall tale.[12] But with a difference, for whenever Thoreau strolls into town from Walden, it's in order to cut American heroism down to size and make it seem craven despite itself. So he prefers to tell what prove to be *small tales* in the end. Witness his conjuring up of the pathetic image of all those propertied but unfortunate young American men pushing their barns and farms before them down the road of life, and getting flattened spiritually by the needless enormity of their possessions. He writes: "How many a poor immortal soul have I met well nigh crushed and smothered under its load, creeping down the road of life, pushing before it a barn seventy-five feet by forty, its Augean stables never cleansed, and one hundred acres of land, tillage, mowing, pasture, and wood-lot!" (W 5).

The larger point that Thoreau is trying to make in moments like this one is that if Americans are exceptional among the world's peoples, as they assume themselves to be, it is only in respect of the fact that their behavior is even more absurd than the incredible behavior sometimes indulged in by individuals of other nationalities. And several of the foreign individuals that Thoreau mentions in the course of his exercise in comparative mythology most likely never really existed anyway, except in fable and story, while the rest were holy men and visionaries. They all had excellent reasons for acting as they did, and can be excused their eccentricities. Americans, who are "comparatively free," don't have good reasons for their unnatural actions and can't be excused for behaving so oddly—and unnaturally (W 6).

Thoreau's jaundiced perspective on the American success story puts him squarely in the tradition or rather the counter-tradition of the disaffected and disenfranchised idler for whom the bustle of life in the United States not only has no charm, but also seems inexplicably weird. This counter-tradition runs from Irving's Rip van Winkle and Cooper's Leatherstocking through to Twain's Huck Finn and beyond, all the way up to the slackers of the present day.[13] Just picture a scruffy, bearded Thoreau sitting in the window of the Concord Starbucks, sipping a decaf organic latte, skimming a dog-eared copy of *How to Stay Alive in the Woods,* doodling on a napkin, and gazing with a mixture of bafflement and contempt at his hardworking but spendthrift neighbors as they pass by on pointless business errands, and you will see what I mean.[14]

I'd also like to suggest, while I'm making a few outré comparisons of my own, that to some extent—a surprising extent, actually—Thoreau's manner, if not his grammar, syntax, and vocabulary, resembles that of later generations of American humorists, men like Twain and Bret Harte and Josh Billings and Will Rogers, or (to really stretch the point) today's stand-up comedians, all of whom offer similarly laconic but sharply drawn observations about the foibles of and the occasional pratfalls taken by their fellow citizens, while posing as both consummate insiders and thoroughly disillusioned outsiders. "Let us not play at kittlybenders," Thoreau writes in the last chapter of *Walden* (kittlybenders is a game in which the competitors run across thin ice): "There is a solid bottom every where." And to illustrate his point, he tells a funny story: "We read that the traveller asked the boy if the swamp before him had a hard bottom. The boy replied that it had. But presently the traveller's horse sank in up to the girths, and he observed to the boy, 'I thought you said that this bog had a hard bottom.' 'So it has,' answered the latter, 'but you have not got half way to it yet.'" The moral of this story, or, if you like, the counter-punch to its punchline (which suggests that there is more than one way to bring a man down from his high horse), is that the same is true of "the bogs and quicksands of society; but he is an old boy that knows it" (W 330). So much, then, for those whippersnappers the social constructionists.[15]

I suppose it can be debated whether Thoreau was humorous in a humor-less way, or humorless in a humorous way: whether a New England humorist isn't too chimerical a creature for us to contemplate. But even if Thoreau's epigrammatic statements sometimes allude to the classics and provoke few if any belly laughs, damning one and all as they do, and even if jokes like the one I've just quoted may have been picked up from his reading, they are still recognizable as one-liners and zingers. They get remembered—and, naturally enough, misremembered and misinterpreted—in much the same way that jokes do, especially bad jokes, the ones that grate upon our cultural sensibili-ties in an irritating or even an offensive way, which is nonetheless pleasurable. Provided, of course, that they don't get censored or at least suppressed by readers who admire Thoreau the New England Transcendentalist (also a rather chimerical creature, it seems to me) more than they admire Thoreau the humorist and comic surrealist, who is much too aggressive, too much of a spoilsport, and much too unsympathetic for their tastes.

The Maine Woods

In order to have a look at some examples of what I mean by "natural decon-struction," let's leave Walden with Thoreau once more, go with him not to Concord but to the Maine woods, and turn our attention to some interesting passages from "Ktaadn." But first a word about the overall character of this text. Since it is largely devoid of philosophical digressions and literary flights of fancy, it has struck some of Thoreau's admirers as a quite conventional and less than satisfying work of art. In "Ktaadn," you are told everything you do not know, or already know only too well and don't wish to be reminded of,

about what it is like to camp out in foul weather with several companions and
only an overturned boat for shelter. Thoreau writes:

> Not far from midnight, we were one after another awakened by
> rain falling on our extremities; and as each was made aware of the
> fact by cold or wet, he drew a long sigh and then drew up his legs,
> until gradually we had all sidled round from lying at right angles
> with the boat, till our bodies formed an acute angle with it, and
> were wholly protected. When next we awoke, the moon and stars
> were shining again, and there were signs of dawn in the east. I
> have been thus particular in order to convey some idea of a night
> in the woods. (*MW* 40–41)

And as if this sort of particularity were not torment enough, you also have
to endure passages like the following, which is burdened with the unpro-
nounceable place names that make the map of the Maine woods almost use-
less to the visitor from elsewhere: "The mountain may be approached more
easily and directly on horseback and on foot from the north-east side, by the
Aroostook road, and the Wassataquoik river; but in that case you see much
less of the wilderness, none of the glorious river and lake scenery, and have no
experience of the batteau and the boatman's life" (*MW* 3). Since so much of
its bulk is composed of guidebook passages of this kind, readers who find
Walden bottomless and transcendental tend to find "Ktaadn" lacking in depth,
bottom-heavy, and much too stolid a text.[16] The very factuality of the account
offered in "Ktaadn" (and in the rest of *The Maine Woods,* too) has been seen
as grounds for complaint.

According to some critics, the Maine woods figure in Thoreau's writing
about them only somewhat peripherally. While many pages of "Ktaadn" are
devoted to these woods, they are not treated figuratively, but literally, unlike
the woods surrounding Concord, which are treated metonymically in *Walden,*
as fragments and living reminders or proxies of a primeval forest long since
vanished. Nor have the Maine woods as depicted in "Ktaadn" been invested
with anything like the symbolic potency of, say, the sea in *Moby-Dick.*
Ishmael went a-whaling and encountered Leviathan, whereas Henry David
only went leaf peeping and encountered some lumbermen, a couple of blanket Indians in Old Town, and a few dozen brook trout, which he promptly
ate—and as facts go, neither the lumbermen nor the blanket Indians nor the

trout are especially impressive, despite Thoreau's best efforts to convince us otherwise. In *Walden* facts seem to be vitalizing, whereas in "Ktaadn" (as in *The Maine Woods* as a whole) they seem obdurate, and pose an impediment to the forces of imagination.[17]

But to devalue the depiction of everyday, mundane factuality as readers who judge "Ktaadn" to be a failure seem to do sends two very simple and commonsensical questions begging for an answer. Why would Thoreau have bothered to go to Maine in the first place, if the day-to-day experience of being there wasn't going to provide him with something more valuable than indifferent filler material for a narrative he otherwise need not have bothered to write at all? And if indifferent filler material is indeed all he was able to gather while he was there—if his trip really was unsuccessful—why did he sit himself down afterwards and write about his Maine travels anyway, and at such length? It's not as if Thoreau had inches to fill, a deadline to meet, and an expense account to justify. He wrote, as he almost always wrote, at a venture.

The few scholarly readers who have deigned to write about "Ktaadn" at all have preferred, almost without exception, to focus their critical attention on Thoreau's account of Mount Katahdin's ascent and descent, which they regard as climactic (despite the fact that, properly speaking, "Ktaadn" has no plot—and therefore has no need for a moment as dramatic as a climax is supposed to be).[18] And by fixating on only one or two more elevated passages of "Ktaadn" while largely ignoring the remainder of its text, which is pitched in a much lower and less inscrutable register, these readers have revealed a preference for the transcendental much more decided than was Thoreau's own. It's almost as if the rest of "Ktaadn" were somehow a digression, or even apocryphal—and almost as if *Walden* had earned its secure place in the canon because its admirers were willing to nudge aside not just other texts, but other texts by the same author.[19]

That Thoreau died with the words "moose" and "Indian" on his lips only makes the interpretive dilemma apparently posed by "Ktaadn" seem even more urgent to readers inclined to fret over his inconsistencies and lapses (rather than to make hay out of them, as I am proposing we ought to do). Thoreau may have picked these words up, like arrowheads and potsherds, at Walden, where he is known to have buried his sizable nose in chronicles of the exploration and settlement of early New England and in volumes of natural history. But "moose" and "Indian" possessed no life for him until he went to Maine and saw the aboriginal beings to whom the words referred—or traces of them—on their native ground.

However, while Thoreau's deathbed utterance may be interesting, it's no more decisive than his earlier announcement of his intention "to front only the essential facts of life" at Walden Pond. On his first trip to Maine, the moose and the Indian proved to be just as fleeting as, well, life itself.[20] And so I'd like to suggest, and will try to demonstrate, that simply because "Ktaadn" is a more down-to-earth and workmanlike text than *Walden* doesn't mean that it fails to express its author's intellectual side and his maverick sensibility. Thoreau may have been on leave from Walden and taking a Transcendental-ist's holiday, but he never forgets to measure the distance he has traveled from Concord as accurately as he possibly can while he is in Maine. And his atti-tude toward his Massachusetts home remains as skeptical as ever. He writes: "If I were to look for a narrow, uninformed, and countrified mind, as opposed to the intelligence and refinement which are thought to emanate from cities, it would be among the rusty inhabitants of an old-settled country, on farms all run out and gone to seed with life-ever-lasting, in the towns about Bos-ton, even on the high-road in Concord, and not in the backwoods of Maine" (*MW* 22–23). Life-everlasting, it seems, is death to the greenery of thought: it is a weed. Consequently Thoreau must devise a new discourse and a new frame of mind lively and sophisticated enough to deal with the difficult reali-ties of a new country, "the backwoods of Maine."

This new discourse and new frame of mind are what I have in mind when I speak of "natural deconstruction." Consider, if you will, Thoreau's account of a discovery he made in a logging camp near the dam above Quakish Lake. There he noticed, strewn about on the departed loggers' "well-flattened, and somewhat faded beds of arbor-vitæ leaves," the following items: "an odd leaf of the Bible, some genealogical chapter out of the Old Testament; and, half buried by the leaves . . . Emerson's Address on West India Emancipa-tion . . . also . . . a pamphlet entitled History of the Erection of the Monu-ment on the grave of Myron Holly. This was the readable, or reading matter, in a lumberer's camp in the Maine woods, thirty miles from a road, which would be given up to the bears in a fortnight. These things were well thumbed and soiled." "Well thumbed and soiled" it may have been, but Emerson's ad-dress, Thoreau is informed, *"had made two converts to the Liberty party here"* (*MW* 34; italics in original). This information he passes on to his reader with a certain glee, since it suggests just where the outermost reaches of the effectiveness of Emersonian discourse might lie.

I wonder: can Emerson's address, along with the chapter of the Old Testament and the pamphlet concerning the monument to the otherwise forgotten Myron Holly, be counted as an intertext in this instance? Or has it become just another text, leaves buried among still more leaves and hence mere *reading matter,* its legibility eroded by the rough thumbs of loggers and its readability all but exhausted by the partisan political uses to which it has been put—and to be exhausted for a fact (pardon the expression) the minute the bears move in? Talk about deconstruction: the Yale School cannot compete. Thoreau and the bears, aided by the organic process of decomposition, have too great a natural advantage, and have already staked a claim to the more cultured and supposedly more radical academicians' territory. Compared to Thoreau and the bears, and the fading and rotting of leaves (which converts them to soil much more systematically than reading "soils" texts), the Derrideans and de Manians and all their patented moves start to seem a bit tame.

Tameness is, however, a relative quality (as I have already tried to demonstrate in my discussion of the men-as-muskrats passage from "The Village"), and there is no inherent reason why deconstruction might not, like Thoreau, attempt to go wild. Jonathan Culler, challenging Umberto Eco's argument against overinterpretation and taking exception to Eco's breezy characterizations of deconstruction, makes an apposite point, and if you listen carefully you will hear an unexpected but distinctly Thoreauvian echo in Culler's words. He writes: "Interpretation is interesting only when it is extreme. Moderate interpretation, which articulates a consensus, though it may have value in some circumstances, is of little interest."[21] One thing that Thoreau cannot be accused of, it seems to me, is moderation, certainly not when it comes to the expression of his opinions and the pressing of interpretations that force us to view the world differently than we do. Hence his sly characterization of Emerson's address, which places it on a par not only with a desecrated text— with that handful of leaves roughly torn from one of the least readable sections of the Old Testament, one concerned precisely with a myth of origins and therefore ripe for questioning or, if you insist, deconstruction—but with a trivial pamphlet on local history of a sort wholly irrelevant to life in a logging camp.[22]

In the context of the Maine woods, Emerson's address may be just as am-
biguous a marker of civilization as the single red brick Thoreau saw at yet
another campsite, the lone ring-bolt driven into a rock he glimpsed on one of
the lakes, or the dingy playing cards he discovered on a stump at another
logging camp, with much the same sort of face value as, say, the joker. Of
course Thoreau understands that all these markers of the increased human
presence in the wilderness, and of human decadence, may be the grim por-
tents of a future in which the Maine woods have been entirely and utterly
deforested. But I think he also sees them, more ambivalently and—dare I say
it—more imaginatively, as part and parcel of the landscape he is traversing, in
which disturbances and disruptions, in the form not only of logging and litter-
ing but also in the form of parties of hunters both red and white, swarms of
black flies, mosquitoes, and no-see-ums, depredations by wolves, wildfires
ignited by lightning strikes, and freezes deep and hard enough to give birth to
glaciers, all come with the territory. To put the point somewhat differently,
the signs dropped from the hand of man strike Thoreau's imagination with
just as much impact as the tracks of moose do. They don't strike his conscience with anything like the same force. The Decline of the West, Down
East, isn't something he rues—not, at any rate, to the point of grieving over
it—since it, too, appears to be part of the nature of things.

Emerson's address also seems to have something in common with the ad-
vertisement that Thoreau found plastered to a tree above the falls at Katep-
skonegan Lake, in that the address also urges something upon the inhabitants
of the north woods—emancipation—which they either already enjoy or for
which they have no readily apparent need. Thoreau writes:

> Half way over this carry, thus far in the Maine wilderness on its
> way to the Provinces, we noticed a large flaming Oak Hall hand-
> bill, about two feet long, wrapped round the trunk of a pine, from
> which the bark had been stript, and to which it was fast glued
> by the pitch. This should be recorded among the advantages
> of this mode of advertising, that so, possibly, even the bears
> and wolves, moose, deer, otter, and beaver, not to mention the
> Indian, may learn where they can fit themselves according to the
> latest fashion, or, at least, recover some of their own lost garments.
> (MW 50)

Thoreau and his companions are moved to commit their one act of naming by this unexpected evidence of the enterprise and ingenuity of commerce, which has introduced a form of mass media, and arguably the most powerful one, into the Maine woods well in advance of settlement, as if the frontier needed first to be pacified not with a military but with an ad campaign. "We christened this," Thoreau writes, "the Oak Hall carry" (*MW* 50). Needless to say this christening is ironic, and it may be an example of how the assignment of place-names can be unsettling rather than settling, which is one of the key themes of natural deconstruction as practiced by Thoreau.

Here is another, and a clearer, example of the same phenomenon and theme. Concluding his narration of the first day's travel north from Bangor, Thoreau writes: "At sundown, leaving the river-road awhile for shortness, we went by way of Enfield, where we stopped for the night. This, like most of the localities bearing names on this road, was a place to name, which, in the midst of the unnamed and unincorporated wilderness, was to make a distinction without a difference, it seemed to me" (*MW* 8). As Thoreau travels through them, the Maine woods are continually receding from his grasp in ways that prevent their being named and incorporated, or constituted as a body that can be recognized and addressed civilly, then confronted as a fact. But let me hasten to add that this disappearing act is the very thing that makes the Maine woods appealing to Thoreau. He doesn't find their unsettledness, their "wildness," especially unsettling, not in a personal way. Far from it: the difficulty of coming to terms and face to face with them poses an intellectual challenge he gladly accepts.

The interplay of the settled and the unsettling in the Maine countryside is similar to the interplay of presence and absence in texts. Notoriously, deconstruction puts more emphasis on the latter, absence, than it does on the former, presence. And as it happens, during his first trip to Maine Thoreau was just as attentive, if not more so, to what wasn't there as he was to what was there. That is precisely why "Ktaadn" seems more notable for the things he didn't see than for the things he did. The most conspicuous sight that Thoreau missed seeing is the summit of Katahdin itself, which was shrouded in mist on the day he climbed the mountain. But he also missed seeing moose, mature white pines standing in the woods (he saw plenty of them tangled in logjams, washed up on lakeshores, or being rendered into lumber as they were run through the mills at Old Town), loggers at work, and the two

Penobscots with whom he and his party had arranged a rendezvous at the outset of their journey up river.[23] It therefore might not be too much to call "Ktaadn" a record, and a fulsome one, of absences, given the close attention its author pays to the many traces left behind them by the denizens, human, nonhuman, and inhuman, year-round and seasonal, of the Maine woods. This means that Thoreau's depiction of these woods is marked by considerable irony and a fair amount of uncertainty from the very outset of his narrative. As often as not, he has to concede that in the Maine woods—as in Oakland—there seems to be no *there* there. And so I'd like to suggest, cautiously, that during his first trip to Maine and the writing and revision of "Ktaadn," Thoreau made an unexpected detour, and took what we now call "the linguistic turn," or something not unlike it. Caution is advised here, I think, because while Thoreau may be aware of the radical untranslatability of certain aspects of his Maine woods experience ("Katahdin," for example, means "highest land," which isn't very edifying), many of the traces that caught his attention were literally traces, or tracks, trails, and piles of trash.[24]

In the Maine woods, the ratio of revelation to concealment tends to be rather low, and Thoreau seems grateful for and amused by such glimpses of the facts, and the artifacts, as he is granted. Describing the scene where he and his companions camped the night before their first attempt at ascending Katahdin, he notes in passing that "there was the skeleton of a moose here, whose bones some Indian hunters had picked on this very spot" (*MW* 55). And he doesn't complain, since this pile of bones is about as close to actual moose flesh as he is going to get on this trip. Though he sees their tracks almost everywhere he looks on the tangled slopes of Katahdin, the moose themselves prove to be entirely elusive. But their elusiveness makes them no less representative of the Maine woods, and it may make them still more so, since much of the "wildness" of wild animals is demonstrated by the fact that whenever we come around, they run away and hide (unless, of course, they decide to test our courage and see if they can't scare us off instead).

See, for example, what happens when Thoreau and his companions become disoriented during their hike down the mountain, and one of the two guides, Tom Fowler, climbs a tree to scout the countryside as best he can, which isn't terribly well. Thoreau writes: "To Tom we cried, where away does the summit bear? where the burnt lands? The last he could only conjecture; he descried, however, a little meadow and pond, lying probably in our course, which we concluded to steer for. On reaching this secluded meadow, we found fresh tracks of moose on the shore of the pond, and the water was still unsettled as if they had fled before us. A little further, in a dense thicket, we seemed to be still on their trail" (*MW* 69). The alert reader will detect in this passage not only the dynamic of settlement and unsettlement being played out in a different way (naturally, this time, instead of culturally), but shades of the hound, the bay horse, and the turtle-dove that Thoreau claims to be seeking in *Walden*. However, the moose of the Maine woods, unlike the hound, the horse, and the turtle-dove, is not depicted as a wholly figurative animal (witness that skeleton left behind by the Indian hunters). Yet given how unwilling it is to show itself, and given the fact that despite its failure to appear it is nevertheless eerily present, or always already—but only just—vanished, the moose seems perfectly suited to evoke the "wildness" it embodies, which as I've suggested is elusive by definition. Paradoxically, what makes the moose of "Ktaadn" literally a moose is that there is really no question of our interpreting it in terms of what Heidegger calls "that thinking that explicitly enters Appropriation in order to say It in terms of It about It."[25] To assert that Thoreau says, as it were, "Moose in terms of Moose about Moose" in "Ktaadn" would be to interpret this animal's nonappearance in that text as, despite everything, an epiphany—and to obey a Kantian impulse ruled out by the spirit of deconstruction as, well, deconstructive.[26]

At this juncture it is tempting to conclude that the Maine woods, covered as they were with marks left by innumerable hands, hooves, and paws (for there are bears on the slopes of Katahdin, too), struck Thoreau as a palimpsest, a scrambled text or rather a scramble of texts, which he could never hope to decipher. The pertinent question then becomes, was this palimpsest a document of barbarity, as he had hoped, or a document of civilization, as he had feared?[27] Given how it is described in "Ktaadn," it actually appears to have been something in between: a treaty marking an uneasy and unstable compromise between barbarity and civilization, a treaty which might be abrogated someday—and torn all to pieces—or not. Thoreau, it seems, was inclined to be an optimist about barbarity and nature, however much of a pessimist he might have been about civilization and culture. He had that interesting option as a practitioner of natural deconstruction, who was against all odds a sort of materialist and who knew how to be literal-minded (which needless to say is incrementally) whenever an occasion called for a degree of literal-mindedness and yet involved a confrontation with a paradoxical reality badly in need of explanation and interpretation. Describing the single clear and almost panoramic view of the Maine woods he was able to obtain partway down the south side of Katahdin, he writes: "There it was, the State of Maine, which we had seen on the map, but not much like that. Immeasurable forest for the sun to shine on, that eastern *stuff* we hear of in Massachusetts. No clearing, no house. It did not look as if a solitary traveller had cut so much as a walking-stick there" (*MW* 66; italics in original). Depending on one's point of view, then, the Maine woods appear in "Ktaadn" less as a palimpsest than as a perennial *tabula rasa*, a slate which—somehow—always manages to wipe itself clean. The tablelands surrounding Mount Katahdin may be covered from time to time with thin overlays and traceries of meaning, with clearings and houses, or even with glaciers, but as the seasons change and the mist clears they are endlessly renewed, and are revealed to be endlessly self-renewing. The lumbermen, the Penobscots, the moose, and last but by no means least the trees: all may go away for a spell. But given world enough, and time, they return.

Their capacity for self-renewal in the wake of destruction gives the Maine woods the qualities of toughness and vulnerability that, however incompatible they may seem when coupled, appear to be two of the defining traits of wilderness. Feel free to quibble with my use of the word "wilderness" as much as you like. I have good authority for it. Thoreau writes: "Thus a man shall lead his life away here on the edge of the wilderness, on Indian Millinocket stream, in a new world, far in the dark of a continent, and have a flute to play at evening here, while his strains echo to the stars, amid the howling of wolves; shall live, as it were, in the primitive age of the world, a primitive man. Yet he shall spend a sunny day, and in this century be my contemporary" (*MW* 78–79). The point is, a few clearings do not deforestation and settlement make, no more than the tootling of a flute conjures up all civilization like the snake charmer conjures up his cobra. Nor, for that matter, do a few howling wolves make for a "howling wilderness." The situation is much more complicated than that, textually, anthropologically, and ecologically.

I would be remiss if I did not add that the situation is equally complicated ideologically. Incorporation, to recall the term Thoreau uses and the point he makes in his description of Enfield, does not necessarily mean that a territory has become a fully functioning organ of the body geopolitic (please excuse the neologism). Thoreau's awareness of this fact is yet another thing setting him apart from the great majority of his American contemporaries, including many of the good citizens of Concord. Of the territorial United States, he writes:

> Have we even so much as discovered and settled the shores? Let a man travel on foot along the coast, from the Passamaquoddy to the Sabine, or to the Rio Bravo, or to wherever the end is now, if he is swift enough to overtake it, faithfully following the windings of every inlet and of every cape, and stepping to the music of the surf,—with a desolate fishing-town once a week, and a city's port once a month to cheer him, and putting up at the light-houses, when there are any, and tell me if it looks like a discovered and settled country, and not rather, for the most part, like a desolate island, and No-man's Land. (*MW* 82)

The State of Maine, it seems, isn't the only one to have been overrun without being settled in anything other than a rough-and-tumble, frontiersman's fashion. Like all the other states, and like the United States, it continually needs to be discovered and then rediscovered. And not by a Transcendentalist apt to leapfrog over difficult passages but by some much humbler and more open-minded voyager who is willing to practice what I have suggested ought to be called "natural deconstruction" along the way, restoring the blankness to the map as he goes. Presumably, it was the necessity of some such practice that compelled Thoreau to return to Bangor and travel northward into the Maine woods again and then again in search of a moose and an Indian, before he finally grew too consumptive to make yet another trip, and only had enough wind left to murmur his dying words.

Walden, Revisited

If the interpretation of *Walden* that I offered in the first part of this essay is at all valid, it's no wonder that an initial reading of the book is apt to puzzle someone—a college sophomore with a love of the outdoors, let us say—who approaches it in the mistaken belief that it tells a simple story of one man's escape from the confines of his culture and of his total immersion in the natural world. Such a reader is going to founder in bewilderment approximately two-thirds of the way through "Economy," at the point in that long opening chapter where its author provides a detailed report of his personal expenses. Thoreau says that his purchase of a watermelon, and of some other foodstuffs including sweet potatoes and a pumpkin, was an experiment "which failed" (*W* 59). Imagine that: a failed watermelon, and to make matters worse, abortive sweet potatoes and an unsuccessful pumpkin, too. So much for nature's bounty, and living off the produce of the land.

It's no secret that Thoreau's economic and agricultural standards were almost impossibly high, despite the modest scale of his personal finances and notwithstanding the self-confessed amateurishness of his efforts as a farmer. Our naïve first-time reader of *Walden* therefore can be forgiven for wondering, as the arguments of "Economy" unfold, if the book's tetchy author doesn't entertain some pretty unreasonable expectations not only of culture but of nature, too. And what is true of "Economy" is also true, albeit to a lesser degree and less obviously, of the rest of the book. There is, as I've shown, an awful lot of grousing about Concord interspersed among and interwoven with all the rhapsodizing about Walden Pond.

Arguably, if *Walden* is in fact an account of "life in the woods," as its subtitle proclaims it to be, it is so largely by way of the many negative comments its author makes about the other sorts of life he might have had to endure from the summer of 1845 to the fall of 1847. A life on a farm, for instance, or the life in town he had experienced as a younger man, and to which he returned at the end of his two years and several months at pondside. That these other lives are given a sizable amount of imaginative consideration in *Walden,* and that taking them into consideration imaginatively is crucial to the book's conception and execution, suggests that its character as an idyllic pastoral perhaps ought to be called into question more, and more strongly, than it has. We need to attend more closely to the several complications of Thoreau's point of view and to his puckish rhetorical strategies, not only in *Walden* but in supposedly more straightforward texts like "Ktaadn," which might not give our poor student the simple and vicarious pleasure he seeks either. The presentation of nature in Thoreau's work is rarely any more straightforward than its presentation of culture, and it is often less.

As the little story in *Walden* about the horseman crossing the bog and as the occasional ineptness of Thoreau's Maine guides illustrate, there can be factitiousness about nature just as much as, if not a lot more than there can be factitiousness about culture, and this factitiousness can be equally absurd and comical, as well as dangerous. I think this is something of which Thoreau, as an experienced traveler in both tame and wild places, was perfectly aware. Hence his insistence, very irksome to Emerson who dismissed it as a rhetorical tic, on describing a wildwood in terms of its domesticity and a swamp in terms of the creature comforts it afforded the human visitor, while denying that town life with its velvet cushions and fresh water drawn from a well provided anything remotely comparable.[28] The point Thoreau is trying to make when he confounds our expectations in this way isn't so much that nature is more luxurious and salubrious than culture as that the relative merits of each are matters open to debate, and that both nature and culture need to be explored more judiciously and open-mindedly than in the past. This explains why, having determined that it was necessary for him to go to Walden, Thoreau determined that it also was necessary for him to leave the pond, not only in the fall of 1847 but on a more or less daily basis right from the moment when he first set up house there. It also explains why he didn't limit his excursions to the area encompassed by the two horizons he could see from his doorstep, but occasionally found it helpful to go much further afield, as when he traveled through the forests of Maine to Mount Katahdin.

I'd like to close by suggesting that because *Walden* contains so many deliberate distortions and exaggerations, not to mention some outright fictions, it seems to be concerned with "essential facts" and Thoreau's "life in the woods" only fitfully and by turns, despite his announced intention to proffer to his reader "a simple and sincere account of his own life, and not merely what he has heard of other men's lives" (W 3). Like a political candidate who hasn't been well coached by his handlers, Thoreau tends to wander off-message. Of course he wasn't running for but away from office, and he does warn us in his book's conclusion that he "left the woods for as good a reason" as he'd gone there. And the reason turns out to have been not only "as good" but just the same. Insensibly, he had fallen into a rut and a routine at Walden, until he remembered that he "did not wish to take a cabin passage, but rather to go before the mast and on the deck of the world," the better to see "the moonlight amid the mountains" (W 323).

As his self-indicting pun on "cabin passage" and his romantic reference to moonlight illustrate, the opportunity for fabulation—and confabulation—that the writing of *Walden* afforded Thoreau was much too tempting for him to play it straight, cranky eccentric and scourge of society that he was. Much of

his account of the facts of his life serves him as a platform for criticizing factitiousness, the very thing he supposedly went to Walden to get away from in
the first place, so that he might focus on matters that seemed more reliably
real, chief among them the matter of his own character considered in relation
to the natural world. But like Diogenes the Cynic in his barrel, Thoreau is
forced to take up residence on the verge of factitiousness and the outskirts of
town. Otherwise there would be no point to his quest for personal honesty
untainted by social prejudice.

Notes

1. Henry David Thoreau, *Walden,* ed. J. Lyndon Shanley (Princeton: Princeton University Press, 1971).
2. James Russell Lowell, "Thoreau," in *Thoreau; A Century of Criticism,* ed. Walter Harding (Dallas: Southern Methodist University Press, 1954), 52; reprinted from *North
   American Review* 101 (October 1865): 597–608. For a much more recent but similarly
   dismissive description of Thoreau by someone who, like Lowell, doesn't really care
   very much for *Walden* or its author, see Leon Edel, "The Mystery of Walden Pond," in
   The Stuff of Sleep and Dreams (New York: Harper & Row, 1982), 47–65.
3. Sacvan Bercovitch, *The American Jeremiad* (Madison: University of Wisconsin Press,
   1978), 190.
4. Michael Gilmore, "*Walden* and the 'Curse of Trade,'" in *Ideology and Classic American
   Literature,* ed. Sacvan Bercovitch and Myra Jehlen (Cambridge: Cambridge University
   Press, 1986), 293, 297, 301.
5. But not as obtuse as a recent newspaper article that appeared in the "House & Home"
   section of the *New York Times.* The article, written by a columnist who specializes in
   design, compares Saddam Hussein's hideout on the Tigris River to "Thoreau's one-
   room cabin on Walden Pond, built by the writer, for $28, as a place 'to front the essen-
   tials of life,' which Mr. Hussein surely found himself doing as well, if by necessity
   rather than choice" (Christopher Hawthorne, "House at the End of the Line," *New
   York Times,* Thursday, December 18, 2003: F8). The article also compares Hussein's
   hideout to Hitler's bunker and to the Unabomber's shack in the woods of Montana (see
   F1, F8). It's amusing, but worrisome, to see Thoreau so blithely associated with such
   dire misfits as Hussein, Hitler, and the Unabomber.
6. It should be noted that readers otherwise sympathetic to Thoreau also are likely to take
   him to task for his lack of community spirit. Lawrence Buell, for instance, praises
   Thoreau for his "environmental sensitivity," but finds "the high degree of social disaf-
   fection that his environmental responsiveness reflected" troubling, since it introduces
   a "potentially escapist element" into his work (*The Environmental Imagination;
   Thoreau, Nature Writing, and the Formation of American Culture* [Cambridge: Harvard
   University Press, 1995], 139, 388, 389). On the immediate political dangers posed by

the combination of Thoreauvian "resistance to civil government" and relative indifference to community, see Jim Corbett, *Goatwalking: A Guide to Wildland Living and a Quest for the Peaceable Kingdom* (New York: Viking, 1991), 98–103.

7. My sense that Thoreau is happy to contradict both himself and others would mark one difference between my treatment of *Walden* and that offered by Walter Benn Michaels in his essay "*Walden*'s False Bottoms," *Glyph* 1 (1977): 132–49, where despite the deconstructive spirit of the analysis, contradictions are seen not as inevitable, much less laudatory, but as an inherent flaw. As Jonathan Culler points out in his commentary on Michaels's essay, "One might think *Walden* too easy a case for the seeker of contradictions. Its narrative line is relatively weak and critics have often thought it a series of spectacular fragments" (*On Deconstruction: Theory and Criticism after Structuralism* [Ithaca, NY: Cornell University Press, 1982], 235). In other words, to deconstruct a text already deconstructed—or never "properly" constructed in the first place—by its author may be to argue beside the point, even if it is excusable as a demonstration of what was, in 1977, still a new and an exciting approach to interpretation.

8. Steve Shapin and Simon Schaffer, *Leviathan and the Air-Pump: Hobbes, Boyle, and the Experimental Life* (Princeton: Princeton University Press, 1985), 225.

9. Steve Fuller, *Philosophy of Science and Its Discontents,* 2nd ed. (New York: Guilford Press, 1993), 8. On the apparent emptiness of many social constructionist claims, see Ian Hacking, *The Social Construction of What?* (Cambridge: Harvard University Press, 1999).

10. Bruno Latour, *Science in Action: How to Follow Scientists and Engineers through Society* (Cambridge: Harvard University Press, 1987), 207, 208.

11. In an article on Thoreau published in 1880, Robert Louis Stevenson wrote: "He adopted poverty like a piece of business. Yet his system is based on one or two ideas that I believe come naturally to all thoughtful youths, and are only pounded out of them by city uncles. Indeed, something essentially youthful distinguishes all Thoreau's knock-down blows at current opinion. Like the posers of a child, they leave the orthodox in a kind of speechless agony. These know the thing is nonsense" ("Henry David Thoreau: His Character and Opinions," in *Thoreau: A Century of Criticism,* 64; reprinted from *Cornhill Magazine* 41 [June 1880]: 665–82). Stevenson later recanted his criticism of Thoreau's ideas about economics in particular and the larger fabric of society in general—criticism that was relatively mild to begin with—but other readers seem much less willing to forgive the author of *Walden* for his book's inconsistencies and his personal peccadilloes. For instance, Edel insists that the actual circumstances of the book's composition were altogether at odds with the "large myth" it contains: "At Walden Pond, Thoreau's ear was cocked to the sounds of Concord. He led neither the solitary nor the Spartan life his book described," but instead conducted "an experiment to prove something in his fancy" ("The Mystery of Walden Pond," 50, 52). Edel seems to think that we ought to find Thoreau's willingness to experiment highly objectionable.

12. For some more thoughts on this subject, see Edward L. Galligan, "The Comedian at Walden Pond," *South Atlantic Quarterly* 69.1 (1970): 20–37.

13. Thoreau's performance in the passage I have been discussing also puts him, albeit somewhat less squarely, in the tradition of the American jeremiad. But since that tradition has been explored by others (most notably, by Bercovitch), and since I am working a different tack here, I will say no more about Thoreau's contribution to it.

14. See Bradford Angier, *How to Stay Alive in the Woods* (New York: Macmillan, 1962). Thoreau is cited, approvingly, several times in Angier's text.

15. For another interpretation of Thoreau's interest in bottoms which, like Walter Benn Michaels's, in some ways resembles and in other ways differs from my own, see Michael Warner, "Thoreau's Bottom," *Raritan* 11.3 (Winter 1992): 53–79.

16. Readers often feel proprietary about books they love, and try to use them as yardsticks not only for measuring everything else their authors might happen to write, but for giving their authors a sharp rap across the knuckles, too, if some portion of the everything else does not measure up. This is especially true of readers of *Walden,* "one of those works that epitomize an author's life and writing, that gather all rays on a single focal point," according to Martin Bickman. "Such books," he adds, "make everything else the author did seem like a preparation or a falling off" (*Walden: Volatile Truths* [New York: Twayne, 1992], 18).

17. According to Lewis H. Miller Jr., as Thoreau describes his travels "through an immense, limitless forest" in *The Maine Woods,* "he is deprived of the 'license' afforded him by his clearly demarcated terrain in *Walden,*" so that "metaphor becomes fact as Thoreau's imagination can no longer dive deeper nor soar higher than Nature goes" ("The Artist as Surveyor in *Walden* and *The Maine Woods," ESQ* 21.2 [1975]: 76, 78). And Frederick Garber argues that each chapter of *The Maine Woods* "recounts a test of consciousness, a pitting of its capacities against the most resistant antagonist available," and maintains that this is a test the book's protagonist does not always pass. "The rocks remain unredeemably rocks," Garber writes, which means that "Thoreau was defeated by the *material* of Ktaadn" (*Thoreau's Redemptive Imagination* [New York: New York University Press, 1977], 75, 83, 101). Clearly Thoreau's great concern for facts, forests, and rocks isn't fully shared even by some of his most ardent admirers.

18. See, in addition to the studies cited in the previous note, Sherman Paul, *The Shores of America: Thoreau's Inward Exploration* (Champaign: University of Illinois Press, 1958), 358 et passim; John G. Blair and Augustus Trowbridge, "Thoreau on Katahdin," *American Quarterly* 12.4 (Winter 1960): 508–17; Roderick Nash, *Wilderness and the American Mind,* 3rd ed. (New Haven: Yale University Press, 1982), 89–91; John Tallmadge, " 'Ktaadn': Thoreau in the Wilderness of Words," *ESQ* 31.3 (1985): 137–48; and Max Oelschlaeger, *The Idea of Wilderness: From Prehistory to the Age of Ecology* (New Haven: Yale University Press, 1991), 145 et passim.

19. The selective reading of "Ktaadn," and of all Thoreau's work including *Walden,* suggests that Howard Horwitz makes a valid point when he states that "criticism has practiced its own protectionism, protecting transcendentalism, or wishing transcendentalism had better protected itself, from the cultural imagination it often challenged. We may say that criticism has retained the purity of classic idealism—thought's tran-

scendence of materiality and contingency—as the necessary condition of change and virtue" (*By the Law of Nature: Form and Value in Nineteenth-Century America* [Oxford: Oxford University Press, 1991], 62–63).

20. Thoreau did have better success on his second and third trips to Maine, during which he spent a considerable amount of time in the company of two Penobscots (Joe Aitteon and Joe Polis) and saw several moose, the first of which was promptly shot and killed by his traveling companion, his cousin George Thatcher.

21. Jonathan Culler, "In Defense of Overinterpretation," in Umberto Eco et al., *Interpretation and Overinterpretation,* ed. Stefan Collini (Cambridge: Cambridge University Press, 1992), 110.

22. In a discussion of deconstruction as a form of "disproportionate" interpretation that "grafts" the margins of texts onto their centers, Culler writes: "Interpretation generally relies on distinctions between the central and the marginal, the essential and the inessential: to interpret is to discover what is central to a text or group of texts. On the one hand, the marginal graft works within these terms to reverse a hierarchy, to show that what had previously been thought marginal is in fact central. But on the other hand, that reversal, attributing importance to the marginal, is usually conducted in such a way that it does not lead simply to the identification of a new center . . . but to a subversion of the distinctions between essential and inessential, inside and outside. What is a center if the marginal can become central? 'Disproportionate' interpretation is unsettling" (*On Deconstruction,* 140; my ellipsis). It seems to me that Culler's words apply equally to Thoreau's slyly sardonic treatment of Emerson's address and to my foregrounding of that treatment in the context of a reading of "Ktaadn" as an ostensible departure from the standard supposedly established by *Walden.*

23. It seems Louis Neptune and his partner decided to get drunk. When they finally turned up, Thoreau and his companions were already well on their way downstream. So the two Penobscots were too late to act as guides, and had long since been replaced by two white men anyway.

24. For the definition of "Katahdin," see the entry for "Katadn" (Thoreau seems to have been unable to decide how to spell this word) in Appendix VII, "A List of Indian Words," in *The Maine Woods,* 840.

25. Martin Heidegger, "Time and Being," in *On Time and Being,* tr. Joan Stambaugh (New York: Harper & Row, 1972), 24.

26. Richard Rorty, whose remarks on this subject alerted me to the cryptic line I have quoted from Heidegger's "Time and Being," writes: "Kantian philosophy, on Derrida's view, is a kind of writing which would like not to be a kind of writing. It is a genre which would like to be a gesture, a clap of thunder, an epiphany" ("Philosophy as a Kind of Writing: An Essay on Derrida," in *Consequences of Pragmatism (Essays 1972–1980)* [Minneapolis: University of Minnesota Press, 1982], 105). For a discussion of *Walden* that entertains precisely the Kantian hope Rorty describes, see Stanley Cavell, *The Senses of Walden: An Expanded Edition* (Chicago: University of Chicago Press, 1981). For a discussion of moose that confirms my assertion of the difficulty of capturing

them by means of representation, see Daniel B. Botkin, "Moose in the Wilderness: Stability and the Growth of Populations," in *Discordant Harmonies: A New Ecology for the Twenty-first Century* (Oxford: Oxford University Press, 1990), 27–49.

27. Here I am alluding to the seventh of Walter Benjamin's "Theses on the Philosophy of History": "There is no document of civilization which is not at the same time a document of barbarism. And just as such a document is not free of barbarism, barbarism taints also the manner in which it was transmitted from one owner to another. A historical materialist therefore dissociates himself from it as far as possible. He regards it as his task to brush history against the grain" (in *Illuminations: Essays and Reflections,* ed. Hannah Arendt [New York: Schocken Books, 1969], 256–57).

28. In his journal for 1843, and in reaction to Thoreau's submission of "A Winter Walk" to the *Dial,* Emerson wrote: "H.D.T. sends me a paper with the old fault of unlimited contradiction. The trick of his rhetoric is soon learned. It consists in substituting for the obvious word & thought its diametrical antagonist. He praises wild mountains & winter forests for their domestic air; snow & ice for their warmth; villagers & wood choppers for their urbanity and the wilderness for resembling Rome & Paris. With the constant inclination to dispraise cities & civilization, he yet can find no way to honour woods & woodmen except by paralleling them with towns & townsmen. W E C declares the piece is excellent: but it makes me nervous & wretched to read it, with all its merits" (*The Journals and Miscellaneous Notebooks of Ralph Waldo Emerson,* vol. 9, *1843–47,* ed. Ralph H. Orth and Alfred R. Ferguson [Cambridge: Harvard University Press, 1971], 9–10). "W E C" refers to William Ellery Channing.

Afterword

SANDRA HARBERT PETRULIONIS
AND LAURA DASSOW WALLS

FOR MORE THAN 150 years, *Walden* and Henry David Thoreau have spoken to that within us that seeks to "front only the essential facts of life . . . to live deep and suck out all the marrow of life . . . to cut a broad swath and shave close, to drive life into a corner, and reduce it to its lowest terms . . . to know it by experience" (*W* 90–91). The contents of this book demonstrate that scholars of Thoreau's magnum opus continue to break new ground as they consider its multifaceted advice. Thoreau asserted that the leaves of the earth's strata were not page upon page to be studied by geologists and antiquaries chiefly, "but living poetry like the leaves of a tree" (*W* 309). The everlasting vitality of *Walden* shows that it, too, is not a fossil book but a living text still putting out green leaves of insight today. Thoreau remains the "father" of both environmental activism and American nature writing, and *Walden* their genesis text. These two facts alone point to the need for continual reexploration of both Thoreau's life and his writing, for each generation must redefine Thoreau's meaning for its own time and conditions, and each perspective supplies new analytical and interpretive tools that can reveal much that is novel about this long-familiar text. As Elizabeth Hall Witherell has noted, "A good general Thoreauvian rule is that a careful reexamination of anything that has been accepted as given will yield new information."[1] Here we would like to offer some directions in which critics can continue profitably attending to *Walden*—a book whose composition, political and historical contexts, and ecohistorical and scientific richness, to name only a few dimensions, provide ongoing and productive ground for new research.

As the essays in this collection attest, scholars today continue to recover *Walden* as a middle ground between polarized terms: the empiricism of particular facts vs. the Emersonian idealism that dissolves facts into a dynamic flux of ever-mutating energy; the single lived instance vs. the generalized, universalizing law; the self in proud isolation withdrawn from the sullied compromises of society vs. the reestablishment of community on a higher plane; culture and nature, civil and wild, Concord at one boundary and all the wild West at the other. "Walden," text and place, becomes a border zone under constant negotiation: not a no-man's-land between warring parties but more like the cambium of a tree, the vital interface that does not separate but bonds and generates the inner wood and the outer bark. Similarly, *Walden* produces two kinds of truths, a spiritual reality found in any location, and a physical reality, a particular New England kettle pond where the rocks are hard as—well, rocks, and where on a good day the water is still clear to the bottom. At a time when few of us can afford the rejuvenating escape to exotic wilderness spaces, Thoreau gives us instead the "wild" of backyard places.

"Walden," pond and book, are themselves "facts," simultaneously brute realities that exist beyond our electronic and hypermediated culture, and constructions of that very culture precisely insofar as we labor to make and keep them alive as facts, elements of our shared world. No longer merely a pastoral retreat for recreation and redemption, *Walden* in the new century is a georgic worksite, coming into being as we, like Thoreau, labor to give our ideas body, and our bodies, thought. As a cultural worksite, then, an ongoing construction zone, *Walden* binds together an immense bundle of relations that still need to be teased out and thought, or rethought.

For example, much recent criticism has reopened the question of Thoreau's involvement with science. As we recover a greater understanding of the scientific context in which Thoreau was immersed, we need more fine-grained, deeply informed studies such as William Rossi's in this volume that examine how Thoreau wrestled with particular scientific concepts. Additionally, we need to foster the ongoing discussion of the nature of Thoreau's idealism in light of this new knowledge, gained both by closer readings of *Walden* and by a continuing effort to address Thoreau's scientific notebooks. How did Thoreau's engagement with science refute, redefine, or extend his early commitment to idealism? The "Two Cultures" divide separating literature from science has long severed Thoreau the poet from Thoreau the scientist, and much work remains if we are to reintegrate the two.

Contemporary ecology has long since abandoned the model of balanced and stable ecosystems progressing in an orderly fashion to mature, climax states. Ecologists explore instead the constant and dynamic change found in all ecosystems, particularly in "shreds and patches," the fragmented ecosystems of today.[2] Thoreau's Walden was both patched and shredded, an abused landscape stressed by many generations of agriculture on poor soil and largely deforested in his lifetime. We need to review our understanding of Thoreau's ecological wisdom in the face of this new ecological science. We also need to reconsider how the very act of writing *Walden* inflects the green space we call Walden Pond, now protected, thanks to Thoreau's inspiration, as a state reserve. How did *Walden* change Walden? How did it change the way we see all green spaces—including those far away from New England's oaks and pine, winter snows, and summer huckleberries?

Far from being alone in nature, much of *Walden* is concerned with the creation of community, both the human society of the town and its outskirts, and the community of humans and nature together in which Thoreau is not the sole Adamic namer or organizer but at various points participant, intruder, competitor, guest, resident. As philosophical, cultural, and ecocritical studies reexamine human-animal relations, there is much to reconsider about Thoreau's own interactions with woodchucks, fishes, foxes, partridges, loons. With how much personhood does Thoreau invest Walden's animals? Are they "lower" than human, proto-human, non-human? Do they have independent agency? Do they, too, build their own worlds, and how do those worlds interface with the human?

On yet another horizon, in an age of searchable hypertexts, the nine-year genesis of *Walden* demands renewed critical attention. Two groundbreaking studies—J. Lyndon Shanley's *The Making of "Walden"* (1957) and Robert Sattelmeyer's "The Remaking of *Walden*" (1990)—elaborate on the chronology of and context in which Thoreau crafted the eight drafts of *Walden*.[3] Ronald Earl Clapper's 1967 doctoral dissertation, a two-volume labor of love titled "The Development of *Walden*: A Genetic Text," is indispensable to any scholar desiring to learn when certain material made it into *Walden*, information essential to biographical, historical, and political studies.[4] But forty years is an overlong time for scholars to rely on a dissertation, however instrumental the work may be. Aided by recent bibliographical and historiographical analyses of *Walden*, scholars could make an extraordinarily important contribution to scholarship on *Walden* by integrating Shanley's, Sattelmeyer's, and Clapper's work; equally beneficial would be a searchable, user-friendly electronic text of the discrete manuscript drafts. As one example, Thoreau turned to science during the pivotal years from 1849 to 1851, and his most substantive revisions to the evolving manuscript of *Walden* occurred largely after that turn was made. Yet we have no complete, detailed analysis to explain exactly how Thoreau's growing confidence in the revelatory nature of scientific fact was inflected in his revisions to *Walden*.

If nature writing is conceived not as an escape from politics but as itself profoundly political, as Lance Newman suggests, then a related research front is opened. How do we read nature and politics together? How does the political in *Walden* engage with the natural? How is *Walden* transformed if we read Thoreau not as the son of privilege but as a working-class radical, pro-posing not retreat but a new form of political engagement? Assessments of Thoreau's political and reformist sentiment typically focus on the more overtly political speeches and essays as well as the antislavery polemics—"Resistance to Civil Government," "Slavery in Massachusetts," and "A Plea for Captain John Brown"—yet *Walden* was also shaped by its time, particularly given the politically turbulent years that elapsed between the book's inception in July 1845, when Thoreau moved to Walden Pond, and its publication in August 1854. Extant scholarship on Thoreau's political thought, such as Bob Pepper-man Taylor's *America's Bachelor Uncle: Thoreau and the American Polity* (1996), has to some degree examined the political rhetoric and sensibility that frames *Walden*, but further evaluation of its political and historical refer-ences—particularly the timing of their insertion into the *Walden* manu-script—is needed. As one example, when we know that Thoreau's claim to have assisted "one real runaway slave . . . toward the northstar" (*W* 152) was added to the "Visitors" chapter in 1852,[5] two years following the Fugitive Slave Law's passage and one year after his family's aid to slave Henry Williams, we can interpret this remark in a specific political, as well as symbolic context.

Additionally, more contextual illumination is needed on the issue of gen-der in *Walden*, since the assumption that Thoreau's "wilderness" excludes the feminine has resulted in far too little attention being paid to this question. As Sarah Wider illustrates, feminist readings can take the very distance between Thoreau and the woman reader and transform it into a kind of charmed space.

Himself unmarried, Thoreau lived nearly all his life in an extended household with many women—his mother, his sisters, his aunts, permanent boarders Prudence Ward and her mother. He played a curiously "feminized" role in town, taking the neighbors' children on nature rambles and refusing his "masculine" responsibilities toward career, home, and family. Certainly Thoreau codes nature as "she," but given this context, what does that mean? How available is his "georgic" labor to women?

Finally, *Walden* itself does not exist in lonely isolation. We need more studies that, like Dana Phillips's, relate *Walden* to Thoreau's other texts. Of them all, *Cape Cod,* arguably Thoreau's second-best book, is perhaps the most underread and undertaught of his works. Thoreau turns herein from the snug enclosure of the pond to the wild and terrible ocean. What kind of worldview emerges when these two texts are put in conversation? How does Thoreau navigate from glacial kettle pond to Concord river, to wilderness mountaintops, to the Atlantic? Facing the ocean, Thoreau asserts that he turns his back on all America—but if so, he fronts all the world. The global is always local at all points. How does Thoreau, master of the local, encounter the global? In his mind's eye he observes the ice of Walden melt into the Ganges. How does the cosmopolitanism of *Walden* link to worlds beyond America? For the immense bundle of relations that make "Walden" real were not bounded by his horizon.

In 1997, Elizabeth Hall Witherell agreed that earlier scholars had correctly suggested that the "definitive" biography of Thoreau would never be written but that each era would generate its own life story.[6] Witherell also urged scholars to attend to Thoreau's relationship with women, particularly those family members, such as his sister Sophia, also a naturalist, with whom he enjoyed close relations.[7] Nearly a decade later, these recommendations loom all the more valid and insistent. Recent cultural biographies of antebellum American figures have augmented and recovered the lives of the canonical (Walt Whitman), the historical (John Brown), and the less well known (Lydia Maria Child, Sarah Alden Ripley, the Peabody sisters), but, remarkably, no study has yet given us the "life and times" of Henry David Thoreau. Particularly in light of recent works reassessing Thoreau's relationship to nineteenth-century science and politics, and two books providing us with his unpublished natural history manuscripts, *Faith in a Seed* and *Wild Fruits,* a new biography for a new century seems quite overdue.

To close with perhaps the most important nexus for continued attention to

Walden—the next generations of readers, scholars, and self-examined lives: the students. Forty years ago, Thoreau was revered on college campuses as a kindred antiwar protestor; twenty years ago, he became the godfather of the new interdisciplinary field of environmental studies. But the twenty-first-century classroom has changed, and its students are far less convinced, in many respects, by Thoreau's experiment in self-culture, with his earnest yearning to "live deliberately." Disgruntled reactions to Thoreau's two years "off" have always existed, but today's young adults have come of age post-9/11, and have been educated primarily by the pedagogical imperative of "teaching to the test." Gone are the leisurely hours of reading *Walden* cover to cover their junior or senior year of high school. Today's college student has often never heard of *Walden* or Henry Thoreau, a dilemma indeed for the instructor who must sandwich Thoreau into the literature survey course. Classroom methodology benefited substantially from Richard Schneider's *Approaches to Teaching Walden and Other Works* (1996), but recent conference sessions attest that interest in learning creative strategies to bring the book alive in the classroom remains high.

In his 1977 study, *Several More Lives to Live: Thoreau's Political Reputation in America,* Michael Meyer laid out the manner in which since the 1920s, Thoreau has become public property, a claim that is just as true today. But there is a danger in this familiarity. We risk seeing Thoreau the cultural icon become Thoreau the caricature, the figurehead of bygone eras and concerns, the poster child of the sixties whose manifold message of "Simplicity, simplicity, simplicity!" is irrelevant to our lives and our increasing dependence on techno-materialism (*W* 91). Yet since its publication in 1854, *Walden,* like an overriding conscience, has beckoned to each new age to consider what we do, acknowledge the basis of our choices, offering its message of renewal and commitment to well-examined, well-earned lives. In our new century, we can capitulate to a vapid frenzy of consumerism and environmental destruction, or we can choose otherwise. But as Thoreau has always reminded us, the choice is ours to make.

Notes

1. Elizabeth Hall Witherell, "Henry David Thoreau," in *Prospects for the Study of American Literature: A Guide for Scholars and Students,* ed. Richard Kopley (New York: New York University Press, 1997), 21–38: 32.

2. See, for example, Daniel Botkin, *Discordant Harmonies: A New Ecology for the Twenty-first Century* (New York: Oxford University Press, 1990).

3. J. Lyndon Shanley, *The Making of "Walden"* (Chicago: University of Chicago Press, 1957); Robert Sattelmeyer, "The Remaking of *Walden*," in *Writing the American Classics,* ed. James Barbour and Tom Quirk (Chapel Hill: University of North Carolina Press, 1990), 53–78.

4. Ronald Earl Clapper, "The Development of *Walden*: A Genetic Text," Diss. in 2 vols., University of California, Los Angeles, 1967.

5. Ibid., 1:31, 434.

6. Witherell, "Henry David Thoreau," 22.

7. Ibid., 23.

Contributors

NINA BAYM is Swanlund Chair and Center for Advanced Study Professor of English and Jubilee Professor of Liberal Arts and Sciences at the Universisty of Illinois, Urbana. She is General Editor of the *Norton Anthology of American Literature* and has written many books and articles on nineteenth-century American literary topics. In 2000 she won the Jay Hubbell Medal from the MLA's American Literature Section for lifetime achievement in advancing the study of American literature. Her interest in Thoreau goes all the way back to her Ph.D. thesis, "The Paradoxical Hero in Thoreau's Writings."

ROBERT E. CUMMINGS received his Ph.D. from the University of Georgia and is assistant professor of English and director of First-Year Composition at Columbus State University in Columbus, Georgia. He studies both American literature and computers and writing, particularly their intersection through sites such as the American Literature Wiki. He has written about environmental concerns as expressed in the works of William Faulkner, particularly in "Go Down, Moses." He is currently coediting a volume of essays examining the advent of wikis in education titled *The Wild, Wild Wiki: Unsettling the Frontiers of Cyberspace* (University of Michigan Press, forthcoming 2007).

ROBERT OSCAR LÓPEZ received his Ph.D. from SUNY Buffalo and currently teaches English as an assistant professor at Rutgers, Camden. He specializes in eighteenth- and nineteenth-century American literature, Classics, and ethnic studies. He is also an active writer about current events for alternative magazines and has been published in *A: Inside Asian America, CounterPunch,* and *Buffalo Report,* among others. He is currently working on two books of literary theory, runs his own website, www.bronzepage.com, and is in the process of completing an additional M.A. in Classics.

LANCE NEWMAN is associate professor of literature and writing studies at California State University at San Marcos, where he teaches courses in early U.S. literature, Romanticism, and the cultural history of nature. He is the author of *Our Common Dwelling: Henry Thoreau, Transcendentalism, and the Class Politics of Nature* (Palgrave, 2006), and editor of *Transatlantic Romanticism: An Anthology of American, British, and Canadian Literature, 1767–1867* (Longman, 2006). His work has appeared in *American Literature, New England Quarterly, The Concord Saunterer, Romanticism on the Net, ISLE: Interdisciplinary Studies in Literature and the Environment,* and elsewhere. He has also worked for fifteen years as a guide on the Colorado and Green Rivers in southeastern Utah and in Grand Canyon.

H. DANIEL PECK is John Guy Vassar Professor of English at Vassar College, where he has directed the American studies program and, more recently, was the founding director of the College's new environmental studies program. He is the author of *Thoreau's Morning Work* and *A World by Itself: The Pastoral Moment in Cooper's Fiction,* both published by Yale University Press, and is a past chairman of the MLA Division on Nineteenth-Century American Literature. His Thoreau publications, in addition to *Thoreau's Morning Work,* include two Penguin Classics editions, *A Week on the Concord and Merrimack Rivers* and *A Year in Thoreau's Journal: 1851.*

SANDRA HARBERT PETRULIONIS is associate professor of English at Pennsylvania State University, Altoona. She is the author of *"To Set This World Right": The Antislavery Movement in Thoreau's Concord* (Cornell University Press, 2006) and the editor of *Journal 8: 1854* in the Princeton University Press series *The Writings of Henry D. Thoreau.* She has also published articles on Melville, Alcott, and other nineteenth-century American authors.

DANA PHILLIPS is an assistant professor of English at Towson University. He has published articles on a variety of topics in American Literature and a book, *The Truth of Ecology: Nature, Culture, and Literature in America* (Oxford, 2003), which in 2004 won the Modern Language Association's prize for best book by an independent scholar.

LARRY J. REYNOLDS is professor of English and Thomas Franklin Mayo Professor of Liberal Arts at Texas A&M University. He is former president of the Hawthorne Society, author of *European Revolutions and the American Literary Renaissance* (Yale University Press, 1988), and editor of the Norton Critical Edition of *Woman in the Nineteenth Century* (1998) and *A Historical Guide to Nathaniel Hawthorne* (Oxford University Press, 2001). His current projects include a study of Hawthorne and slavery and of political violence in the American Renaissance.

DAVID M. ROBINSON is Oregon Professor of English and director of the Center for the Humanities at Oregon State University. He is author of *Emerson and the Conduct of Life* (Cambridge University Press, 1993), and editor of two recent Emerson collections occasioned by the Emerson Bicentennial, *The Spiritual Emerson* (Beacon Press, 2003) and *The Political Emerson* (Beacon Press, 2004). His contribution to the present collection is drawn from his book *Natural Life: Thoreau's Worldly Transcendentalism* (Cornell University Press, 2004).

WILLIAM ROSSI is associate professor in English at the University of Oregon. He is a coeditor of *Journal 3: 1848–1851* and *Journal 6: 1853* for the Princeton edition of Thoreau's *Writings,* the editor of *"Wild Apples" and Other Natural History Essays* (University of Georgia Press, 2002), and the author of several essays on Emerson, Thoreau, and others.

ROBERT SATTELMEYER is Regents Professor of English and director of the Honors Program at Georgia State University. He has been an editor of Thoreau's Journals for the Princeton University Press edition of Thoreau's *Writings,* and is the author of *Thoreau's Reading* and many articles on Thoreau.

LAURA DASSOW WALLS is John H. Bennett, Jr., Professor of Southern Letters at the University of South Carolina, where she teaches courses in early American literature, Transcendentalism, and literature and science. She is the author of *Seeing New Worlds: Henry David Thoreau and Nineteenth-Century Natural Science* (Wisconsin University Press, 1995) and more recently of *Emerson's Life in Science: The Culture of Truth* (Cornell University

Press, 2003), as well as various essays on Thoreau, Emerson, Alexander von
Humboldt, and others.

SARAH ANN WIDER is professor of English and women's studies at Colgate
University, where she teaches courses in nineteenth-century American literature and contemporary Native American literature. She is the author of *Anna
Tilden, Unitarian Culture, and the Problem of Self-Representation* (University
of Georgia Press, 1997), and *The Critical Reception of Emerson: Unsettling All
Things* (Camden House, 2000), and is currently working on a study of late
nineteenth- and early twentieth-century women writers, artists, and activists
who took Thoreau's and Emerson's work as a central element in their intellectual platform.

MICHAEL G. ZISER is assistant professor of English at the University of
California, Davis, where he specializes in environmental writing and early
American literature. His dissertation, "Continent Ajar: Early American Writing and Environmental Practice," is an environmental literary history of early
American letters from Hariot to Cooper. His current work includes turning
that dissertation into a book, as well as researching scientific writers (especially botanists and ornithologists) operating in America before 1820.